ANSWERS FOR THE QUESTIONS YOU NEED TO ASK:

Do children blame themselves for the death of a family member?
Many children believe they caused the death of a parent or sibling. The consequences of guilt can be deep and long-reaching, so learn to spot the signs that your child is struggling with this powerful emotion.

When is a child too young to attend a wake or funeral?
No child is too young—if your child is well prepared and well supported. Learn why attending such events may actually help your child and how you can provide needed support.

Can a preschooler understand the concept of death?
Yes, with concrete explanations and language. Learn how to best break bad news to your youngster.

Should I worry about a child committing suicide after a family death?
Although uncommon, there are signals no parent dare miss when it comes to an extreme reaction to grief . . . especially among adolescents.

My child has been yelling, slamming doors, and storming off. How do I cope?
Discover why anger is a common reaction to grief . . . and how to help a child channel these normal feelings into constructive activities.

My child has become the "perfect" kid. Should I be concerned?
Yes. Find out how this behavior may be a mask for depression and anxiety or may predict an increased risk of alcohol or drug abuse.

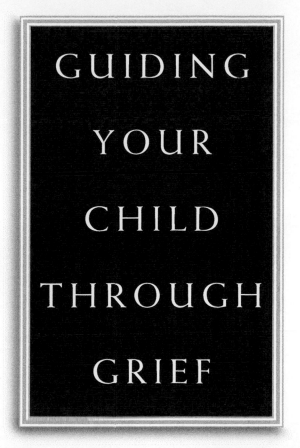

GUIDING

YOUR

CHILD

THROUGH

GRIEF

MARY ANN EMSWILER,
M.A., M.P.S.
&
JAMES P. EMSWILER,
M.A., M.ED.

BANTAM BOOKS
NEW YORK TORONTO LONDON SYDNEY AUCKLAND

GUIDING YOUR CHILD THROUGH GRIEF
A Bantam Book / August 2000

Book design by Glen M. Edelstein.

Library of Congress Cataloging-in-Publication Data

Emswiler, Mary Ann.
Guiding your child through grief / Mary Ann Emswiler and James P. Emswiler.
p.   cm.
Includes index.
ISBN 978-0-553-38025-5
1. Grief in children.   2. Grief in adolescence.   3. Bereavement in children.
4. Bereavement in adolescence.   5. Loss (Psychology) in children.   6. Loss (Psychology) in
adolescence.   7. Children and death.   8. Teenagers and death.   9. Child rearing.
I. Emswiler, James P.   II. Title.

BF723.G75 E57 2000
155.9′37′083—dc21   00-023645

Published simultaneously in the United States and Canada

Bantam Books are published by Bantam Books, a division of Random House, Inc. Its trade-
mark, consisting of the words "Bantam Books" and the portrayal of a rooster, is Registered in
U.S. Patent and Trademark Office and in other countries. Marca Registrada. Bantam Books,
New York, New York.

PRINTED IN THE UNITED STATES OF AMERICA

To Pat, Greg, and Kate
with all our love

CONTENTS

GUIDING

YOUR

CHILD

THROUGH

GRIEF

Chapter 1

WILL MY CHILD BE OKAY?

BOTH OF US WROTE THIS BOOK, BUT IT BEGAN WITH JIM'S STORY. Here it is in his own words:

June 24, 1989, was a beautiful summer morning with the sweet smell of flowers in the air. Our family had just completed a stressful week as we had gone through the death, wake, and funeral of my father-in-law. This was the first death of a loved one for my children. They adored their grandfather and would miss his bear hugs and tenderness and guidance. As they peered at his lifeless body at the wake and joined in the prayers at the funeral, I could see them struggle with this new concept, death.

Little did they know just how deep and long-lasting that struggle would be.

The day after the funeral, we climbed into the car for the one-hour drive home. My wife, Mary, sat next to me, and our eleven-year-old,

Greg, and our eight-year-old, Katie, were in the backseat. Patrick, our fourteen-year-old, had gone home with a friend the night before.

As we drove down the highway, I told Mary about a potential job promotion, which would mean more income for us but also more travel and time away from the family for me. I asked her what she thought about the idea, but she didn't respond. I glanced over and saw her head cocked back. I thought she had a bloody nose and asked if she was all right. When she still didn't respond, I knew something was terribly wrong. She just stared at the ceiling, her body stiff, the fingers of her left hand opening and closing as if to communicate in some way. I shouted, "Hold on, Mary!" and floored it. Mary kept breathing in and breathing in until she could hold no more air within her. And then she exhaled deeply—the same ghostly exhale I had seen her father take just a few days before. The kids screamed from the backseat, "What's wrong, Dad? What's wrong?!" Mary slumped onto my shoulder, and a single tear fell slowly down her left cheek.

I pulled off the highway and into a hotel parking lot. Someone called an ambulance while I performed mouth-to-mouth resuscitation, thinking this had to be some kind of absurd nightmare. But there was no pulse and no heartbeat in my wife's limp body. A doctor and nurse came out of the hotel and began CPR on Mary until the ambulance arrived. The paramedics pulled out the defibrillator and revived her silent heart. But it was too late. That silent heart, now revived, was twice its normal size when it gave out. Mary would be able to live with the help of tubes and machines, but she was brain-dead.

The day after Mary's heart attack, the doctor informed me that there was no hope of recovery for Mary. I gathered myself together as best I could, then went home to get the kids. I brought them to the hospital, and we stood around Mary's bed, the sound of air being pumped into her lungs echoing in our ears. What I did next was the most difficult thing I have ever done in my life. I looked down at our three children, their innocent faces shivering with fear, their arms gripping my legs as tightly as they could. I took a deep breath and somehow the words came out: "Your mom's not going to make it. She's going to die."

The outburst of primal wails that followed seemed to last forever. We just stood there as a wounded family and let the tears flow and gush until there was nothing left inside. Each child then walked over to Mary, kissed her on the cheek, and said, "Good-bye, Mommy. I love you."

Their aunt escorted them out of the room; I remained behind as the nurse disconnected the life-support system. I looked down at Mary, and I looked deep within myself; both looks were stares of disbelief. My thirty-nine-year-old wife of eighteen years and the mother of our three wonderful kids was dead.

I walked out of the room and down the hospital hallway. I had never felt so alone. I remember that moment as if it were yesterday. I will never forget it, never.

Mary had no apparent medical problems, nor had she complained of any difficulties. Her health had seemed as perfect as our life. We both had good jobs, a home in the suburbs, three children, two cars, and a strong 401(k). In sixty seconds on June 24, 1989, however, my life and the lives of my children changed forever. In a matter of moments, I went from being a husband to a widower, from sharing the responsibilities of raising children to being a single parent. Before, I had been a sales manager, traveling up and down the East Coast; afterward, I left that position to take care of my three young ones. In a matter of moments, my world turned upside down.

As deep as my pain was at losing Mary, it spiraled even lower whenever I thought about my children. They were so young and would have to grow up without a mom. No mother would hold them or tuck them in at night, no mom would cook for them or shop for clothes that matched. My thoughts jumped ahead to the junior prom, graduation from high school, choosing a college, getting married, and having babies—all without their mother to help them and guide them. This was not what I had planned.

But I have discovered since then that life is no more a trip to be planned than grief is a problem to be solved. Both are journeys to be traveled. And what a journey it has been.

A few years after Mary died, I remarried. A mutual friend had introduced me to Mary Ann, and we all went to the theater one evening. After the play, I offered to drive Mary Ann home. "But first," I told her, whipping out coupons from my shirt pocket, "I need to stop at the grocery store to pick up a few things for the kids' breakfast." How rusty I was at the dating game—what an outstanding romantic overture! Fortunately, Mary Ann thought it was amusing to grocery-shop at eleven-thirty P.M. No doubt she realized that I was a man who could introduce her to new experiences in life!

And she was right. When we married in 1991, Mary Ann, a business executive, entered a family with two teenage boys and one preteen girl who had experienced the sudden, untimely death of their mother.

As Jim walked down the hospital corridor after Mary died, the first thought that entered his mind was: "Will my kids be okay?" The looks on his three children's faces as they learned about their mother's death were nothing short of traumatic. Would this experience—so sudden and so unnatural—ruin their lives forever?

For both of us, the question of how to help children through grief became a driving passion. Soon after we married, we both left our jobs in the corporate world to found the New England Center for Loss and Transition, a nonprofit organization dedicated to helping those who grieve the loss of a loved one, particularly children.

After Mary died, Jim had discovered that many mental health professionals knew little about issues of grief and loss. When he talked to one therapist about his feelings, she said, "I'd like to help you more, but I really don't know very much about grief and loss." Another family counselor, who did stimulate some useful communication among family members, told Jim the same thing.

When we opened the center, most of our direct service work focused on bereavement counseling and support groups for adults. Jim's personal tragedy and our own experience of raising three grieving children quickly attracted a number of young widows and widowers, in their thirties and forties, seeking counsel. We listened to these parents and shared stories with them. Grateful for the help and support they received, nearly every parent raised the same concern: "This is really helpful for me as I work on my grief, but what about my kids? Do you have anything that will help them?"

In the summer of 1994, we asked two other therapists to join us in creating a children's grief support program. Similar groups that already existed at that time were the excellent program at the Dougy Center in Portland, Oregon; the Center for Grieving Children in Portland, Maine; and Fernside in Cincinnati. In the spring of 1995, modeling our program on what we saw as the best aspects of each, we opened The Cove, a program for grieving children and their families in Guilford, Connecticut. Six families initially signed up, and by the end of the year, the original group had grown to more than seventy-five. As the program expanded, other mental health professionals used our model to start Coves in other parts of the state. Within four years, that little program with six families in Guilford had grown to six sites serving hundreds of grieving children and their parents.

The need for such programs is great. Approximately 38,000 children under the age of eighteen have experienced the death of a parent in the state of Connecticut alone. Nationwide, an estimated 3.5 million grieving children are struggling to make sense of the frightening new world created by the loss of a parent.

In the past seven years at the center, we have worked with countless grieving parents and children, and the lessons we have learned from them as well as from our own personal experience constitute the heart of this book. These chapters are the result of years of the pain and promise, trial and error, failure and success in raising grieving children.

THE FIRST PRIORITY

Most parents of grieving children share the same immediate pressing concern that Jim felt: *Will my child be okay?* As one young widow, whose husband had died two months earlier, said to us, "Death has already taken my husband from me. I don't want it to suck the life from my children as well."

When a family experiences a death, it is natural for the parent or parents to be concerned about the children first. She wants to protect her children and shelter them from pain and fear. She wants to take it away, "replay the tape," and return to life as it was before this tragedy took place. But she can't. So she looks for ways to help her children get through it in the best way possible.

The parents' concern is often so strong that they will put their own grief on hold until they're satisfied that their kids will get through the crisis. Many parents of grieving children have told us that the second year after the spouse died was worse than the first year. A young widower joined our support group eighteen months after his wife died of cancer. "I thought I really had it together," he told the group on the first night. "I more or less sailed through the first year after Sharon died. No stages of grief, no major depressions. I missed her a lot, but I didn't feel destroyed by her death. Everyone was telling me how terrible the holidays would be and how hard the anniversary of her death would be, but they really weren't that bad. I had one focus and one focus only during that first year: that my kids weren't going to be damaged by this. I worked day and night to make sure everything would be the same as it was before Sharon died. When the anniversary of her death arrived, I breathed a sigh of relief and said, 'We made it!' I had achieved the goal of keeping the ship sailing smoothly. My kids were going to be fine. But as soon as I breathed that sigh of relief, an overwhelming feeling of pain hit me like a ton of bricks; my own grief just leveled me. It's like Sharon just died, and I've just realized it."

Will your own child be okay?

To answer that question, we need to define what *okay* means. If it means "returned to normal," to the way life was before your spouse or child died, the answer is no. Your child's life will not be the same. *Your* life will not be the same. And the life of your family will not be the same. Death changes individuals and families forever. But just because life will never be the same doesn't mean you will never again have happiness or joy or pleasure. You will, as impossible as that may seem now.

If *okay* means "coming through the experience of grief without serious damage to physical, mental, emotional, and spiritual well-being," the answer is maybe. Many factors determine this outcome. The child whose parents have both died in an auto accident and is sent to live with relatives in a community filled with gangs and drugs is less likely to come through it "okay" than the child whose parent has died of cancer and is surrounded by caring family and friends. And how a child experiences and copes with grief often depends on his coping skills before the death occurred.

The reason parents worry so deeply about whether their children will be okay after the death of a loved one is that most feel like they've landed in foreign territory. When you had your first child, you may have prepared for parenting by reading Dr. Spock, Dr. Brazelton, or other child-care experts. But when a death occurs in a family, there hasn't been much written to help you.

"When Bud died," Florence told the other parents at The Cove, "I felt so alone and insecure. Up until then, I thought I was doing a good job of raising my boys. If I ever had questions or concerns about their behavior, I'd just ask my friends how they would handle the situation.

But if I have a question about how the kids are reacting to their father's death, I have nowhere to turn. None of my friends have had a spouse die, and when I ask them a question, they just tell me I should go to a counselor."

Advice on helping children process grief *is* available. With knowledge and attention from their parent or caregiver, children can get through this painful, scary experience and, in many cases, become stronger as a result. The purpose of *Guiding Your Child Through Grief* is to give parents, grandparents, and other caregivers the skills and techniques to help children cope with the death of a family member in a healthy way over the months and years ahead.

Guiding Your Child Through Grief focuses on children who are grieving for a parent or sibling, but its suggestions also apply to those grieving for a grandparent, other relative, a friend, or even a pet. Even though children's grief arises from a variety of causes—accidents, chronic illness, suicide, homicide—many feelings of loss are similar. By understanding how children grieve and what you can do to help them, you can help make sure your grieving child will be okay in the best sense.

Here's what you'll find in the chapters that follow.

Chapters 2 and 3 focus on how children grieve. When a loved one dies, children experience many of the same feelings that adults do: fear, anger, sadness, and confusion. But the key difference is in how children comprehend death and the way they express their grief. Chapter 2 explains how grief is expressed at every stage of childhood development and how children grieve in their own way and in their own time. It also explores the ways in which children revisit their grief throughout their lives. Chapter 3 examines the way kids feel, describing the variety of emotions that children may have, and the way they express their feelings through their behavior. Here, you will find several approaches for figuring out what's going on inside your child.

When a death occurs, the entire family structure changes, not just the individuals. Chapter 4 illustrates this shift in family dynamics and offers helpful insights for parents as they redefine the structure. We've identified three goals of grieving families and suggest how you can fulfill them, as well as describe six key factors that affect how well a family copes with a death.

In our own personal and professional experience, we have identified five challenges that children face in order to heal from their loss and move forward with their lives. Chapter 5 describes these challenges and gives parents concrete methods of helping their children meet them.

Chapter 6 provides specific guidance on discussing death and grief with children. Perhaps the most important aspect of processing children's grief is communication. This chapter shows how to communicate both verbally and nonverbally with a grieving child now and in the future. It explains how to get kids to talk about their feelings and what to do if a child never talks about the loss.

A century ago, when a death occurred in a family, grandparents, uncles, aunts, and other members of the extended family would gather to provide support for the widow or widower and the children for months or even years. Today, with the extended family spread out across the country, it is less likely that they will be able to offer a supportive presence over the long term. Instead, a grieving family today often relies upon the local community for support. Friends, teachers, coaches, Scout leaders, and members of religious congregations can form a "holding community" to keep the family stable and secure during the months of intense grief. Chapter 7 offers suggestions for finding and using holding communities as your family grieves. It also describes children's grief support programs and how to know if a group is right for your child.

Some of the most difficult times for grieving families are holidays and other special days during the year. Parents often wonder how to help bereaved children celebrate these special days. In Chapter 8, we explain why the holidays appear to be so difficult and offer tips to help you and your child cope with them in an appropriate way. We also explain the power of rituals for children and list some practical rituals that you can use for holidays, birthdays, and anniversaries.

Chapter 9 concentrates on adolescents and grief. Beyond childhood but not yet adults, teenagers often grieve alone because parents don't know how to treat them as mourners. Adolescence is a tumultuous stage of development in and of itself; losing a loved one can make life even more confusing for both teens and parents. In this chapter, we address the question we hear most often from parents of teens, "How do we know if his behavior is a phase of adolescence or a grief reaction?" We then describe the six needs of grieving teens and suggest practical methods of helping them through their grief.

How do you know whether your child's behavior is the result of normal grieving or he needs some extra help from a professional? Chapter 10 takes a look at when grief goes wrong and what you can do about it. It examines the risk factors for complicated mourning and lists twelve signs of grief gone wrong—signs that you can watch for and act upon before they become more serious. We suggest how to choose a mental health professional if the need arises.

How does the loss of a parent or sibling affect a child over the years ahead? She will certainly change, but will that change be positive or negative? Two factors appear to make the difference: a child's resilience and her interpretation of what happened. Chapter 11 explores the long-term effects of childhood grief and presents the latest research from experts who have been studying this impact over the years.

If you are considering remarriage, either now or in the future, we share in Chapter 12 our professional advice and personal wisdom on stepparenting a grieving child. There *is* a difference between stepparenting after a divorce and stepparenting after a death in the family. Knowing the difference and knowing what to expect and how to respond can be crucial to the well-being of your family. We offer practical strategies for stepparenting a grieving family. This is a wealth of information you won't find anywhere else. We know; we've tried.

Parents of grieving children are often so concerned about their kids' well-being that they neglect their own. But it has been our experience that parents who don't take care of themselves can't take care of their kids. In Chapter 13, we present ten tips for self-care and a personal checklist to indicate whether you might benefit from some outside help.

Chapter 14 includes questions that parents of grieving children frequently ask. Chances are, they are questions that you have asked as well, or may ask in the future—questions such as how to explain cremation, heart attacks, suicide, murder, and the death of a pet.

Little did Jim know when he turned to his kids in the hospital and told them, "Your mom's not going to make it; she's going to die," that that ending was also a beginning. It was the beginning of a new, mysterious life—frightening at some times, peaceful at others, but always educational.

It is that education that we share with you in this book. We offer you all the insights and lessons we learned from the grieving children and families with whom we've worked and from our own grieving family. We share the pain, the joy, the heartache, and the wonders of raising a grieving child.

This book presents the latest research and advice from the world's finest bereavement experts. It also includes the stories and struggles of the grieving parents and children who continue to live their lives with courage and inspiration. They know that there's nothing they can do about the past, but that there is much they can do about the future.

And so can you. Read the pages that follow and begin to shape your future and the future of your grieving child. Learn all you can about how children grieve and how you can help them confront the challenges they face. By doing so, you can rest assured that your grieving child will be okay.

Chapter 2

HOW CHILDREN GRIEVE

A year or so after my husband died, my ten-year-old son began to "act out" at school. The teacher wanted to discipline him, our pediatrician wanted to medicate him, and the school psychologist wanted to evaluate him. I was just confused. What does it all mean?

—Shannon, 39 years old

F ORTY-FIVE-YEAR-OLD ADAM* HAD FINALLY FOUND HIS DREAM job: selling heavy machinery internationally. He thrived on the challenge and the opportunity to travel in countries he'd only read about. His e-mails to friends glowed with happiness. Family photographs reflected his renewed zest for life. So his wife, Donna, didn't understand when she received a call two days before Thanksgiving saying that Adam had died in Belgium from an overdose of Valium. "Was he feeling too stressed out?" Donna wondered in anguish. "I know sometimes he'd take an over-the-counter stimulant because of all the time changes. Did he take too much Valium to help him sleep? Was he depressed and hiding it from us? Did we miss something? We'll never know, but the questions haunt me."

Over time, as Adam's children responded to his death in surprising ways, the confusion mounted. Joe, an eighteen-year-old freshman

* Names and circumstances of the case study subjects in this book have been changed to protect their privacy.

who'd received a hockey scholarship to the college of his dreams, decided to return home and commute to a nearby state school. He spent most of his time with his old girlfriend, a high school senior, and with his family. Sixteen-year-old Andrew, whom Donna described as a "dedicated couch potato," signed up for both the school play and the town's spring soccer league. "We never see him," Donna commented. And Marcie, at eleven, hounded her mother to take her to a local support group for grieving kids.

"What do I do with all this?" Donna asked. "I'm not really concerned with Marcie. She seems to have found a place with other kids who are grieving. She says she feels like she fits in there and can really talk—which is what she does all the time anyway! Sometimes I think I should just permanently attach the telephone to her ear." Donna paused, reflecting.

"But I wonder if I should have let Joe return home," she continued. "He seems to be moving backward instead of forward. And although I'm glad Andrew's exercising—we always tried to get him to do that, as he keeps pointing out—it seems like too much. Should I force him to slow down? Is he just avoiding dealing with it all? Meanwhile, I don't want to do *anything*. I feel like we're in a quicksand of sadness, and the more we try to climb out, the more we're sucked down into it. We're just walking through the world like zombies. I'd just as soon take the phone off the hook or run away."

Grief, Donna was learning, expresses itself in a multitude of ways, as her children mourn Adam's death differently from one another and from their mother. Each child's grief pattern produces a different set of responses. But before we examine these differences, let's consider what the experience of grief has in common for all children.

A CHILD'S GRIEF

Contrary to what others may tell you, your child will experience many of the same thoughts and emotions as you. She'll be sad, and she'll cry—although she may not let you see it. She'll worry about this new set of circumstances. She'll be angry and lonely and preoccupied, just as you are.

The difference is that she's still a child. She lacks your adult skills for understanding, coping with, and expressing what she's going through. She feels even less in control of her world than you do. Thus, she'll handle and work through her grief differently from you.

A child's process of mourning differs from that of an adult in eight specific ways.

YOUR CHILD'S GRIEF REFLECTS HIS CURRENT STAGE OF DEVELOPMENT

Even at four years of age, Josh was very clear: He did *not* want to attend his grandfather's wake. Finally, after his parents made several attempts to learn why, the reason came out. He was scared to view his grandpa's body because he had been told, "We've lost the head of the family." At four, Josh's thinking was literal—he thought he'd see his grandfather without a head, and that prospect frightened him too much.

Young children are still trying to figure out how the world works, and now they must also struggle to understand the death of a loved one. Even adults struggle with that, so consider how hard it must be for your child, with her limited life experiences and cognitive development. Depending on her age, she may not quite grasp concepts such as *cancer* or *heart attack* or *soul* or *forever*. Nor does she necessarily have the words to express what she is feeling or the emotional ability to understand feelings like regret, ambivalence, numbness, or even sorrow.

Your child's grief reaction will also be colored by what's important to him at this stage of life. Three-year-olds often feel anxious when their parents leave for a night out. A *grieving* three-year-old may struggle even more with that situation, since someone dear to him has left and never come back. He may fear that you'll do the same. By contrast, while your grieving adolescent may want to know where you're going when you leave to attend another child's sporting event or go on a camping trip, she'll usually cope just fine without you. In fact, she may enjoy the freedom! But since teens seek peer acceptance, she may struggle more with feeling different, since she may be the only teenager she knows who's grieving. She may crave a chance to talk with kids her own age who are immersed in the same pain she is.

The following sections describe common thoughts of grieving children at various developmental stages.

Grief in infancy Some people mistakenly equate not understanding with not grieving. "Thankfully," they'll say, "she's too little to understand her mommy's gone. She'll be spared that pain." But as any mother who has nursed can tell you, even very young infants know when something's wrong. They know when Mom's upset—and they won't nurse when she is.

Babies know their parents by their smell, the sound of their voice, the way they hold them. They know the rhythms of the day. They know what responses they can count on when they coo or cry.

So as you grieve the death of someone you love, your baby notices. Maybe you're more quiet with her, or a little less playful. Perhaps you have less time to spend with her, or you respond more slowly to her crankiness. Her schedule changes. Such small changes, inevitable as they are, matter enormously to infants.

Your baby also experiences a sense of "gone-ness" that's simply baffling. Without being able to articulate it, he notices that that deeper voice, that scratchy beard, that "bouncer" is no longer around.

So yes, infants grieve. Their world, as they know it, isn't the same. The "rules" they've come to rely on no longer work the same way; nor does the world feel as safe or as comforting. You may notice your baby "grieving" with changes in eating, bowel, or bladder habits. She may fall asleep earlier or later, wake up more often, or nap more or less frequently. Your normally contented baby may be less easy to soothe for a time or be less responsive and playful than usual. She may be less tolerant of being passed around among "strange" adults and may fuss until you hold her again.

Two- to six-year-olds Sandy's husband, Rick, died after two years of intense cancer treatment. "At least we saw it coming," Sandy told a friend at the early December wake. "We had time to say everything we wanted to say. We were able to enjoy Richie together, and we prepared him as best we could."

Richie, at three, talked about death a lot. So it shocked some people at the wake when Richie bounced up to Sandy and said, "Mommy, Daddy's dead, right?"

"Yes, honey, he is," Sandy replied, stooping down to eye level.

"So when will he take me to see the trains this year?" Richie asked.

"Honey, he can't. His body doesn't work anymore, remember?" Sandy continued.

"But he'll be home for Christmas, won't he?"

Sandy winced. She had just come up against Richie's "three-year-old-ness." Despite her best efforts to explain to her son what happened, there were just some aspects of death that Richie was not going to grasp at his age.

Compare telling a child about death to teaching a baby to walk. We stand our babies on their feet, holding their hands, and move their legs through walking motions. But no matter how often we do this, the baby can't walk until his little body is ready and able to. Still, it's important to exercise their muscles as training for the day when they are ready. Similarly, understanding death develops over time, as we continue to talk about it and as children develop the mental readiness to understand.

Dr. David Schonfeld, an associate professor at Yale University School of Medicine, observes that preschoolers struggle with three key concepts.[1] The first is what he terms the "nonfunctionality" of the body: kids need to learn that death means the body doesn't work anymore. Death is not, as young children sometimes believe, being a little "less alive." It means bodies don't feel, hearts don't beat, lungs don't breathe, eyes don't see, ears don't hear, and so on.

The second concept is that death is final. Little ones, like Richie, think death is reversible, that dead people can return to the land of the living. After all, isn't that what we sometimes see on television? Wile E. Coyote gets smashed by an anvil and, seconds later, pops back up.

Third, children need to learn that death is universal. Everybody dies. But little ones may think death is like an accident: people can live forever if they are very careful.

As they struggle with these concepts, preschoolers are concrete and literal in their thinking. They may open a window so that Mom or Dad can hear their prayers "up in heaven." If the legs of your loved one are covered by the casket cover, your preschooler may ask, "What did they do with the legs?" What he sees, what he hears, is what exists to him.

Further, your preschooler still grapples with separating fantasy from reality—what he has power over from what he doesn't. Child development specialists often describe preschoolers as egocentric magical thinkers. Preschoolers believe that if they think something, it will happen.

As a result, death may cause a lot of confusion for your child. "Why would Daddy die if I didn't want him to?" he may ask. Or more poignantly, he ponders, often in silence, *If I wished Mommy dead, did I kill her?*

Six- to nine-year-olds Between six and nine years of age, your child will begin to understand that death is final and permanent, although she still may not grasp her own vulnerability to it. Unless she's experienced the death of a classmate or a young sibling, she may still believe that death happens only to "older people." (And "older" generally means anyone who's not a child. In kids' minds, we parents are ancient!)

At this age, many children think of death as something physical—as a spirit, perhaps. Often it's something violent—a burglar or ghost that comes to get you. Or it's something bad—a punishment for bad behavior.

Some six-to-nine-year-olds think death is contagious, that you can "catch" it from another child who has experienced a death in his family. So your child may be shunned or teased by classmates who believe this.

Also at this age, children are fascinated by the biological details of death. One nine-year-old described to an adult friend all the tubes in her mom's body before she died, as well as the color of the bodily fluids passing through them. Your child may want to know the specifics about cremation, how bodies decay, embalming, and the like.

As difficult as it may be for you to discuss these details, honesty is usually the best policy. If no one answers your child's questions, he'll fill in the answers with his imagination—and a child's imagination can conjure up ideas that are far scarier than reality. Death education should be like sex education. If your seven-year-old asks how babies are born, you can answer his question simply, without discussing foreplay or conception—information for which he may be developmentally unprepared. You can answer his questions about death simply as well.

Of course, you'll want to make sure your child understands what *dead* means (that the body doesn't work anymore—no feeling, no seeing, no breathing) before you explain subjects like cremation or embalming.

Further, it's best to follow your child's lead, supplying her with only the details she's asked about. Finally, remember that it's okay to say, "I don't know. Let's go find out together." (In Appendix A, we list several excellent resources on death facts. A funeral director, one who can discuss such subjects on a child's wavelength, is a good source of information as well. See also Chapter 14.)

Ten- to thirteen-year-olds Between the ages of ten and thirteen, most children begin thinking more abstractly. Your child now knows what *dead* means, that everyone dies, and that death is irreversible. Now he'll struggle with *why* it happens. He's learning, in a more profound way, the rules about how the world works (and much to our chagrin as parents, he's challenging them).

As a result, he'll experiment with ideas and theories about death. Is death a way to get rid of people in order to make room for the new ones? Is it true, as Aunt Matilda said, that every time there's a birth, there's a death, or that death comes in threes?

Your child will also consider how death affects relationships. He'll say and understand things like "Grandpa won't be able to take me fishing anymore."

Children in this age group may now identify more strongly with adults of their own gender. They may tap into spoken or unspoken cultural rules about how men are "supposed" to grieve (by themselves, quietly, strongly, without tears) or how women are "supposed" to do it (with others, with tears, taking care of others). Lines like "big boys don't cry" may force a young boy into a terrible choice: to deny his feelings or to deny being "one of the guys." Girls may learn to take care of others at the expense of taking care of themselves. But although your child may be influenced by what others say, what you encourage and demonstrate at home still carries the most weight. (We discuss more specific differences between the grief of boys and girls in Chapter 14.)

Teens and grief Adolescents think about death the way adults think about death—in some respects. They understand death intellectually, even though they may still feel invincible. So instead of struggling with the basics of death, your teenager is probably struggling with life's larger questions: *Why do bad things happen to good people? Why me?* Yet he's still a child. Adolescent mourning, which mixes both child and adult types of responses, can be complicated, so we've dedicated Chapter 9 to the topic.

CHILDREN GRIEVE IN THE MIDDLE OF EVERYDAY LIFE

You've probably already noticed that children don't grieve on cue, when we expect or want them to, when it would be convenient for us, or when everyone else is grieving. Children grieve in the course of their daily lives, when something triggers their grief and when they feel safe enough to express it.

What triggers grief? It could be seeing all the other dads at a sports event, making a card or gift for a parent in school, hearing about the illness of another parent or friend's sibling, or just a fleeting memory. Whatever the reason, grief washes over your child, and it can be pretty scary for her.

She'll also wonder if her parents can accept and hold her in her grief. Often the key factor in whether a child feels safe enough to grieve is whether the adults around her can tolerate it. Many kids shy away from talking to their parents about their grief. Why? It's a survival strategy. Unconsciously, your child may worry that if she talks about the death, you may fall apart. And if you fall apart, then who will take care of *her*? No, many grieving kids reason, it's better not to talk about this grief stuff with Mom or Dad.

That's one reason why children may be more able to express their grief in school settings. Many kids sense that a particular teacher or coach can tolerate whatever they have to say about their grief. This points to the importance of *holding communities*, other adults who can support a grieving child, which we discuss in Chapter 7.

If a child does talk to her parent about her grief, she may do so in a specific setting that feels safe—at night, perhaps, in the quiet of her own room and her own bed, or perhaps during the lulling safety of a long car ride.

GRIEF IN KIDS COMES OUT IN BRIEF BUT INTENSE "EPISODES"

When twelve-year-old Caitlin's parents died in a car crash, her grandmother Rose dreaded telling her the news. She waited until Caitlin returned from school, put her arm around her grandchild, and then, crying a bit herself, told Caitlin what had happened. As Rose expected, Caitlin began sobbing. But after a few minutes, Caitlin wiped her eyes and asked, "Can I go over to Jessica's?"

Rose hesitated before saying yes, because she was confused. Part of Rose felt relieved: *Maybe kids* are *resilient,* she thought, *and maybe the loss wouldn't be so bad for Caitlin after all.* But she also felt angry. Both of the girl's parents had died, and all she could think about was playing with a friend? How selfish!

What Rose didn't understand is that Caitlin's reaction was perfectly normal. Children dip in and out of grief. They know how much pain they can tolerate at any given moment, and when they reach their limit, they simply shut it off and do something else. This defense mechanism is a healthy way for them to pace themselves through their grief.

As adults, we react similarly. We distract ourselves with television, or we take a nap, or we change the subject. Perhaps we are simply less abrupt and more gracious about it than children are.

There's bad news and good news about this aspect of your child's grief. The bad news is that when a grief spasm hits, the extent of the pain your child is experiencing will probably blow you away. It's hard to watch. The good news is that the grief spasm will be brief. If you can be present and help your child to feel his pain without running away from it, this too *will* pass. And every time your child lets those feelings of grief run their course, he will be that much closer to healing.

Elaine Gustafson, an instructor at Yale School of Nursing, shared this story with us. One morning as a four-year-old girl headed down a staircase with her mother, she looked up at her mom and asked, "Mommy, why did Grandma have to die?" At the *bottom* step, while her mom was still struggling to formulate an answer, the little girl piped up again: "And Mommy," she asked, "how do they put the air in the air conditioner?"

SOMETIMES CHILDREN TEMPORARILY REGRESS AFTER A DEATH

Three-year-old Jeremy had just been toilet-trained when his dad died of a heart attack. Months later, he reverted to diapers for a short period.

Sometimes even twelve-year-olds periodically suck their thumbs for a while after a death. Normally independent children may turn clingy, and articulate kids may start stuttering. Your child may become possessive again, "forgetting" temporarily how to share her toys. She may want you to feed or dress her again. Night-lights may become a standard room accessory once more. Older kids, who normally spend their free time with numerous activities, may want to spend more time with the family, just hanging around. Grieving adolescents may resurrect crayons and coloring books or pick fights with brothers or sisters whom they normally would protect. Even college-age kids may regress, hanging out with younger kids or returning to prior hobbies or activities. One of our kids slept with a particular stuffed duck and baby blanket until late adolescence, taking them off to college along with a credit card and a stereo system.

Rather than see regression as a problem, think of it as taking a break from grief. For a while, your child is using behavior to return to a time in his life when things seemed safer and less complicated, a time when Mom and Dad took care of him completely.

Regressing can also be a legitimate cry for more attention. After all, most grieving parents juggle many balls, and your child may need more than you have to give at a particular moment. Regressing may be a way for your child to refocus you on *her* needs for a time.

CHILDREN EXPRESS THEIR GRIEF IN THEIR ACTIONS

Emily, at nine, loved coming to The Cove, because meeting with other kids who'd lost a family member was comforting to her. The grief support program offered art projects and games, each designed to encourage grieving kids to express what the experience was like for them; it also gave Emily a chance to discuss the death of her dad with kids her own age. And she enjoyed the focused time she spent with her mother during the family activity and snack. But one Sunday before the meeting, Emily's mom found her etching designs into the wooden kitchen tabletop with a pen.

That wasn't like Emily, so her mom pulled her close and asked her what was wrong. Emily, it turned out, had been etching almost absent-mindedly while she thought about The Cove. As much as she loved The Cove, she told her mom, it was still scary sometimes to talk about her grief. So like an adult who, when nervous, unconsciously grinds his teeth, clicks a pen, or doodles heavily on a pad of paper, Emily used her pen and the kitchen table to act out her anxiety. Once Emily's mother knew her daughter was anxious, she helped her find less destructive ways to express it.

Emily was fortunate to have a mother so insightful and so patient with her grief process. But even if you're less philosophical about such things, simply understanding can help you remain calm.

As adults, we often talk out our grief or simply think about what's happening. But young children don't have the verbal skills or mental abilities necessary for those methods of coping. Instead, they "act out" their grief, either through play or through interacting with other people (which we discuss in the next chapter).

Sometimes your child's play may seem odd or even eerie to you. For example, children often play "dead" by lying quietly, arms stiff and body rigid on a bed, or they play "buried," by covering each other in sand. Your child may also play "funeral" or "hospital" or "emergency room." Such play is a way of figuring out what has happened, of trying to understand it, much like a child who plays school at three or four in order to get a sense of what that experience is all about.

Understanding, for most of us, is power. It makes us feel more in control. It helps us feel safe. It helps us feel normal in the midst of an experience that would otherwise make us feel as if we were going crazy.

As a parent or caregiver, if you understand and expect behaviors like playing dead, you'll feel less queasy when you see them in your child. Try to be patient, and use those occasions as a catalyst for talking about death. By talking about it, you can help your child put words to his experience, helping him master the events of his life.

Children act out their *feelings* of grief as well. Anger, for example, a normal grief reaction, might surface as teasing or as seemingly unreasonable outbursts, complete with yelling, slamming doors, and storming off. Or your child may channel her anger into aggressiveness in sports, playing the drums loudly, pounding clay, or some other physical activity. One lucky mother described how her adolescent daughter's anger came out in a room-cleaning frenzy!

Whatever behavior you see, recognize that it may well mean something significant. If it represents an ongoing issue that jeopardizes the long-term well-being of your child, get extra help for him. If it does not, you may not need to respond at all. Just recognize that whatever you see holds clues to understanding your child more fully.

CHILDREN OFTEN POSTPONE THEIR GRIEF (OR PARTS OF IT)

In the Boston-based Child Bereavement Study, William Worden and Phyllis Silverman followed 70 families and their 125 children who were grieving the death of a parent.[2] Their study found that in many children, grief reactions don't surface until at least the second year after the death. Similarly, when a sibling dies, the surviving siblings may experience behavior changes starting as late as five years after the death, according to Bridie Tracy, cofounder of the southern Connecticut chapter of Compassionate Friends, a nationwide network of support groups for bereaved parents.[3]

Why do kids postpone parts of their grief for so long? Grief can be scary—for adults as well as for children—and your child needs to feel safe before he'll be willing to risk confronting the chaotic thoughts and feelings he carries inside. He needs to know that, when he does, his basic needs will still be taken care of. He needs answers to basic questions: *If Mom dies, who will pack my lunch? Who will take me to Scouts? Who will do the laundry? Will the family still have enough income?* Beyond the practical concerns, he needs to know whether you, the surviving parent, are "strong" enough to make sure his world holds together.

You may feel similar strains in yourself. Many widows and widowers need to complete all the paperwork and set their financial world straight before they can start to deal with their emotions. One young widow, for example, exclaimed in a burst of frustration, "How am I *feeling*? How am I *feeling*?! Who knows and who cares! I can't even figure out how I'm going to buy Pampers for my baby!"

Taking care of the house, the insurance, the hospital and funeral bills, and the will, not to mention the food shopping, the cleaning, and the laundry—all these practical details can overwhelm you, crowding out your grief, at least for a time. Like many grievers, you may need to deal with the chaos *outside* before you can deal with the chaos *inside*.

Adults usually settle many of those details within the first few weeks after the death. At that point, their grief starts to resurface in a more pronounced way. But your grieving child may need a year or two to feel secure again after a parent dies, or two to five years after a brother or sister dies. Only then might he be able to tackle some of the more frightening aspects of his grief—the seemingly bottomless sadness, the anger, the relief, the regrets.

In the meantime, your children may try to avoid reminders of the person who died and refuse any discussion of feelings. Adolescents may become extremely busy, essentially pushing aside their grief with activity. Don't doubt, however, that they are carefully watching *you*. They know intuitively when you're "okay enough" for them to grieve. They sense when *you* can deal with the pain *they* feel inside. They know, somehow, when you'll be able to help. And often they'll wait until that time to grieve.

Of course, as we discuss in Chapter 10, if your child never has any reaction at all to the death or acts as if nothing's changed, you may want to find some extra help for her. But if she is confronting her loss in bite-sized pieces and putting off some parts of her grief for a while, don't worry. That's how kids grieve. They take it at their own pace, in their own time, when they figure they can handle it. Parents can invite them to acknowledge and express what the experience is like for them (doing what grief counselors call *grief work*). But forcing that work on them before they're ready can be scary. It can cause them to clam up even more. Ultimately, it can do more harm than good.

Remember too, as we mentioned before, that children often share different parts of their grief with other people, whom they themselves carefully select. If your child senses that you can't handle his fear or anger, he may talk to a teacher or grandfather instead. You can help him by encouraging him to do so and by educating the other adults in his world so that they're ready for whatever he needs to say.

CHILDREN REGRIEVE WHEN LIFE CHANGES SIGNIFICANTLY FOR THEM

Sometimes you'll be able to predict when your child will revisit her grief: for example, when you move from the house that holds so many memories.

At other times, it will surprise you. For months before our son Greg left for college, our youngest child, Kate, celebrated. She *knew* life would be *so* much better when he left: no more arguments about which television show to watch, no more looking for her shampoo only to realize that Greg had borrowed it, no more debates about whose turn it was to use the phone.

But within a month after Greg left, Kate became extremely sad. He had been a touchstone for her in their high school. His absence at the dinner table meant a *further* shrinkage in her family.

Greg's leaving represented another loss for Kate. And this new loss resurrected the old one. At this time, she revisited her grief over her mother.

Happy events can trigger fresh grief as well. Bar mitzvahs and graduations, for example, call for celebration, but family members may feel a certain sadness that Mom or Dad or a particular brother or sister is not there to applaud as well.

Finally, when a child undergoes a new emotional or mental growth spurt, she'll often regrieve the old loss. She now understands the loss differently. She appreciates its significance more fully. Such changes bring forth new emotions and new grief.

CHILDHOOD GRIEF LASTS THROUGHOUT CHILDHOOD, AND PIECES OF IT LAST INTO ADULTHOOD

When a child experiences the death of a parent or sibling, it's a watershed event. Her life will never be the same. The loss will unquestionably shape her in profound but also sometimes subtle ways, and it will be one of the primary lenses through which she sees and interprets life. (See Chapter 11.)

Nevertheless, you can use the concrete steps suggested in this book to help your child cope with the death. Will these steps enable her to step back in time, to a place where her heart was whole and her world still wonderful? No, that's no longer possible. Will they take away her pain? No, unfortunately not.

But once tragedy strikes, our job as parents is to help our children integrate the tragedy into their life stories in ways that leave them competent, contributing, and compassionate. Our job is to teach them how to choose hope over despair—to choose life in the face of death.

Chapter 3

WHAT GRIEVING CHILDREN

FEEL AND DO

Right after Mom died, I used to wonder why she left us. I mean, didn't she love us? Then later I figured out that it just *happened*—she didn't *mean* to have a stroke. But that was scary too: What if Dad couldn't help it and he died? What would we do then?

—Ben, 14 years old, reflecting on his grief at 7

I S IT NORMAL FOR A GRIEVING CHILD TO . . . ?" PARENTS FREQUENTLY ask us. As adults, we know how *we* feel when we're grieving: scared, angry, relieved, jealous, guilty, lonely, and on and on. We know what *we* do to cope: cry, talk, withdraw from the world, work a lot or as little as possible. But then we watch our kids, hear what they say, and see what they do. If it doesn't match what we expect, we wonder, "Is this okay?"

The truth is that among children, grief reactions vary widely. Basically, though, their responses fall into two categories: what children feel and what children do to express those feelings.

WHAT GRIEVING KIDS FEEL

When a death occurs, children of all ages feel what we feel. Mostly they just express it differently: more with actions than with words. Remember, children are still learning to pick apart and label all those jumbled feelings. It's hard work.

Sometimes it's difficult even for adults, with all of our life experience and coping skills, to decipher what's going on inside of us. Remember the last time you had a falling out with a friend or colleague? Maybe you knew you were mad, but there was more to it than that. Only after thinking and talking about it (and perhaps even sleeping on it) were you able to figure out your feelings and say "I'm hurt," "I'm frustrated," "I'm scared," or "I'm jealous." If *we* sometimes struggle with complex situations, imagine what it must be like for grieving kids. They *feel* all the feelings but have to wrestle with words to express them.

COMMON EMOTIONAL REACTIONS TO DEATH AMONG CHILDREN	
Sadness, sorrow, depression	Apathy, lack of enjoyment,
Fear, insecurity, anxiety	emotional "flatness"
Relief	Powerlessness, helplessness
Ambivalence	Guilt and regret, shame, lowered
Longing, loneliness, alienation,	self-esteem
jealousy	Shock, feelings of unreality
Hypersensitivity, emotional ups	Anger, irritation, impatience,
and downs	frustration

Because you love your child, you hate to see her experience *any* of the emotions identified in the box above. But you may really flinch if she experiences certain feelings: shame, relief, fear, guilt, or anger. No doubt you flinch for a loving reason: You can't stand to see her in so much pain. It's incredibly difficult to watch. But if you deny these feelings in your child in order to make *yourself* more comfortable, then you abandon her and force her to deal with them all by herself. Loving your child means tolerating your own discomfort so that she can heal within the circle of your embrace.

Throughout this book we explore how to respond to these particularly difficult feelings. But for now let's focus on understanding why they occur and a few of the many ways in which each feeling might be expressed.

Sadness, sorrow, depression Of course children feel sad when someone they love dies. Most kids, in the immediate aftermath of the death, show their sadness with tears. According to the Child Bereavement Study, two-thirds of grieving kids cried during the first weeks after the death; but only 13 percent cried after the one-year anniversary of the death.

Some parents report that their children never cry. Early on, they wonder if their child is even sad. How can we reconcile the data with these observations? Kids often tell us they don't like to cry in front of their parents. "My mom says she just wants me to be happy," sixteen-year-old Genna confided one day. "So I cry in my car or when I'm hiking. That way Mom doesn't have to see it."

Some kids cry a lot, some just a little, and some not at all. Regardless, grieving children feel sorrow just as adults do, and their sadness may last long after the crying stops.

You may also see sorrow in your child in any of several other forms: withdrawal from friends or family; eating more or less; a loss of interest in hobbies or school; sighing; waking in the middle of the night or sleeping more or less; or irritation and frustration with other people or situations.

Your child may also try to deal with his sorrow by avoiding reminders of the person who died. Eighteen months after Mary died, we were decorating the Christmas tree when Greg quietly left the room. As we considered his behavior, we realized that many ornaments had a "Mom" story attached: ornaments given when one of the kids was born; Crayola ornaments because she loved crayons; ornaments made by the kids in school and given to her as gifts; and so on. Those stories, which we recalled with laughter and tears while decorating the tree, proved too much for Greg, who chose to avoid the painful reminders.

In our experience, most grieving children ultimately cope well with their sorrow. For a few children, however, grief triggers the illness of depression. While some symptoms of grief and depression are the same, depression is a disease that is best treated by a mental health professional. The guidelines in Chapter 10 can help you to distinguish between grief and depression and to figure out where to go for extra help if the situation calls for it.

Fear, insecurity, anxiety Anxiety shows up in grieving children as often as sadness, according to the Child Bereavement Study. Research on adults comes to the same conclusion: Grief can be terrifying as well as sad. How so? When all your assumptions about how the world works have been shattered, you worry about how you'll get along.

That's probably why your child wants to know your schedule in precise detail: she's fretting over whether you'll be safe, whether you'll come back to care for her. Sixty-two percent of children grieving a parent's death worry that the surviving parent will die as well, according to the Child Bereavement Study. If your child suddenly hounds you to wear your seat belt, to stop smoking, or to eat more healthfully, this may explain why.

Children sometimes also fear for their own health. Josie, a high school junior, came to us four months after her mother's death from uterine cancer. We described to Josie the many reactions that her body might have to such stress. When we noted that menstrual changes can occur, she brightened. "I haven't had a period in three months," she said. "I was afraid I might have uterine cancer too." Clearly, such information is no substitute for a good health exam by a qualified physician, but a health professional's report that there's nothing physically wrong *can* help calm children's fears.

COMMON PHYSICAL REACTIONS TO STRESS AND ANXIETY	
Headaches	Fatigue
Grinding teeth, jaw tightness or pain	Muscle tension
	Cold, clammy hands
Throat tightness, feeling like something is stuck in the throat	Need to urinate frequently
	Shortness of breath
	Dry mouth
Heart palpitations	Neck or shoulder pain
Numb or tingling sensations	Nervous tics
Dizziness, faintness	Tight or heavy chest
Feeling smothered	Sweating
Nausea, diarrhea, or stomach pains	Menstrual changes

Some children fear being abandoned by or separated from their family or friends. If your child is clingy, resists going to school or camp, or wants to sleep with you or a sibling, that may be the reason. Your child may also worry that there won't be enough money to live on and that you'll need to sell the house and move away from the school and friends they know.

Many grieving children go through a period of waiting for the other shoe to drop. It's as if they're thinking, *Now I know that life can be totally unpredictable, so I'd better watch carefully in order to protect myself and the other people in my family.* Sometimes this constant state of vigilance causes grieving children to be distracted, absentminded, and unable to concentrate on whatever task lies at hand. As a result, they may be less productive in school for a time.

Anxiety can also show up as changes in eating (eating more or less), a nervous restlessness or hyperactivity, sleeping more or less, or a tendency to be more easily startled.

Relief We don't often acknowledge any feelings of relief when someone dies. It somehow seems disloyal. If we do express it, others may question our love, we fear. But truthfully, although many of us would give anything to have our loved ones back, certain aspects of life may just be easier without them. You no longer have to discuss with anyone how to raise the kids or how to spend your money. Toothpaste tubes remain capped. Socks end up in the proper place without any effort on your part.

As fifteen-year-old Jake explained, "Sure, I miss Dad. But the pressure's off some now. I don't have to dread every time I bring home a B on my report card. And maybe I can become a firefighter instead of going to college like Dad wanted."

If the person who died in your family struggled with a long illness, you and your children may feel relief that his pain is finally over. As much as you would like to have him back in a healthy state, you may also feel relieved of the stress and physical exertion required to care for him. Many people express relief that they no longer have to go to the hospital every day.

Your child may feel relieved that she no longer has to share a bedroom with a sister who died. She may be glad that Mom and Dad are no longer caught up in caring for a terminally ill child and now will have more time for her. He may be relieved that he no longer has to live up to his older brother's academic or sports reputation or answer to his demands. Old-fashioned, before-death sibling rivalry often becomes unspoken, after-death relief.

Feelings of relief, then, are normal. And in a family that has been struggling (with the normal friction of adolescence, with severe conflict between the parents, with drugs or alcohol use, with physical or sexual abuse, for example), relief comes to the fore even more prominently. A physically abused sixteen-year-old expressed it this way after her father died: "I loved him and I hated him. I miss him, and I'm totally glad he's gone from my life."

Ambivalence One reason relief is so hard to acknowledge when we're grieving is that we mistakenly think that a person can hold only one feeling about someone at a time. Children, because they think in such concrete, black-and-white terms, fall victim to this error even more than adults do. "Either you like me or you don't," a little girl might say on the playground. "You're either *my* friend or you're *her* friend."

Similarly, your grieving child may feel, *Either I loved my dad, or I'm angry with him. Either I loved having him around, or I'm relieved that he's gone.* We need to teach our children that we can have many feelings about the same person all at the same time.

You can teach your child about ambivalence by identifying nongrief situations in which he might have multiple feelings. At the end of a school vacation, he might still enjoy being off school but miss his friends. If your child has a fight with her best friend and they're no longer playing together, you might point out that she's still angry at her friend but bored since she misses her company.

You can also talk about your own mix of feelings. Dixie explained it this way to her kids: "I miss Daddy so much, it hurts sometimes. And I'm angry, too, that he's not here to help me mow the lawn."

Longing, loneliness, alienation, jealousy Like adults, most children long for the dead person to return. "There's a hole in my heart without Duane," explained Timmy, an eight-year-old grieving the death of his twin brother.

Many grieving children feel alienated from friends who have *both* parents or *all* their brothers and sisters. Sometimes, in an attempt to fit in with the other kids, they try to pretend that nothing's happened. They don't want their loneliness to be compounded by problems with their friendships.

And feelings of alienation can be compounded by other kids isolating the grieving child. In elementary school, children may worry that a disease like cancer is contagious and avoid the child whose parent or sibling died of cancer. Preadolescent cliques, searching for any criterion by which to classify peers as "in" or "out," may isolate the grieving child as "different." Teens, as they move away from their parents and identify more with their peers, often attempt to sand down any differences between themselves and other teens: they dress alike, use the same slang, and watch the same TV shows. Unfortunately, "griever status" is not so easily changed.

Out of these feelings of loneliness and alienation, jealousy sometimes grows. "I was jealous that other kids had moms to cheer them on at swim meets, sleep over at Girl Scout campouts and make Halloween costumes," remembers Lila, who is now twenty-three but was nine when her mother died. "In high school, I imagined that everybody *else's* mom was teaching them how to dress so their hips didn't look so big and taking them shopping for prom dresses. Even now, I'm jealous when I see moms and daughters shopping together or having lunch. How would that be if my mom were still around?"

Hypersensitivity, emotional ups and downs After a death, grievers often feel vulnerable. Julio, a twenty-eight-year-old widower, described it as "feeling like my skin had been peeled off." His ten-year-old son, Enrique, said, "It's like everybody's watching me now. I'm living in a glass house, and people are throwing huge rocks at me."

That heightened sense of vulnerability can lead to hypersensitivity, in which the merest slight produces an outburst of anger or tears or withdrawal. Frequently, in both adult and child grievers, emotional lulls follow such outbursts. The grief comes in waves—emotional ups followed by emotional downs.

Apathy, lack of enjoyment, emotional "flatness" In contrast to hypersensitive grievers, some kids mourn in emotional monotones for a short while. They describe this as:

- "It's like the whole world is just gray."

- "I feel empty inside, like there's just this big, hollow room in my body."

- "I wish I could have fun with my friends or even cry—that would be better than this—but I can't. I just don't feel anything."

- "Nothing matters anymore. What difference does it make? Who cares?"

- "Blah, blah, blah, blah, blah—that's what it's like."

Powerlessness, helplessness After her brother collapsed on the basketball court, fourteen-year-old Karin admitted, "I just feel so helpless. I couldn't save T.J., and I can't do anything to make my parents feel better. My friends say, 'Just don't think about it,' but I can't even do that. I can't control my thoughts. They just come in whenever they feel like it."

Like you, perhaps, your child may feel that his world is spinning out of control. Feelings he's never felt before wash over him unexpectedly. People he barely knows—teachers, neighbors, distant relatives—may "intrude," expecting hugs or kisses, demanding to know how he feels, fixing strange meals for him, sometimes even rearranging kitchen cabinets or cleaning out closets without asking. Such behavior may add to your child's anxiety, or it may simply make him angry.

Guilt and regret, shame, lowered self-esteem Regardless of the facts, children often feel that they are responsible for a death in the family. If your child is very young, at that "magical egocentric" age when she thinks the world acts according to her wishes and unspoken thoughts, she may think that wishing someone dead can actually kill them. And the closer in time the thought or wish was to the death, the more likely it is that your child will believe it was her fault.

Further, as with adults, *maybes* and *if onlys* haunt children, causing guilt. "Maybe," we muse, "if only I had . . . then she would still be alive." Family members may contribute to those feelings of guilt if, prior to the death, they used phrases like "you'll be the death of me yet" or "you'll give me a heart attack."

At any age, children search for the reasons for a death. And like the rest of us, they may find it less scary to think that their actions were somehow responsible for the death than to believe that bad things happen randomly in the world or that someone they trust may hold more of the blame. When six-year-old Bobby's little brother climbed out of bed, fell out the window, and died while his mom was changing the new baby's diaper, Bobby felt he was responsible. He should have watched his little brother more carefully. In play therapy, the deeper truth came out. Bobby couldn't afford to believe that his brother's death was simply a tragic accident or that Mom was too distracted. After all, if Mom or Dad could "let" a brother or sister die, then maybe they could "let" him die too.

Guilt manifests itself in many ways. A child may feel so bad about her actions that her school or sports performance suffers. Or she may turn into the "perfect" kid, always polite, always helpful, always looking for ways to "make it right."

If your child feels guilty, she may withdraw from others. *After all,* she may think, *who would want to associate with someone who did something like that?* Or she may take the anger she feels at herself and redirect it against others, becoming aggressive and hostile.

While only some grieving kids feel guilty, almost all grieving kids feel regret. They may know the death wasn't their fault, but they wish the situation could have turned out differently: that the drugs had worked; that the emergency technicians had restored a heartbeat; that the drunken driver had been traveling on a different road.

Even when kids regret something about their own actions, they usually recognize that those actions reflect normal human limitations. "I wish I could have done a tracheotomy like George Clooney on *ER,*" whispered Angel after her brother choked to death at a local fast-food restaurant. "I would have done it. I swear I would. I just didn't know how."

Finally, many children feel regret over words unspoken and experiences that can never be shared. "I just wish my mom could have been there to see me graduate from high school," José said. "She was always pushing me to stay in school, stay in school, because she never got to. I remember being frustrated that she kept saying it. I'd say, '*Okay,*

Mom, I *will*. I *hear* you.' If she could just see me now, she'd be really proud."

Regret, however painful, is not unhealthy. Shame, however, like guilt, is more problematic. While guilt means "I believe I *did* something bad, that my *actions* caused harm," shame means "I *myself* am bad." A shameful person feels, "If I were just a better person, my mom or dad or brother or sister would still be alive."

In our experience, children who feel shame after a death often suffered from poor self-esteem before the death. The fact that Mom or Dad died just reconfirms their own unworthiness. Unconsciously, these children blame themselves for the fact that Mom or Dad "left." Eleven-year-old Desiree knew that her mother often "forgot" to take her medicine for diabetes. When her mom died after falling into a diabetic coma, Desiree reasoned, "If I'd been a better kid, then Mom would have taken her medicine. She would have wanted to stay around and be with me."

Even children with good self-esteem can fall prey to shame after a death. Most often, these are the kids who feel isolated and alienated from their peers, as if there were something wrong with them simply because they come from a grieving family.

If your child is feeling shame, he may exhibit many of the same behaviors as if he were feeling guilty. He may apologize a lot, even when the problems are clearly not his fault. His self-esteem may seem low or may plummet further.

According to the Child Bereavement Study, though, such issues may not show up until the second year after the death. Unfortunately, the research doesn't explain why. Perhaps, over time, kids feel less and less supported and more and more isolated from their peer group. Maybe they feel abandoned by the person who died and eventually start to wonder if that abandonment was because of their own worthlessness. Finally, their inability to prevent the death of someone they love or to influence the consequences may reduce their feelings of self-worth. For whatever reason, grieving children often report lowered self-esteem.

How does lowered self-esteem show up? In addition to the behaviors outlined above, your child may back off from normal challenges, feeling he's not up to the task at hand. He may withdraw from his peer group, believing he no longer fits in. Some children may attempt to prove superiority over their peers through verbal or physical outbursts.

Shock, feelings of unreality Shortly after someone dies, grievers often feel numb or shocked. The new reality just doesn't square with what "ought" to be. "I can't believe it really happened," many grievers say.

When a griever is in shock, the feelings you'd expect after a death—like sadness—sometimes don't surface for a while. That's why wakes are sometimes filled with reminiscing and laughter, and why children, early on, may deny that a death has occurred.

Later on, children may have a heightened sense of unreality. We've heard older kids talk about it in these ways:

• "I feel like I'm living in a dream (or cloud). Everything's hazy."

• "I feel like I'm walking around inside myself."

• "It's like I'm trying to touch people through Jell-O (or cotton gauze). I can see it all out there, but I can't reach it. I feel disconnected from the rest of the world."

• "I don't fit in my own skin anymore."

• "Everything's distant. Even voices sound like they're coming from so far away."

Anger, irritation, impatience, frustration Sometimes when a parent dies, children feel angry at that parent, simply for dying. (As unreasonable as that may be, it's a common experience.) Or they feel anger at their surviving parent for not preventing it somehow. Or they feel anger at other kids who enjoy two living parents. They may feel anger at the medical personnel, or at God. While anger is normal, in some families, anger, even in its milder forms of irritation, impatience, and frustration, can be a difficult emotion for people to admit having. You yourself may feel that there's something wrong about being angry when someone has died. Kids pick up on parents' disapproval, and they may feel guilty about their own feelings of anger.

But regardless of your own attitudes, your children may never be able to admit to you that they're angry. Being angry at you or at the person who died may feel risky. What if you object to their anger? How can they risk losing your emotional support at a time they are so insecure?

Instead of admitting it to you, your kids may display their anger by fighting, teasing, yelling, or cynicism. According to the Child Bereavement Study, children who express their anger more aggressively often are more fearful for the safety of their parents, feel less able to talk about the person who died, and have a greater sense of being out of control. In other words, their sense of powerlessness, their unspoken and unresolved fears, evolve into anger. William Worden concludes, "It may be that such behavior was a means of getting a strong reaction from the surviving parent as well as giving the child a greater sense of empowerment."[1]

Some kids may channel their anger into sports, art, or writing (whether prose, poetry, or music/lyrical composition). Others may try to douse their anger through drug or alcohol use or other delinquent activities. Finally, some kids may deny their anger altogether, mask it with a perpetually cheerful expression, and instead turn their anger inward, against themselves. When that happens, the risk of lowered self-esteem and depression increases dramatically.

WHAT GRIEVING KIDS DO

How grieving kids act reflects what they are thinking and feeling. Sometimes their actions are a direct expression of what's happening inside them, and sometimes they're a defense against it.

Sean, a nine-year-old grieving child, fell asleep in school one day. His teacher, knowing his brother had died recently of sudden infant death syndrome, gently awakened him. She thought no more of it, but when it became an almost daily occurrence, she called his mother. Sean's mother puzzled over her son's sleepiness. "I'll admit I'm not very organized these days," she reflected to the teacher, "but I *always* get the kids to bed on time."

That night Sean's mom poked her head in every half hour to see what was happening and was stunned to see that Sean stayed awake until three A.M. No wonder he fell asleep in school. When she spoke with him about it, Sean admitted that he deliberately tried to stay awake at night because his little brother's death terrified him. Might he, too, go to sleep and never wake up?

COMMON BEHAVIORAL AND PHYSICAL RESPONSES TO GRIEF IN CHILDREN	
Crying, weepiness	Paranormal experiences
Restlessness	Hyperactivity, sleep changes
Withdrawal	Clinginess, avoiding being alone
Lack of concentration	Less productive in school
Eating changes	Lack of interest in hobbies,
Physical complaints	school
Fatigue	Absentmindedness
Avoiding reminders of person	Easily startled
who died	Regression (bed-wetting, thumb-
Headaches, stomachaches	sucking, etc.)
Hiding grief	Sexual acting out
Accident-proneness	Risky behaviors
Boredom	Physical weakness
Dreams	Sighing
Stress reactions	

It's important to understand that a single behavior may have any of several different causes. Crying may indicate longing for a dead parent, or it may be an expression of fear that the surviving parent may die too. Eating less may mean your child is too sad to feel like eating, or it may mean she's too anxious to eat. Overachieving may indicate that she has a lot of anxious energy, or it may mean that she's trying to overcompensate for guilt, shame, or low self-esteem.

It would be so much easier if we could do behavior-interpretation-by-number: "If a child acts this way, then it means he's in this kind of bind." Unfortunately, understanding behavior doesn't work that way. At a time when you yourself have the fewest inner resources because of your own grief, you need your best powers of detection and care to help your grieving child.

We've covered many of the common behaviors of grieving children in the previous sections. Let's focus now on three behaviors that we have not yet discussed above: dreams and paranormal experiences; accident-proneness; and risky behaviors.

Dreams and paranormal experiences Across all age groups, more than half of the children in the Child Bereavement Study reported dreaming about the parent who died. For children, such dreams may be either comforting or frightening.

And it may take a while for your child to open up and admit it, but many children say they've seen or heard the person who died. That's not surprising since, according to a 1971 study by W. D. Rees, almost 40 percent of adults sense the presence of a dead loved one at some point in time, and 14 percent say they've actually seen or heard the person who died.[2]

Some adults will interpret such experiences as tricks of the mind as a result of extreme longing. Others believe they're a spiritual manifestation of their loved ones. Make of it what you will, but children report paranormal experiences of loved ones who died. They're common for a grieving child. They're normal.

Accident-proneness According to the Child Bereavement Study, in the months shortly after the death of a parent, 25 percent of grieving children (mostly adolescent boys) experience an accident. As they move through the first year of bereavement, moreover, the percentage jumps to 34 percent for all children and 45 percent for adolescent boys. Roughly one-third of these accidents require medical attention. In the second year of bereavement, the rate drops back to the rate for nonbereaved children.

Why are grieving children more accident-prone? Some experts think that children who feel guilty may experience accidents to punish themselves for what they see as their role in the death. Others say accidents may be an unconscious effort to get the dead parent to return—after all, Mom always came to apply Band-Aids and comfort before. Still other grief theorists venture that accidents among adolescents may reflect depression and subconscious suicidal behavior.

But what makes the most sense to us is that grieving children are often preoccupied and anxious. Their attention may simply be more focused on their fears and on figuring out what has happened than on what they're doing. They may not be paying attention to the here and now, and that lack of concentration may result in injury. This theory is supported by the study's finding that children who experience accidents are more insecure and more often feel personally unsafe.

Risky behaviors The most disturbing of all behaviors of grieving children are the risky ones: drug and alcohol use, fast driving, sexual activity, and—every caregiver's worst nightmare—suicidal ideas and gestures. Of course, we can't ignore such risky behaviors. It's the parents' job to help kids make safer choices. And yet over our years of counseling grieving adolescents, we've come to appreciate what's behind these behaviors.

Drugs and alcohol, for example, provide escape from pain. Adults use them for the same reason—and they work, however temporarily. Think of it as a form of self-medication. Grieving kids who use drugs and alcohol in this way are not "bad" kids. They are kids who need guidance and help to grieve in more appropriate ways.

Fast driving (and engaging in high-risk or adventure sports) can be a way of challenging death, believing that if you can survive an extreme experience, you can survive anything. Sometimes it's also an unconscious death wish. Either way, if your child engages in such behavior, it deserves attention.

If your teen suddenly becomes very active sexually (or even promiscuous), take a deep breath. Despite what others may think, it's not about you, your values, or your parenting. More than likely, your child needs something she's not getting. She may crave intimacy and not know of any other way to get it. She may feel isolated from her peers and see sexuality as a way to feel included again. Or she herself may feel dead inside and rely on sexual excitement to feel alive once more.

Finally, having already lost one person to death, you may find it difficult to even think about the possibility of suicide in your child. If your child is ten or younger, it may help you to know that children rarely attempt suicide at such a young age. Obviously, if you see really concerning behavior, talk to a mental health professional immediately, but according to the American Foundation for Suicide Prevention, only six children in the United States under the age of ten killed themselves in 1993 (the last year for which we have data).[3]

Suicide is a greater concern among struggling preteens and adolescents. Between eleven and fourteen years of age, the number of U.S. children who killed themselves was still relatively small—315 in total (230 boys and 85 girls). But between fifteen and nineteen, the rate of suicide climbs to one per every thousand teens in that age group, with almost five times as many young men killing themselves as young women. So when your child reaches puberty and regrieves his loss, you'll want to watch for the signs of depression that usually precede suicide attempts. (See Chapter 10.)

Many grieving adults think about death (including their own) a great deal. So it's not surprising that children do as well. Sometimes a child may simply wish he *could* die in order to be rid of the emotional pain. At other times, she may entertain fantasies about dying in order to reunite with the person who died. Again, this is a problem only if it turns to suicidal thoughts, plans, and actions.

Wishes to die and fantasies about it are not the same thing as suicidal thoughts, in which one thinks about actually taking steps to cause one's own death. Obviously, though, if your child is *stuck* in death thoughts or fantasies, you'll want to get extra help for him. Prolonged death wishes can be a sign of underlying depressive disease.

If your child engages in risky behavior on an ongoing basis, follow the guidelines in Chapter 10 to find a mental health professional with whom you and your child are comfortable. Risky behavior following grief is highly treatable by mental health professionals who are knowledgeable about grief.

DEFENSES

Sometimes the behavior of a grieving child may not be a direct expression of how she's feeling, but rather a defense mechanism. Defenses have received a bum rap over the years. We accuse others of being "defensive" or "in denial." We shake our heads, calling it avoidance, when someone won't face up to the facts as *we* see them.

But the truth is that defense mechanisms serve a valuable purpose: In the face of deep trouble, they keep us afloat. They do so in two key ways. First, they help us take in a difficult reality a little bit at a time, only as much as we can handle right now. Second, they help us manage the reality we *do* take in, often making it more acceptable by slightly distorting it.

In his memoir *Growing Up,* commentator Russell Baker relates how his defenses kicked in at the age of five, when his cousin Kenneth told him his father had died.

When Kenneth walked right up to me, . . . he stared at me with such a stare as I'd never seen.

"Your father's dead," he said.

It was like an accusation that my father had done something criminal, and I came to my father's defense.

"He is not," I said.

But of course they didn't know the situation. I started to explain. He was sick. In the hospital. My mother was bringing him home right now . . .

"He's dead," Kenneth said.

His assurance slid an icicle into my heart.

"He is not either!" I shouted.[4]

Children's defenses are more basic than those of adults. In general, young kids primarily use three defenses: denial, splitting, and devaluing.

Denial You've no doubt seen denial in your own child. Remember that time when you walked into the kitchen, found your three-year-old grabbing a cookie, and yelled, "I said no cookies now. It's too close to dinner"? His response was, "I didn't take a cookie." He knows he's in trouble, so despite being caught red-handed, he denies his involvement. It's too scary to think of the consequences otherwise.

Like Russell Baker, your grieving child may for a time deny that the death occurred. Even more likely, he may deny some of his feelings. Fear, rage, and guilt, are frightening emotions for many of us. As normal as they are, they can make us feel like we're going crazy. So sometimes your child may deny such feelings on the surface and instead take them underground. Then when they resurface, it's in a hidden form.

Your child, for example, may complain of a physical ailment: a headache, a stomachache, or symptoms that mimic those of the person who died (like breathing difficulties or heart palpitations). Underneath it all, he may be afraid that he'll die from the same ailment. Or he may be concentrating so hard on pushing away his emotions that he gets a headache. Thirteen-year-old Erica, raised in a home of deeply committed pacifists, was enraged when a truck driver fell asleep at the wheel and ran into the family car, killing her brother. She dreamed of revenge, of finding the truck driver and shooting him. Afraid that her parents would not love her if they found out about her violent fantasy, she kept it inside. Eventually, the stress of hiding her anger came out in stomach pains.

Splitting In splitting, children claim to have only the feelings that seem acceptable to other people and that are manageable. The rest of their feelings—the ones not socially acceptable (relief, for example) or the ones that feel too overwhelming to acknowledge—they attribute to other people or to toys. (They "split" off those feelings from themselves, not claiming them as their own.)

Kristen was four when her dad died of a heart attack. One day her mom noticed Kristen with her stuffed bunny. Shaking the bunny violently, Kristen growled through gritted teeth, "Bad bunny! Don't do that! You'll be the death of me yet!" Her mom recognized the phrase as one used commonly by her mother-in-law and realized that Kristen felt responsible for her dad's death. But instead of saying, "I feel guilty," Kristen attributed the guilt to her bunny.

Some children split or divide up their emotions among different objects. One child, for example, may split her sadness from her anger, feeling sadness about the parent who died and directing all her anger at the parent who survived. After all, she might reason, one cannot be angry at a person who died. And besides, the parent is a safe person to be angry at: the child knows she can count on the parent to continue to love her no matter what she says or does. Another child, in contrast, might be angry at the person who died, feeling that he can't afford to be angry at the only parent he has left.

Devaluing The third defense that children commonly use is devaluing. It reveals itself as boredom and in expressions like "I don't care" or "It doesn't really matter." It's a way for your child to try to back away from the situation, to ignore it, in the hope that it won't affect her as much. Like the other defenses, it won't work in the long run, but it will help a child feel safe here and now.

One summer, eleven-year-old Trista witnessed the death of her brother in a boating accident. The next several months proved highly emotional for her. During basketball practice the following winter, a teammate taunted her, yelling, "Don't pass it to Trista! She can't play.

All she ever does is cry!" The coach penalized the teammate, then turned to Trista and asked her how she felt. "I don't care," Trista replied. Of course, Trista *did* care. Insults hurt. But Trista wasn't ready to deal with that pain, so she backed away, claiming it didn't matter. She was defending herself emotionally. Only when a child persistently avoids painful realities or emotions does a parent need to be concerned. If a child periodically uses defenses as a tool to manage her world, that's perfectly normal.

GETTING INSIDE YOUR CHILD'S WORLD

Children express themselves far more eloquently in actions than in words. Or as mental health professionals say, "Behavior has meaning." For the most part, the meaning of your grieving child's behavior is simple: It's her best attempt to get what she thinks she needs, whether you understand it or not.

The Barker family provides a good example. Six months after her husband died of a rare infectious disease, Victoria panicked. She slept poorly, overate, and felt constantly on edge with her kids. "I don't know if I can do this on my own," she confessed. "David—he's not quite two—he wants to be held constantly. Paul's eight. He just hides in his room after school and sleeps. John's nine. His latest thing is to line up all his toy soldiers at the door to his room. There's hell to pay if you try to cross that line or knock one over! Meanwhile, I need to pay the bills."

Over weeks of grief work together, it became clear that everyone in the Barker family was scared. Victoria worried about the kids and the bills. John feared that death was going to come get him, too, just as he'd seen in the movie *The Christmas Carol.* He fantasized about fighting off the bad guy, "Death," with his toy soldiers. Paul dreamed repeatedly that he opened a door and his dad punched him in the face. Afraid of another such dream, he fought to stay awake until the wee hours of the morning. That's why he napped in the afternoon. And David, at two, couldn't talk about what was wrong, but only Victoria's holding comforted him.

The same feeling, then, can come out in many different ways. Likewise, the same actions can reflect many different emotions. That's why it's important to discover what's at the root of your child's behavior. Is she sad? Angry? Ashamed? Guilty? Until you figure out the reason your child is behaving the way she is, you won't know how to best respond.

We suggest several approaches for figuring out what's going on inside your child. First, of course, talk to him about the situation. What can he tell you about what he's feeling? Can he recall all the times he's felt this way?

Second, look for patterns in her behavior. When did the behavior start? Did a significant event precede it the first time? Does it occur throughout the day or only at specific times? In any situation or only in certain situations (at school, at home, or at play)? With anyone or only with certain people? What do those situations and people have in common?

Now review the list of "Common Emotional Reactions to Death Among Children" among grieving kids on page 27. Would any of those emotions explain the behavioral pattern that you're seeing? If not, review how children of various ages understand death (Chapter 2). Is there a belief that your child might be hanging on to, one that might explain his behavioral pattern? How is he interpreting what's going on in his world? How might that be influencing his behavior?

What do other people (teachers, school social workers, neighbors, coaches, scout leaders, and so on) notice about your child's behavior? Share your observations with them. Then ask if they have any thoughts on the behavior's possible cause.

Ray, for example, couldn't help but notice the changes in his eight-year-old daughter's behavior after her mother died. Willa quit Little League. She still played with her best friend in the after-school program, but she refused to go to her house on weekends. Instead, she spent Saturdays at the nearby house of a divorced neighbor and her child.

Ray talked to Willa's teacher. The only change she'd noticed was that Willa had gone to the school nurse's office a number of times the week before, during art class. The school nurse finally shed light on the situation. "Willa said she didn't like art," the nurse said. "But I think what she really didn't like was the fact that everyone else in class was making a card for their moms on Mother's Day but she couldn't." Ray realized that in all of the situations Willa was avoiding, she was the "odd one out," the only child without a mom.

A third way to figure out what's going on inside your child is to watch him play. Since children often "play out" what's uppermost in their minds, make-believe can often give you clues. What themes come up again and again in his make-believe? What situations does he act out with friends or dolls? What pictures does he draw, and how does he describe the situations they portray? Do you see any parallels between his play activities and what might be going on inside him?

Alex, a five-year-old, was normally drawn to art and to playing cars in elaborate cities that he built in his sandbox. After his little brother died, he began watching superhero cartoons. Gradually, his play reflected his television interests. More and more, he played with Ninja Turtles and G.I. Joe. He began drawing only fighter jets and tanks.

After talking to the family's pediatrician, Alex's mother realized that he might be scared and trying to figure out how to be strong enough to ward off more catastrophes. At the suggestion of the social worker where Alex would attend kindergarten, she enrolled him in a summer martial arts program.

"I wouldn't say he's back to normal," Alex's mother said at the end of the summer. "He still plays superhero and sometimes draws military vehicles. But now he draws other things as well, and it's good to see him back in the sandbox again."

Whatever patterns you see in your child's behavior, don't panic. As difficult as the behavior may be to watch, chances are you will be able to lessen it, especially if you take some time to figure out what's happening and how best to respond.

Finally, remember that you don't have to deal with your child and her grief by yourself. Follow the guidelines in Chapter 7 on using the surrounding community to "hold" your child. If you're concerned or stuck, know that many resources are available: schools, child guidance clinics, children's hospitals, hospices, and children's grief support centers. Call them, and ask them to refer you to a mental health professional who works with grief in children.

HOW GRIEF AFFECTS FAMILIES

Since my husband died in a drunk driving crash, my family's become a mixed blessing. On the one hand, a lot of times I wish they would all just go away. I don't feel like cooking meals or doing laundry or listening to one more school story. On the other hand, my kids are the only reason I get out of bed in the morning. Without them, I think I'd just curl up in my bed and die.

—Anita, 46 years old

I F YOUR GRIEVING FAMILY FEELS LIKE BOTH A BLESSING AND A curse, you're certainly not alone. When death occurs in a family, all hell breaks loose. The balance between change and stability is disrupted. *Everything* is different. Family therapist Murray Bowen describes grief in the family as a shock wave: the death of one person initiates an entire series of disruptions, affecting who does what in the family (the roles they fill), how folks communicate, how the family copes with stress, and how it sees itself.[1]

THE THREE GOALS OF FAMILY GRIEVING

"Ever since our son was killed in a boating accident," Joanna related, near her wit's end, "our home has turned into a war zone. The kids are constantly at each other's throats, my husband is angry at me for crying so much and thinks I should 'move on,' and I'm angry at my husband for being so insensitive. The whole thing is out of control!"

"Chaotic," "out of balance," "out of control"—we hear these descriptions time and again after a death in the family. Often, clouded by chaos, family members feel that they are making no progress in their grief. They interpret the chaos as evidence that their family life will never again be "okay." Yet the feeling that life has become chaotic is a predictable part of grief.

That's why it's important to understand that family grieving has three primary goals: reestablishing stability; acknowledging the experience and implications of the loss for each person and for the family as a whole; and supporting each person and the family as a whole in their efforts to start growing again. By understanding and accomplishing each of these goals, parents and other caregivers can help create a family environment that fosters healing in grieving children—regardless of how turbulent the situation still feels.

GOAL 1: REESTABLISH STABILITY

In the early days following a death, families and friends usually focus on doing the necessary chores. They cook meals, answer the phone, and help plan funeral services. Family togetherness is the norm, and everyone tolerates a high level of emotionality.

As the demands of normal life return, however, families must work out new routines, compensating for the loss of the loved one's contribution. Who will take out the trash now? Who will chauffeur the kids to baseball practice? Who will help with homework? Who will care for the kids after school? Who will make the rules? Who will enforce them? Who will talk to teachers, Scout leaders, coaches?

Compensating for Who's Missing After a death, roles shift, often dramatically, as a family attempts to find a "new normal," a pattern of life that's predictable and therefore a bit calmer.

Because of these role shifts, grievers often ask, "Which is the worst when you're a kid—losing a mother, a father, a brother, or a sister?" In fact, they're all lousy. With each one, a child loses something different but something significant. Much of what he loses reflects the roles that person filled for him.

For instance, if your child's mother died, she probably lost the person most active in her everyday care as well as in the household. Many mothers take a larger share of the responsibility for enforcing rules. These role losses create disorder in home life.

Mothers also more often act as the bearers of memories (answering questions like "What was I like as a baby?") and as emotional guides: they help the other family members focus on feelings, identify them, and process them.

On the other hand, for many families, losing a father means losing the larger source of income, with all the ramifications for housing, schooling, recreation, and so on, that that implies. Even if plenty of money remains, many children whose fathers die worry about money: they know that Dad was a significant financial contributor.

Fathers also tend to function as the family's "coach." As one young woman reflected retrospectively on her loss, "Dad taught my older brother and sister how to ski. But after he died, when I was ready to learn, no one was left to teach me. So I've missed him a lot over the years. Sometimes, though, I think I miss him even more now: he would have helped me buy my first car, figure out which job offer to take— the kind of stuff I see my friends going to *their* fathers for."

Losing a brother or sister wreaks havoc as well. Kids miss the companionship, the guidance, and the "trailblazing" of an older sibling; the self-esteem that comes from mentoring a younger child; and all the many bonds of connection that tie brothers and sisters together. "I'm not a big brother anymore," complained six-year-old Danny when his soon-to-be-born brother died in the womb. "I had it all figured out. I was going to teach him how to fish, and I was even going to let him pet my dog sometimes."

Most importantly, when a sibling dies, the surviving children may "lose" both their parents to grief. Under normal circumstances, we cope with disturbing realities and emotions in part by using others as resources. We turn to a few trusted souls for advice, comfort, and perspective. For children, those few others are most often parents. They become, in effect, emotional "shock absorbers."

Tragically, however, grief can so consume parents that they understandably may lose touch with their other children's emotional needs. As an adult, Shelley vividly remembers her parents' reactions when, at five, her two-year-old brother died. "All they could talk about was

Jimmy," she recalls. "It was like when he died, he took all of their love with him. There was none left for me. I used to think that it would have been better if I had died. I figured they would have missed me less than they missed him. And they would have had love left over for my other brothers and sisters."

Further, parents grieving the death of a child may not have the internal resources for their other kids—even if they understand what those children need. They may have to struggle so profoundly to survive each day that they have little energy left over simply for being there for the rest of the family. Under these circumstances, the children must develop new sources of advice, comfort, and perspective.

As we discuss in Chapter 7, this is why communities are so important to grieving families: often they can compensate to some degree when parents are overwhelmed by practicalities or by their own grief.

Creating New Communication Patterns After a death, children may talk more with a parent, each other, or adults outside the family, or they may talk less. They may express their feelings more, or they may hold back over time. They may communicate directly, or they may rely on others to relate their experiences.

These changes alter the pattern of communication in the family. Sometimes the person who died was the family member who kept everyone informed of news and plans. Or she may have been the one who broached the more difficult subjects in the family. In the Lane family, Frankie (at seventeen, the second oldest of four adolescent boys), stood out as the argumentative one.

"My husband was really strict with all the boys," Frankie's mother, Faith, recalls. "But Frankie fought him tooth and nail. He challenged every rule. The rest of the boys just went along. Then after Frankie died, it seemed like they all did it—they all fought about the rules."

Frankie's brothers remember it differently. "Dad's rules frustrated all of us," says Lee, the oldest brother. "We'd bitch about it pretty much nonstop when we were together. But Frankie was always ready for a fight. So he took Dad on. Sometimes Dad got tired of arguing and gave in. Sometimes he didn't. But either way, Frankie was the best one to fight it out because he sort of enjoyed it. Now, without Frankie, we all kind of have to fight our own battles."

Nineteen-year-old Shana reflected on the changes in her family's communication patterns. "The day after I got back to college from Christmas break, Dad called me to say Mom had died from a massive stroke. I think it was a three-minute phone call. And that's what it's been like ever since. When Dad and I talk every Sunday, it's like *CNN Headline News*: 'School's going well'; 'Still love Artie'; 'Think I'll work at Perfect Parties this summer.'

"Mom would have wanted to know the details. Sometimes I resented that—it seemed like she was prying. But now I miss it. I miss having her take on things. I miss knowing that someone cares enough to listen, even to the stuff that, after I've said it, seems unimportant. Now my sister and I try to do that for each other, but I don't know—it's not quite the same," Shana said.

Over time, just as a body develops new nerve pathways after an injury, most families develop new communication pathways after a death. As always, the important thing is to pay attention to the needs of each individual and of the family as a whole.

How can you determine which needs are going unmet in your family? Look at the sources of friction. Usually, cranky, combative, or angry kids aren't acting that way for the fun of it.

Over and over, we hear of school-age children who say to surviving parents, "I hate you! I wish you had died instead!" They may even strike out physically. Typically, such children just don't know of any other way to focus attention on their needs.

Clearly, in such an instance, the hitting needs to stop. But if we say the *feeling* needs to stop, then we're telling the child that he can't trust his innermost self, that there's something wrong with him. A casual observer might be tempted to respond, "Don't say that! That's terrible! Of course you don't hate your parent." But then the child would have to deal with guilt and shame as well as his anger. Instead, it's more helpful to explore why he's angry and what needs of his are not being met.

Troublesome behaviors thus may signal deeper needs. Ask yourself, "What does my child need right now? Does she need to know what the plans are? Does she need to talk about her feelings? Does she need to hear how much I love her?"

Creating an Emotionally Safe Environment In addition to reestablishing practical routines and communication patterns, families need to reestablish emotional stability or balance. It's uncomfortable and impractical to sustain the high level of intense emotions experienced right after the death. And it's not so easy to continue being tolerant of the strong emotions that sporadically pop up in other family members. But as everyone knows, there's also no going back to the emotional climate before the death. A new stable yet flexible emotional climate must be established.

Some families create such a climate easily. They seem unafraid of turbulent emotions. They are able to be intimate with each other while respecting each person's different emotional experiences. They balance being *me,* being an individual, with being *together,* being a family.

Other families try to create a "safe" emotional climate in less helpful ways, such as by becoming overly involved in each other's lives. When Julia's older sister, Meg, was raped and murdered at college, her parents feared for Julia's safety as well. Although she herself was nearly eighteen, her parents increasingly wanted to know in great detail where Julia was going and with whom, what she would be doing, and for how long. They encouraged her to stay home on weekend evenings. They changed her curfew to eleven P.M. They restricted her driving radius to her own hometown, which as Julia reminded them had "no shopping mall and no movie theater!"

Her parents transformed Julia's search for a college into a search for one they felt was safe: small, rural, and all female. Finally, Julia rebelled. "I love my folks and I know they're just trying to protect me," she said, "but if it comes down to a choice between them and me, I'll choose me. I have a right to my own life, and I want to study music at Juilliard in New York City!"

Understandably, Julia's parents were frightened for her. But their mistake was to try to manage *their* fears by controlling the details of *her* life. What worked for them in the short term wasn't going to work for Julia in the long term.

Some parents try to create a "safe" environment for their children by overinvolving themselves in their childrens' emotional lives as well. You might find yourself presuming that your child has certain emotions rather than helping him identify his own emotions. You might be tempted to push him toward certain common behaviors (talking about the death, for example) rather than encouraging him to find his own expression (in art or music, for example). Or you might try to force him to confront aspects of his grief that he's simply not ready to confront, rather than inviting him to explore his own grief in his own way on his own timetable.

For some parents, this emotional overinvolvement is a way of avoiding their own pain. It's easier to take care of your child's needs than to experience your own. A successful businesswoman once asked us how she could help her three school-age daughters cope with the death of their father two months earlier. "It's taken a lot of time and a lot of work, but I think I finally have it all worked out," Carrie reported. "I've lined up individual counseling for each of them. The two younger ones are in grief groups at school. I heard that kids get things out in art and drama, so I found a two-week creative workshop this summer for all of them. Every night, when I tuck the girls in bed, I really push them to talk about how they're feeling. On weekends, we work together on this grief workbook that I found. Can you think of anything more that I can do?" She didn't like our response: How was she handling her own grief?

Clearly, grieving children need special attention. They rely on their parents to help them get through such an overwhelming experience. But as in every other aspect of growing up, they need a balance between being themselves and being part of a family. At every age, people resemble toddlers: We venture out to explore the world, and we return home to reconnect and catch our emotional breath. In mourning, we reach out and touch our pain, then "come home" to the safety and solace of the people who love us.

After a death, our tendency is to hold one another close. Naturally, we want to minimize the pain for our children. But in the end, it's their grief and theirs alone. We can't know what it's like for them. We can't control their experience. We can't force their healing. In short, we can't live their lives for them. They have to grieve their own grief, "grow" their own lives, develop as their own persons. All we can do is provide a home for them in which it's safe to think and feel whatever is in their minds and hearts—no matter how sad, scary, or "ugly" those thoughts or feelings may be to us or anyone else.

Because some thoughts and feelings are so difficult for parents to acknowledge, one of the most common but problematic ways some parents try to reestablish an emotional balance is simply to push the emotions away, walling them off, trying not to feel them.

When Alice Hathaway Lee Roosevelt, Theodore Roosevelt's first wife, died, he tore up all pictures of her and never again mentioned her name to their daughter, Alice, or to friends. In essence, he regained his emotional stability by avoiding the pain associated with his memories. Other families do the same by avoiding information about the death itself or by immediately making changes in the home (converting the bedroom to another use, getting rid of pictures or artwork) to wipe out reminders of the person who died.

While this strategy may work for a short time, it usually breaks down simply because the reminders are too constant and the emotions too powerful. Further, this strategy actually hurts family members and especially children, who need to feel the feelings of grief in order to heal and who gain comfort and perspective from staying connected to the person who died.

Sometimes families accept certain feelings and reject others. After her husband and son drowned in a fishing accident, Gail tried to help her five-year-old daughter, Chrissy, through the pain. "We talk about them a lot," Gail said, "but I always try to do it while we're busy doing something. Otherwise Chrissy starts to cry, and I can't stand that."

What Gail was teaching Chrissy was that it's okay to remember—but if she wanted Mom to hold it together, she'd better not cry. So Chrissy simply built a wall around her sadness. She blocked it off.

Sometimes families reject certain feelings because of what the parents learned in their *own* childhoods. When Gina, as a child, expressed anger, a severe beating usually followed. She learned, in order to survive, not to get angry. As an adult with a family of her own, however, she still kept a lid on her anger. It still conjured up too much anxiety. Her children learned to do the same.

When Gina's husband died, the kids knew they could be sad or lonely, cry and cuddle. But they couldn't get mad at their dad for dying, or at their mom for not preventing it somehow, or at other kids who enjoyed two living parents. Anger, they unconsciously feared, might push Mom over the edge. In order to keep Mom "in working order" and to maintain some family stability, they avoided the angry grief feelings at all costs.

Unfortunately, walling off emotions is like trying to put a lid on a volcano. For a while, the lid might prevent an eruption. But over time the pressure builds, and eventually the volcano will blow in unpredictable and potentially damaging ways, such as drug use or other risky behaviors.

In extreme cases, families will cut off those who continue to bring up memories or emotions that are unacceptable to the rest of the family. When Amy, nineteen, expressed relief that her cocaine-addicted father had died, her mother rebuked her, saying, "Come on, Amy, it wasn't *that* bad. How can you be glad your dad is dead?" Her mother refused even to talk about Amy's feelings or experience, eventually not talking to Amy at all.

Amy herself had become a painful reminder of a disastrous family life. Rather than face the truth and experience the resulting pain, Amy's mother chose to whitewash the entire situation, avoid talking about the addiction, and create a family secret about it. Amy's younger brothers and sister followed her mom's lead.

After college, Amy moved out of state. She reasoned, "What's left for me here? I have no family left."

Clearly, avoidance strategies reestablish a feeling of emotional safety, but they do so at the expense of emotional expression and even, at times, entire relationships. That in turn inhibits healing and normal growth in children and the family.

Nevertheless, all families, even healthy ones, have some emotional rules: how much importance is given to emotions; which expressions of emotions are tolerated and which are not. Some rules are clearly stated, while others are unspoken but enforced. One lawyer, for example, constantly told his grieving sixteen-year-old son, "I know your mom died, but if you want to get into a good college, you have to be in the top ten of your class. Colleges look at the facts of your record. They don't care that you're not feeling up to par. Feelings aren't facts." He gave his son a clear message that emotions should never get in the way of success.

Whatever the rules, the healthiest families permit children to experience and acknowledge all their feelings, albeit with appropriate limits on where and how those feelings get expressed.

One of our sons was angry for much of his junior year in high school: his mom had died, and he felt nothing else was going his way either. One particular day, his wrath fell on his brother. He threw a hardcover book at him and stormed up the stairs. Halfway up, Mary Ann grabbed him around the knees. "In this family," she explained, "we don't solve problems through violence. It's okay to be angry, but we express it without physically hurting each other."

Since anger is such a common part of the grief process, yet is a feeling that can be difficult to deal with, here are some emotional "rules" that we've found work:

• You can be angry, but you can't destroy property.

• You can yell and scream, alone and in your own bedroom, but you can't verbally abuse your brothers and sisters.

• You can rant and rave about whatever it is that's making you angry, but you can't use "foul" language in this house.

• You can be angry and express it, but you still have to do your homework—just like you can be sad, but you still have to go to school.

You may implement these rules or not, depending on your own comfort level and values. Or you may have to make up rules of your own. Be patient—it may take some time before your children learn the rules, remember them, and accept them.

If your children have feelings that you yourself find it difficult to deal with—feelings like regret, ambivalence, jealousy, relief, guilt, or anger—you'll need a conscious strategy for helping your children through them.

First of all, you can talk to your children about the feeling you find difficult. Tell them directly that many kids feel that way when a person dies. Tell them you feel it too. Help them understand that all feelings are acceptable, even those that are difficult. Sometimes it helps to describe contrasting feelings as "hard" or "soft," or as "sweet" or "sour."

Next, find ways for them to express the feeling, ways that feel tolerable to you. Maybe, for example, you can't stand to see your child's sadness, but she can express it to a grandparent who lives nearby or to members of a peer support group. If so, suggest to that grandparent or support group facilitator that your child may want to discuss her sadness.

Maybe angry outbursts push every button inside you. In that case, you could suggest that your child write an angry letter. Other activities for expressing anger are outlined in Chapter 5. Look for those that meet your child's needs while being acceptable to you.

Sometimes, despite your best efforts, everyone's emotions will begin to bounce off each other and clash. For example, one child may get angry because another is tired and doesn't want to play. Their ongoing bickering about the situation leaves you feeling defeated and depressed. You may sense that the situation is spiraling out of control. That's a good time to take a family time-out, with each person retreating to his or her own bedroom for a brief, specified time period. A few minutes alone can act as an emotional "circuit breaker" for everyone and give you time to begin to figure out what's behind the outburst and how best to deal with it.

Being Flexible Whatever voids a death creates, somehow those empty spaces get filled—either poorly or well. But even the changes necessary to restabilize the family in the long run may in the short run add significantly to the shock wave created by the death itself.

That's why families sometimes try to reestablish stability by rigidly sticking to old habits. Unfortunately, old patterns seldom fit anymore after a death. Too much has changed. Too many new needs emerge over time. So while at first old practices may feel comfortable and soothing in an otherwise overwhelming situation, ultimately they cause more tension because they don't meet the needs of everyone in the family.

Instead, the ability to think and plan flexibly proves much more helpful in the long run. It ensures that no individual's needs are lost in the shuffle of meeting the needs of the family as a whole.

When he turned fourteen and his mom returned to work four days each week, Lewis began minding his ten- and twelve-year-old brothers after school. It was his job, as the oldest, to make sure they were safe and completed their homework. Lewis joked sometimes about becoming "Mr. Mom."

Eighteen months later, Lewis's mom died. His dad began relying on Lewis to do the household chores his mom had performed: laundry, cleaning, cooking dinner, and fixing the next day's lunches. Somebody had to do it, and as the oldest, Lewis, at nearly sixteen, was already shouldering much of the parental role. The arrangement seemed practical to Lewis's dad, who this way could avoid the hassle and pain of losing the homemaker.

At first, Lewis relished the authority that these new roles lent him. But as his sixteenth birthday approached, he dreamed about getting a job at a local restaurant. He'd make some money. He'd be working with friends. And anyway, he felt he'd outgrown the baby-sitting role. He was ready for a *real* job. His younger brothers were now twelve and fourteen—wasn't it time they took on those duties?

His dad didn't see it that way. "I need you to hold things together at home," the father argued. "But since you need more spending money, I'd be willing to increase your allowance." Money, however, was only part of the issue for Lewis. He wanted to step into more adult roles *outside* the family. His dad, in contrast, clung to the old roles and patterns as a means of ensuring stability in the family. Over time, Lewis came to resent his father's dictates and began to act out his resentment through high-risk sports, activities that his father deplored.

Clearly, someone needed to do the laundry, cook the meals, take out the trash. But flexibility is usually more helpful than rigidity. A few simple questions can help you assess your family's needs and develop openness to other options.

First, ask yourself how important the need is in the first place. Must it really be done? Two widowers, we recall, were comparing notes about housekeeping chores. One widower said, "Even with a couple of little kids, I can usually get meals done and dishes finished and laundry washed. I fold it during the eleven o'clock news. But I just *can't* figure out when to do the ironing!" To which the second widower replied in amazement, "Wait a minute—you *fold* the laundry?!" Not only did ironing never make the second widower's to-do list, neither did folding clothes.

A second helpful question is, can your family do this less often? Bess's husband, Tony, relished weekends of playing soccer with his son. But when Tony died, Bess came to hate watching the soccer games. "I was never a soccer parent in the first place," she says. "It basically takes up your whole weekend, which I *never* had time for. And now it's painful to see all the other 'whole' families there. My solution has been to ask my son each week which day of the weekend, Saturday or Sunday, he'd like me to watch. It's not ideal, but it seems to work okay for both of us."

This strategy can be used for household chores as well. Using paper

plates and cups means fewer dishwashing chores. Buying more under-
wear, socks, or towels may mean fewer, larger loads of laundry. How
often, really, do beds need to be changed? Maybe bathrooms need to be
cleaned more regularly, but do you really need to vacuum and dust every
week?

Third, ask yourself who else might be available to help. Maybe
Grandpa would throw your daughter's birthday party this year. A neighbor might be willing to cut your grass, take out the trash cans each week,
or pack another couple of lunches for your kids. Close friends could
provide laundry service for a year. Relatives and friends often want to
help and appreciate finding out concrete ways they can lighten your
load.

Finally, you can ask your friends to brainstorm with you about how
to rearrange your life to make it more manageable. They may see
options that, in your grief and in the stress of the moment, you are
unable to identify.

"But how do I know if the options I develop are good ones?" you
might wonder. "After all, some strategies are helpful and some are not."

Fortunately, you can figure out for yourself whether the options are
good ones by asking yourself three questions. First, do your choices for
reestablishing stability fit the age and maturity of your children? It
would be unhealthy for your six- to ten-year-old to bear the burden
of significant household tasks or for your preteen or teen to become
your personal grief "sounding board." But even school-age kids can
take on a few extra chores. And periodically it's perfectly reasonable to
ask your teen to watch younger children while you visit with a friend
who listens.

Second, will your actions help your child acknowledge and integrate
her mourning into her life? If not, if your actions deny some aspect of
the death or its consequences, then that strategy for stability is likely to
backfire in the end. Ultimately, it will complicate your child's grief
rather than helping to heal it.

Third, will your plans nurture future growth for yourself and your
child? For the initial months after the death, for example, having everyone stay at home may work for your four-year-old. But over time, both
you and your child need to move out into the world in order to continue developing as individuals.

GOAL 2: ACKNOWLEDGE THE EXPERIENCE AND IMPLICATIONS OF THE LOSS FOR EACH PERSON AND FOR THE FAMILY AS A WHOLE

Once you and your children reestablish some stability, then you may feel ready to explore that scary, dark experience called death. Although grieving as a family sounds straightforward, it's actually a complicated matter. First, the grief experience of each person, each child, is unique, both in the emotions it brings up and in its timetable. Second, adults and children cope with grief in significantly different ways.

The Uniqueness of Death for Each Person   Rod was seventeen, first-born in his family, a strong personality, a high school sports star, and a Naval Academy appointee, with dreams of becoming a doctor. When his diagnosis of inoperable kidney cancer came through, no family member was a good donor match. So his family devoted themselves to looking for and signing up potential organ donors. They mounted a series of statewide campaigns, in search of the right donor for Rod. His father, mother, younger brother, and sister each played a part, but Rod himself led the charge.

In campaign after campaign, he enrolled thousands of people. He seemed to do it all: making countless phone calls, spending unending hours greeting potential donors, writing note upon note of thanks to journalists and other volunteers. He was driven.

His cause became a town cause. Volunteers publicized the campaigns. Others staffed the refreshment table. Silently, the town believed that "together, we can sign up enough people. We can find a donor for Rod. We can save him."

So when Rod died before a kidney came through for him, the community felt it had lost its own son, a local hero of sorts. They mourned loud and long. In addition to the church ceremony, a crowded event, a community remembrance service packed the local YMCA. The local bank organized a scholarship fund for high school students aiming for careers in medicine. The garden club planted a perennial garden at the town library in his honor.

But beneath the surface, strong undercurrents were at play. Everyone in the family shared the town's sadness. But Rod's father, who had given up his own studies in medicine to pay the bills after Rod was born, felt bitter that his dream was shattered once again. Rod's mother felt pride in her son's life, mixed with profound sadness. Rod's younger brother, at fourteen an aspiring writer, resented the constant question: "Are you going to be a doctor too?"

Rod's younger sister, age thirteen, felt relieved that it was all over and angry at her brother's drive. What others had experienced as Rod's leadership in the battle against the cancer "enemy," she experienced as tyranny on his part, crushing everything and everyone standing in his way. As she told friends, "His attempts to find a kidney donor were no different from the rest of our lives together. He was always telling me what to do!"

Everybody in Rod's family lost someone when Rod died, but no one lost the same person. His parents lost their first-born star-child. His father lost the bearer of his own dreams. His brother lost the buffer for family expectations: Rod had upheld the family honor, leaving the other two kids the freedom to be whatever they chose. Rod's sister lost a boss she resented.

So each family member experienced different emotions, some contradictory to each other. His mother's pride cannot be reconciled with his sister's resentment, for example. Each feeling was real for the person who experienced it.

And even when individuals share similar feelings, they often experience them on a different time schedule. When Jean's husband killed himself, her first reaction was anger. "How could he leave me like this— with a couple of kids to raise by myself!" she stormed. It took her nine months to reconcile herself to his mental illness and touch the sadness inside her as well. Her children, by contrast, started off mostly sad and moved to anger only after several years.

Sometimes emotional changes reflect the person's deeper understanding of what was lost by the death. Your child first may be sad, with her sadness giving way to anxiety as she realizes that her parent will never come back and that she has lost the security of believing that both parents will always be available to her. Eventually, as she watches other children with both parents, she may feel jealous and angry. Later still, she may return to sadness or anxiety or yet another feeling, depending on circumstances.

As you try to facilitate your family's mourning, it's important to help each of your children explore his own experience over time—

without insisting that he feel the same from one day to the next. Simply accepting each child, wherever he finds himself at this particular moment, grants him the permission to examine what's happened, to make sense of it as well as he can right now, and to integrate it into his life story.

Sometimes this acceptance requires great skill and great patience on your part. Your child may have a wildly different, perhaps even strange, interpretation of past events or of what the dead person was like. When she comes out with such a statement, you may be inclined to correct her, to point out the errors in her reasoning. Instead, bite your tongue. Remember that it's more important that she explore the experience than that she "get it right" immediately. Sure, she'll explore some dead ends along the way, but in the process she'll resolve those aspects of the death that she needs to resolve.

Instead of correcting her, you need to find a way to acknowledge her feelings and supply alternative explanations. Responses that say "So, you understand it *that* way.... It's interesting: I understand it *this* way" are most helpful. (See "What Helps a Grieving Family," pages 68–74.)

After twelve-year-old Clarissa's mother died of brain cancer, the girl overheard her two aunts talking. She related the conversation to her dad late one night on the drive home from her grandparents. "Daddy?" she started tentatively, clearly nervous about raising the subject. "Auntie Gwen says that Mom got cancer because we live under a power line. Why did we move there if power lines cause cancer?"

For a moment, his daughter's question raised Fred's own doubts: Should he have insisted that his wife see a doctor as soon as her symptoms surfaced? Why had he agreed that they probably just meant she was "getting older"? Would it have made a difference?

But that's not what Clarissa asked, so he replied, "Honey, I know Auntie Gwen believes that, and sometimes I wonder, too, why Mom had to get cancer. In talking to Dr. Kristoff, though, I learned that a bunch of scientists have researched whether or not power lines cause brain cancer, and they've found that it doesn't. So no, I don't know what caused your mom to get it. We may never know, as frustrating as that is. I wonder what you think about it all."

Hearing your child's thoughts can be especially difficult if you were at odds in some way with the parent who died. Julie and Jack's divorce proceedings came to a halt when doctors found that Julie was dying of an enlarged heart. But her dying didn't eliminate Jack's anger at her spending habits and the debts she'd piled up. When she died, their four-year-old son, Jon, missed her terribly. After all, he knew her only as the loving mother who took care of him all day until Jack came home.

Jack struggled to acknowledge his own anger while also allowing Jon to miss his mother. He worked hard to encourage Jon's ongoing connection with Julie and to share memories with him, even though he was ready to move on from that chapter in his own life. Jack's willingness to tolerate Jon's expressions of love and yearning stands as a testimony to his love for his son.

Differing Coping Styles Even when you and your children seem to be on the same emotional wavelength, your differing coping styles can complicate matters. For most adults, grief initiates a period of retreat and reflection. To a greater or lesser degree, adults need to withdraw in order to digest what's happening, lick their wounds a bit, and figure out how to move on.

Unfortunately, while you may need to withdraw, your kids may need your active presence more than ever. Just as they ask you for help with their homework, they need you to help them figure out this problem called grief. They need your help in order to interpret the experience. They need to watch how *you* do it. They need your sheer presence to help them feel safe and less isolated. And they need your memories to stay connected with the person who died and to construct a more complete picture of her.

Yet grieving parents still need to make time for their grief. Here are some ways parents have carved out time for themselves:

• "I put my preschoolers to bed an hour earlier so that I can have some time for myself before I collapse from exhaustion."

• "My baby-sitter comes every Wednesday night, whether I have specific plans or not. Sometimes I'll just take a long walk or go sit at the lake or sit in a corner of the food court at the mall. Whatever I do, it's not errands. It's not kid-related. It's my time, just for me."

• "Instead of sending the kids to school on the bus each morning at 8:15, I drop them off at school when it opens at 7:30. They're safe, and I have an extra forty-five minutes to do what I please."

• "You know all those people who said, 'If there's ever anything I can do . . .'? Well, I've taken them up on it. The first weekend of each month, two different families take one of my two boys for an overnight. I used to feel it might be an imposition, but now I feel like it saves my sanity."

• "I set my alarm on weekends, even though the kids sleep in later. It's the best time each week for me to have a few hours alone. Then I take a nap in the afternoon."

• "I used to run errands while my daughter was at gymnastics each week. Now I drop her off and get a cup of coffee at the diner next door."

• "We initiated Quiet Time at our house each weeknight. For one hour after dinner, everyone goes to his room and does something quiet—homework if that's not finished yet, reading, a hobby. But importantly, there's no TV, no radio, no phone, no interaction."

• "I do Bath Time every night. For half an hour or so after the dinner dishes are done, I relax in hot water up to my neck. The kids know that's *my* time: woe unto the child who interrupts for anything less than serious bodily injury!"

• "Lunchtime at work used to be a time for socializing, and sometimes it still is. But often these days, I'll get in my car, eat lunch behind the wheel, drive to the nearest church, and just sit there."

Whatever strategy you devise, realize that your needs are as legitimate as those of your children. You need to cope, and your coping well helps your children cope well too.

GOAL 3: SUPPORT EACH PERSON AND THE FAMILY AS A WHOLE IN THEIR EFFORTS TO START GROWING AGAIN

Just when you think you've got the rhythms down, just when you've accepted the waves of pain and have figured out how to ride them—just then something changes. It may be that your child grows up a bit: changes schools, makes the varsity team, hits puberty, or has her first sleepover. When these milestones occur soon after a parent's death, they may throw you off completely, casting you back into overwhelming feelings. *Why isn't my partner here to share this?* you moan inside.

Later, though, such changes seem less heartwrenching—sad perhaps, poignant even, but not emotionally shattering. That's how growth always happens, with or without a death. We're confronted with new experiences, and with them comes an invitation to grow. Such invitations always involve risk and choice. We can either ignore the invitation, set it aside, and remain in a predictable pattern that feels safe, if not completely comfortable. Or we can accept the invitation and risk becoming something more than we are. The choice is ours, both as individuals and as a family.

You, too, will be offered an invitation to grow as a person after someone important to you dies. You may find yourself asking who you are now that your spouse or child has died: *What does it mean to be alone again after years of marriage?* Or: *Am I still my child's mother even though he's died?* In the process of answering these questions, you may discover parts of yourself—emotions, skills, thoughts—that you never suspected you had.

You may also notice a change in who you are close to. Strangers may become friends. Friends may become mere memories. You may find yourself searching for those people and groups and places where you fit, where you belong, *now*.

Finally, you may anguish over what it all means as well. Why do people die, especially so young? Where's the fairness? Where's God? And if we all just die in the end anyway, why bother trying to build anything? What sense does it all make?

As a family, you'll wrestle with similar questions: who you are now as a family; where you fit in socially; and how this horrendous event fits in your family's story.

"How many are in your family?" a new acquaintance may innocently ask. You fumble for an answer. Do you count the person who died or not? A telemarketer may call asking for the person who died. Again, you hesitate. These are usually signs that you're struggling with who you are now as a family. There's no right or wrong answer to these very painful questions. There's only an answer that works for you, right now, in this situation. At another time, in another place, you or someone else in your family might answer them differently. Each person needs permission to answer such questions however she wishes at any given moment.

You may find that your family's interests change. You no longer enjoy the beach where you all used to go. Or perhaps your family's personality has changed. You're more serious or more sensitive or more open or more affectionate.

Sometimes a simple everyday episode may drive home the realization that you're different. Two years after Naomi's husband died, her mother asked for an updated family picture, since the children had changed so much. Naomi couldn't respond immediately, and she later reflected, "I'm really feeling funny about having that picture taken! I can't say why, except that it seems like the final acknowledgment that we're not who we used to be. We're a different family. Having a new 'family' picture taken feels like the last nail in the coffin."

For some families, fitting in socially remains a difficult problem. First of all, there's the in-law question. As a spouse, you're no longer related to them, but your kids are. What does that mean to you? To your in-laws? How do you fit? How often will you see them? How involved will they be in your children's lives? (Read more on this topic in Chapter 7.)

And how do you and your children fit now in community groups like the Girl Scouts, the soccer league, or a family-based religious education program? When Jim's wife, Mary, died, Jim joked that he'd become a Girl Scout mom. But his joking didn't change the fact that he didn't really fit. He eventually found his niche working on the camping equipment.

While some families find it comforting to be with old friends, others find it painful to be around "whole" families. They may be more comfortable with others who share their situation. Bill and Nancy were in their late twenties when a car sideswiped them, instantly killing their infant daughter, Tasha. Afterward, as much as they still loved their friends, they found it difficult to socialize with them. "We all went to college together. We got married around the same time. And all of us started having kids last year. Now they all have little babies, but our Tasha is dead," Nancy commented. "For us, get-togethers were a constant reminder of what happened, of how they're whole families and we're not. And I think we made them uncomfortable, too, because we were a symbol of just how vulnerable we all are."

Bill continued, "Sometimes we'd try to help them feel more comfortable by acting like nothing had ever happened. But then we'd just come home exhausted and depressed. It's different when we socialize with the friends we've made at support groups. We've all gone through the same experience, so we don't have to pretend in any way."

Finally, families grapple with questions of how their tragedy fits in with their family history. How can you explain it? You may find your struggle in one of the following common family stories.

• The Chosen: "God provides. And on our side, our family always tries to do what's right. Did God screw up, or did we?"

• The Survivors: "Our family has dealt with a lot of problems, but we've always cared enough and worked hard enough to avoid a real catastrophe. What happened this time?"

• The Protectors: "We're family people, totally committed to our kids. We do whatever it takes to ensure that they have a good life. What did we do wrong?"

• The Charmed: "Our family is lucky enough to have tremendous resources: intelligence, good jobs, building retirement accounts. We're Americans, reaching the American Dream. This doesn't fit."

Figuring out who you are as a family after a death involves rewriting the family's story to incorporate the death and its aftermath. Eventually, many families choose to make meaning out of what they see as an otherwise meaningless loss. (See Chapter 11.)

Thirty-year-old Matthew remembers what happened in the years after his mother's death from cancer fifteen years ago. "It just galvanized us," he says, speaking of his family. "We became very determined people. My dad moved from practicing law for a food company to working for a biomedical firm. Now he works for FDA approval of anti-cancer drugs. My brother is an instructor with an adventure-based training company. He works with groups of people from all over the country, helping them confront their fears, overcome them, and work together as a team. I tried law school but hated it. Now I'm finishing my medical residency and hope to work in oncology.

"When I was a teenager, I struggled for a long time with why God let this happen to us," he concludes. "Finally, I've come to believe that there's no meaning in Mom's death except for the meaning we create out of it. I guess all of us have become determined to make a difference in the world as a result."

As your family contends with questions of identity, social fit, and meaning, what's a parent to do?

WHAT HELPS A GRIEVING FAMILY

Six key factors affect how well a family copes with a death. Two of them—the circumstances of the death and how close your family was to the person who died—you can do nothing to change. Obviously, witnessing the murder of a parent will traumatize a griever more than a peaceful death after a long, predictable illness. (See Chapter 14 for a discussion of various types of death.) Likewise, the death of a grandparent who was raising a child will prove more upsetting for a child than the death of a grandparent who lived three thousand miles away and who saw the child only once or twice each year. As much as you'd like to soften the effect of these factors, they're really out of your hands.

Fortunately, you *can* have an impact on the remaining four determinants: the level of mutual respect for differences among those in the family; the strategies your family uses to handle stress together; the openness of your family; and the balance of stress versus resources available for coping.

MUTUAL RESPECT

Parents often marvel at the differences among their children, so it's no surprise that each family member grieves and copes in her own way, on her own schedule. Families cope best when all the differences among them can be respected and even honored.

You can communicate your respect for differences in simple ways. First of all, you can openly discuss the fact that people grieve in different ways and that that's okay. You can list some of the many thoughts, feelings, and experiences that your children may or may not have.

When your child expresses a feeling, such as sadness, you can acknowledge it by saying, "Oh, you feel sad today." Make sure your child knows that you heard him and that you accept what he's saying.

Sometimes you can build on that acceptance by saying, "Sometimes I feel sad, and then sometimes I feel angry. I wonder if you ever feel angry as well as sad." Or if you're lucky enough to have a conversation with several people in the family, you can model respect by saying, "So Greg feels sad when we go to Grandma's. I feel sad too. I wonder if that's the only feeling we have, or if some of us have other feelings to add."

Be especially sensitive to the body language and nonword sounds that you project. You may laugh or turn your back simply because you're distracted by something, such as a commercial on television. Your child may not understand that, however, and may think you mean, *What you're expressing is silly or unimportant.*

When your grieving child is talking to you about an emotionally loaded topic, put down the newspaper. Stop chopping the vegetables. Turn off the television. You can always return to them, and frankly, they're not as important as helping your child emotionally. Your grieving child may stop sharing if he thinks you consider his innermost thoughts and feelings unimportant.

HEALTHY STRATEGIES FOR MANAGING STRESS

We've already discussed two unhealthy ways some families handle stress: cutting off emotions and cutting off people. A third unhealthy method that some families use is blaming. For these families, placing the blame on somebody, *anybody,* gives them a target for all their anger and pent-up emotions and restores their faith that the world is a fair place. Somebody just messed up horribly. When James died from cancer of the esophagus at the age of forty-four, everybody in his family had a different target of blame. Nine-year-old Kenny blamed him for smoking. Keisha, fourteen, blamed her mother: if only she had fed James a totally vegetarian diet and insisted on meditation, Keisha was sure he would have survived. And James's wife, Clare, blamed the doctors. "Why didn't they catch it at his last checkup nine months ago?" she complained.

A blaming coping style usually pervades a family's grief. Tension in the house may be compounded when some family members blame another for not doing his share of the work, for example.

Families who don't rely on blame seem to be able to say, "The death was no one's fault. It's just a terrible situation, stressful for all of us, and we're each doing the best that we can." Often they incorporate five elements into their stress management processes.

Be aware of stress First, they're aware of when they're feeling stressed. They can identify their own moments of vulnerability. After Mike died at age forty-eight, Celeste, his wife, began to refer to her stressful times as "Mike moments" to friends. One day Celeste's temper ran particularly short with her youngest son, a preschooler. Her older ten-year-old son said, "Mom, I think you're having a 'Mike moment.' " Celeste relates, "I just started laughing. Of course, he was right. My preschooler was just being a four-year-old, and I was just stressed from having all the responsibility twenty-four hours a day, seven days a week, without Mike to relieve any of the pressure. Hearing it out of such a young mouth put it all in perspective. From then on, that phrase became our code for saying, 'Hey, this isn't really about what you're reacting to. It's about being stressed out because Daddy died.' "

Identify the sources of stress A second helpful stress strategy is to identify the sources of stress. Just naming what's bothersome can relieve some of the pressure, partly because it tells you that your family is not falling apart and partly because there's a clear "enemy." Sometimes it takes a while to figure out what's causing the stress. Just as it's helpful to look for patterns in your kids' behavior as a means of deciphering what's happening inside them, so too it's helpful to look for patterns in your family's stress. Does it always appear at a particular time of day, or day of the week? After a certain activity? Are there circumstances in which the pattern doesn't hold?

Jerre found that going back to work from ten to five on Monday and

Tuesday caused a stress overload in her family. As soon as she walked in the door at five-thirty, each child vied for her attention. At the same time, they were all hungry, and she felt the pressure of getting dinner on the table. Jerre finally solved the problem by fixing a fruit or vegetable salad first thing each morning, then sitting down with the kids to eat it as soon as she got home. Sometimes salad time lasted an hour, sometimes only thirty minutes. Only afterward did she start preparing dinner. That way everyone's immediate hunger was satisfied, and at the same time, each child received his "family fix." Dinner at seven seemed late, but the process worked.

Respect everyone's needs Jerre's approach to her family's stress also illustrates the third element of successful stress strategies: respecting the needs and feelings of each person while remaining focused on the source of the stress itself. If Jerre had ignored her family's feelings, the chaos would have escalated. On the other hand, preparing food without addressing their feelings would not have worked either. Jerre solved the dilemma by balancing both.

Generate potential solutions, then choose one The fourth strategy is to generate lots of potential solutions before picking one. Jerre debated several options before settling on "salad time." She thought of switching her work hours to 8:30 to 3:30. But she rejected this option because she counted on those early hours each day for her own quiet time. Quitting the job was another option, or cutting back to one day each week. With money tight, however, Jerre felt she'd just be replacing family stress with financial stress.

Ultimately, Jerre's own mom provided the solution. She reminded Jerre that they had all eaten together as a family, even though Jerre's dad never came home from work till 6:30. A late afternoon snack of vegetables and dip carried them through early hunger pangs.

Be patient Developing helpful strategies for dealing with stress takes time. Sometimes you need to sleep on the problem, solicit ideas from others, let it all percolate in your mind, and see what develops naturally in your heart and head.

FLEXIBILITY AND OPENNESS

In addition to mutual respect and healthy stress management, flexibility and openness characterize families who end up functioning well after a loss. As we have seen, families will benefit if they're open to letting others help. Some families try to handle it all themselves, but sooner or later, they usually find they can't do it all themselves, at least not without increased stress. (And stress in a family is often contagious: you "catch" it from your kids and vice versa.)

Additionally, if your family communicates openly about what each of you feels and needs, you're more likely to find solutions that fit.

Be open to the trial-and-error nature of the grief process. Recognize that your family may not "get it right" the first time. Interpretations of the family story, for example, may change over the course of the years, as further ramifications of the death come to light. Working out new relationships with in-laws and new groups of friends may take some time. Remember, the ultimate goal is not to find the perfect solution, once and for all, but to create a space in which each person in the family can fulfill his or her own potential as a human being.

RESOURCES FOR COPING

Since stress is contagious, grieving families who function well find ways to keep stress to a minimum for each family member. For example, even though the children are not *directly* affected, this is not the best time for you to change jobs. Your increased stress may increase their stress as well.

The resources your family has for coping, such as financial stability and a strong network of family and friends, can also offset the stress your family experiences.

Having financial resources obviously helps. First, being able to make ends meet eliminates one source of stress. Second, it increases your options for finding workable solutions. You can hire baby-sitters more often, for example, while you take some private time or visit with friends. Third, it enables you to maintain traditional leisure activities and school choices.

"But I don't *have* any financial resources," you object. And perhaps that's true. But many grievers find that in addition to working full or part time to generate income, they have "hidden" financial assets, assets beyond insurance monies or cash in the bank. They "downsize" from a larger home or car to a less expensive one, thereby freeing up some cash. They ask family members or friends to make a long-term, interest-free loan. They liquidate equity in a house by moving to a rental property. They tap into retirement funds (even though a penalty must be paid). Of course, these may be the last places you want to look for money, but they *are* options for reducing your family's short-term stress.

Sometimes grievers try to put aside their insurance or social security money, saving it for college or the rainy day that they fear will come later on—even though insufficient cash is coming in to pay the bills pouring in today. In the first four months after Chris died, Heather felt she was living under a very dark cloud: the septic system needed to be dug up and repaired, the washer and dryer needed to be replaced after shorting out in a storm, and the family car (after 200,000 miles) was on its last legs. "Chris's insurance policy paid off $50,000," she explained, "but I felt that if I spent that money, where would I ever find the money to send the kids to college? Meanwhile, my accountant friend kept encouraging me to invest it somehow. Finally, my dad pointed out that I could spend $30,000 on repairs and a newer used car and still have $20,000 left to invest. *And* I'll be able to work full time long before any of the kids reaches college age."

One practical question that parents often struggle with is how much of their financial situation to share with the kids. Kids of all ages worry that there won't be enough money. When they ask you about it, how specific should you get? In our experience, it's best to avoid talking in specific dollar amounts. A hundred dollars is a gold mine to an eight-year-old. Twenty thousand sounds like overwhelming riches! If you share specific dollar amounts, your younger child may not understand why she can't buy the latest gadget.

In contrast, your older child may unnecessarily worry about the big-ticket items such as college tuition. He may not understand all the options you have at your disposal for paying the bills.

We suggest that (if it's true) you simply reassure your child by saying, "We have enough money to stay in this house, have plenty to eat, and so on. We may have to cut back on new school clothes or Christmas gifts a little this year. You may have to choose between soccer and visiting Grandma this summer. But we're going to be just fine overall."

Besides financial resources, a strong support network also helps offset the stresses that come with grief. You may enjoy such a network already, or you may need to develop one for your family, as we'll discuss in Chapter 7.

Whatever resources your family now possesses, whatever challenges you now face, practice having patience with yourself, your kids, and with the grief process overall. Just as your child will revisit his grief at each new growth spurt and with each significant change in her world, so too will your family rework their grief over time. Together you'll experience new learning, new ways of adapting, and new means of integrating your grief into your life. You don't have to know it all now. You will have time to work it out together, as a family.

Chapter 5

FIVE CHALLENGES OF A GRIEVING CHILD: HOW YOU CAN HELP

> I woke up the morning Mom died, and it was so quiet—kinda scary quiet. I thought it was weird, but I knew something was *really* wrong when we were allowed to eat Hostess cupcakes and Coca-Cola for breakfast!
>
> —Sarah, 10 years old

IF YOU'VE LIVED THROUGH THE DEATH OF A LOVED ONE, YOU know that death is a twister. It sucks you in, twists you around, then crashes you back to earth in a strange, new land—one that may look fine on the outside but also seems filled with danger. Sound a bit like *The Wizard of Oz*? We think so.

Let's face it. This new land is scary, filled with people we think we know but who are now acting in very strange ways. They may ask us questions that we don't know how to answer. And we're alone, without someone important in our lives.

Like Dorothy in Oz, children and adults alike want to go home—go back to a better time, before their loved one died. We ache to return to the familiar, where we were surrounded by everyone we love and all the people we can count on, where we were safe. "But which is the way back to Kansas?" we cry with Dorothy. "I can't go back the way I came." We'd give anything to get out of the Oz of grief.

Confused by all the crossroads we encounter on the way down the road, like Dorothy we ask, "*Now* which way do we go?" A voice we don't recognize answers, "Pardon me, but that way is a very nice way. . . . It's pleasant down that way, too. . . . Of course, people *do* go both ways!"

Like the scarecrow, our heads are full of straw, unable to understand what's happened. Like the tin man, we're oiled up and functioning but feel empty inside. Like the lion, we put on a brave face when we go out into the world, but where's the nerve we need, the determination? Why do we feel so scared?

Children, especially, silently wish for anyone—a wizard, a God, a surviving parent, a new sibling or stepparent—with the brains, the heart, and the courage to supply the answers and support them through emotional upheaval.

Of course, in the end, there is no wizard.

Grieving children have to find their own way through the land of grief. But they need us to help them discover their own power to do so: to help them figure out their own understanding of what's happened, experience their own feelings of grief, develop their courage, and find their way home to a new place that feels safe yet is still connected to their old life and to the person who died.

We've identified five challenges that grieving children face. Let's explore each one and discuss how caring adults can help grieving kids meet these challenges.

FEELING SAFE IN THEIR WORLD AGAIN

Six-year-old Susan became an only child overnight when a tractor trailer crashed into the family's Toyota, instantly killing her father and brother on their way home from a Boy Scout camping trip. Ever since then, she bounces into her mom's bed every morning with the very same question: "So Mom, what's the plan for today?"

Susan, like most grieving children, has a seemingly insatiable need to know exactly what's happening in order to feel safe again. She needs to know what and whom she can trust. After all, she *thought* Dad would always be there. She *thought* her parents would always protect her and her brother. She *thought* hospitals could make everybody better after an accident.

But that tractor trailer destroyed not only her father and brother but all her assumptions about how the world works. Now she approaches life more tentatively, wondering, "What can I count on? What's predictable? Who can I trust, *really*? My mother? My teachers? Myself?"

Here's how you can help your child reestablish a sense of safety.

DEAL WITH YOUR OWN WORRIES

Anxiety is contagious. During the World War II bombing raids in London, researchers asked, "What is it about this experience that renders some children terrified and some children calm in the face of it?" Much to their surprise, the most critical factor, they found, was the anxiety level of the mother. Calm children seemed to say to themselves, "If Mom's comfortable that everything's going to be fine, then I'm comfortable too."

So how do you stay relatively calm when *your* whole world has blown up too? Here are suggestions from other parents of grieving children:

• "I've started running again. I think it relaxes me in two ways. First, I say to myself, 'If I can make it up this damn hill, I can do anything!' And second, by the time I'm finished with a couple of miles, I'm too *tired* to worry. And I'm just so happy not to be running anymore."

• "Being in touch with nature has always put things in perspective for me. I take a walk in the woods, watch the buds develop or the leaves fall, watch the water trickle by in the stream—and it reminds me that everything happens in its own time. Eventually everything will work out, even though I can't figure out how just now."

• "I didn't set out to do this, but somehow I found myself with a 'worry partner,' another woman who was widowed a few years back. She just listens to it all, makes me feel normal because she worried about all the same things, and helps me think up solutions."

• "Every morning over my cup of coffee, I sit and think about all the hardest times in my life and how I got through them. I list for myself how much better prepared I am to deal with this now than I would have been ten years ago. I think about all the ways in which this could have been worse."

• "I'm getting into spirituality—not religion exactly, but developing the inner side of me. So I'm reading books and trying out meditation. It makes me feel like everything that's happening is part of something bigger, and that it's okay."

As you work to alleviate your own worries, remember: Your confidence that everything will be okay (not wonderful perhaps, but okay) will rub off on your child.

ACTIVELY MANAGE THE LEVEL OF CHANGE IN YOUR CHILD'S LIFE

Obviously, you can't control everything. Sometimes circumstances force us to make changes we'd rather not make. Even when they do, however, there are steps you can take.

Maintain as many routines as you can. This may seem a minor point, but before you doubt its importance, think about what happens when your own morning routine is thrown off. A temperamental coffeepot at breakfast time can sour your mood all morning. And a car that won't start can ruin your day.

Routines that may really matter to your kids include:

• *Morning routines:* how they are awakened in the morning (by an alarm clock, a gentle nudge, or a holler up the stairs) as well as by whom; the details of dressing (who gets their clothes ready, and when—the night before or each morning); which comes first, washing up, dressing, or eating; eating routines (who prepares the food, who eats with whom, who takes care of the dishes, who prepares lunches); who gets the bathroom when; how they are sent off to school; who says good-bye and how (with a wave, a kiss, a hug, a walk to the bus stop)

• *After-school routines:* where they spend their after-school hours, in what activities, and with whom; how they travel home; when they are expected to complete homework, with whose help, and with whose oversight; who fixes dinner, what time it's regularly served, and who cleans up afterward

• *Evening routines:* television rituals; snacks; bathing rituals (who draws the bath and whether it's a time for playing or talking or holding afterward); bedtimes; how they go to bed (at what time, with a story or "talk time," or a tuck-in, or a kiss goodnight); night sights and sounds (nightlights on, music playing, shades drawn or not)

These routines may seem small to us as adults, but to your children, they are the stuff that life is made of.

Make as few major changes as possible. For instance, most of the time it's best not to move your household unless financial pressures force you to. If you do have to move, try to stay in the same town, so your kids can go to the same school and keep the same friends. Stay on the same bus route if possible. In other words, in the face of major change, try to stick to as many routines as possible.

Likewise, if your spouse died and you never worked outside the home, delay returning to work for a while if you can. If you have to start working, try to arrange your schedule in a way that lets your child follow his routine: Pick him up after school still, or be home when he walks through the door. Or if your child always played sports after school or attended an after-school play group, try to keep that up as well.

Many people don't have the luxury of staying in the same locale or setting their own work schedule. And some major changes, tough as they are, may actually help meet your kids' needs. Some parents decide to move closer to relatives who will watch the kids after school. So much as a steady course is reassuring to a grieving child, new needs and new constraints can force change. How do you handle changes that *must* be made?

Communicate.
Explain to your child what's going to change because of the death and, equally important, what's *not* going to change. An amazing number of

kids silently worry, after a parent dies, that they'll be forced to move out of town and that there won't be enough money to survive. Just knowing they will live in the same place for a few more years (even if it means you'll return to work) or that there's enough money to live on (even though it means you have to move) can reassure a child. He will feel better knowing you have a survival strategy.

On the other hand, don't overpromise. And if something may change, tell your child.

Give notice.
Give your children as much notice as possible of a coming change. If you have to move, tell them well before you talk to anyone else about it. Answer their questions and concerns, again and again if necessary.

You'll benefit by getting a chance to help your child figure out how to cope with the change well in advance. And your child will realize you've been honest with him. It's scarier to wonder if your parent is telling you the truth than to know you have to plan for a major change. In the midst of all this change, one thing remains predictable: the parent's trustworthiness.

Space out changes.
Space out major changes if you can, so that your children can get used to them one at a time.

Involve your children.
Involve your children in the change process so they feel some sense of control. Take them with you when house-hunting. Discuss whether their new bedroom should look exactly like the old one or if they'd like to decorate it differently. Encourage them to think with you about what's really important in a house or a prospective after-school babysitter. Encourage them to ask questions.

Recognize your own limits.
Don't take on more changes than you can handle—if you feel overwhelmed, your child will feel overwhelmed as well. Ask others for help if necessary so you can still be present and helpful to your child, even during a major transition.

Move in late summer.
If you have to switch your child's school, try to schedule the move for late summer. This will allow her to spend most of the summer with her existing friends, yet also give her a bit of time to acclimate to a new home before school starts in the fall. When it does start, help her explore the social and recreational opportunities available, but resist the temptation to be overly protective.

Maintain the same rules of discipline and the same expectations for your child. It's tempting to lower expectations for grieving kids; to cut them significant slack in their school effort and attendance, in their courtesy toward others, and so on. Sometimes, especially in the first days and perhaps weeks after the death, that makes sense. But as weeks turn into months, your child needs to return to some sense of normalcy, and that means lovingly and consistently applying the same expectations as before.

Caring discipline, reasonably applied, makes children feel safe. At sixteen years of age, our daughter Kate came back from a church trip to repair homes in Appalachia. She told us about another young man on the trip, whose father had abandoned the family and whose mother had died recently as well. Kate, comparing her situation to his, reflected, "Sometimes you guys and your rules are a pain in the neck, but at least you're around and I know that you're not going to let me do anything really stupid."

Even at sixteen, Kate appreciated what we were trying to do. While she didn't like all of our rules, and she certainly disagreed with many of them, she also recognized their purpose: to keep her safe. So despite the pressure you may feel now to relax the controls, it's especially important to stick to your guns.

ACTIVELY INCREASE THE LEVEL OF PREDICTABILITY IN THEIR LIVES

Not everything is predictable, and frankly, your child needs to deal with some unexpected change as well, in order to grow into a competent adult. But generally, life hands kids enough surprises to teach them flexibility. Now's the time to help them feel like the world is returning from chaos to a place where things happen in predictable ways. Here are some suggestions that other parents have found helpful.

Make sure your child knows where you are and how to reach you. If she's very young, teach her how to use the phone to call you. Always tuck change into her shoe, pocket, or backpack. Instruct her teachers, coaches, Scout leaders, and baby-sitters to let her call. She may use the privilege a great deal at first, but over time that will taper off. And meanwhile, she'll have learned that you are available. Even older kids appreciate knowing where you are and when you'll return. To this day, our college-age kids ask where we are if one of us isn't home.

Do what you say you're going to do. This simple act reinforces to her that she can trust you. It's especially important to be on time when you arrange to meet your child: if you're late, she may worry that something has happened to you too.

Sometimes making these arrangements requires careful communication. Almost two years after Mary died, Mary Ann accompanied Kate on a Girl Scout campout. Before Mary Ann left for a few hours to give a talk, she promised Kate she'd be back at the campground before dark. She returned at dusk to find Kate sobbing, afraid Mary Ann wasn't coming back. Kate and Mary Ann had defined *before dark* differently. For Kate, it meant when the sun set. For Mary Ann, it meant when you couldn't see outside.

Help your child anticipate both what will happen and how he might feel. If you're visiting the cemetery together for the first time, for example, explain what a cemetery is ("where dead bodies are kept"). Talk about gravestones and decorations. Explain why people visit and what people do there (leave mementos, talk to the person who died, sit on the ground and rest). Most important, talk about how he may feel and make sure he knows that all sorts of varied feelings and thoughts are normal.

Also, take time to help your child through regular life transitions, such as changing schools, either from a move or a "graduation" to middle or high school. You may want to visit the new school ahead of time, so your child can find his new classrooms, the lunchroom, gym, bathroom, nurse's office, and telephone. (He may want to call you, especially the first couple of days.) Getting to know key people at the school (teachers, the nurse, the principal) will also give your child a better sense that he's safe and that he has resources if something goes wrong. Teenagers too, as they take on new responsibilities (a first job and paycheck, a checking account or credit card) or prepare for college, appreciate but might not ask for help anticipating and planning for the practical and emotional challenges ahead.

It's also helpful to ask other adults who have raised grieving kids what experiences proved tough for them. While some are universally difficult, such as Mother's Day, Father's Day, Scout campouts, and father-daughter dances, some may be unique to your town. In our town, grade school mothers traditionally help prepare the school's float for the annual town parade. For one grieving youngster we know, working on the float without her "own mom" proved tough. Once such events are identified, you can anticipate these sore spots for your child, and together you can brainstorm the best way to handle them, giving her some sense of control.

Finally, you can predict—and let your child know—that emotions are sometimes unpredictable! One minute you'll be feeling fine; the next minute a wave of sadness will hit as a bittersweet memory surfaces. Just knowing that that happens to everyone can be reassuring, so your child won't worry that he's "going crazy." And you can share with him how to cope with unpredictable emotions when they arise.

BE PRESENT

Nothing is as reassuring to your grieving child as your sheer presence. Express your love more frequently, both in words and in hugs and kisses.

On a regular basis, spend time just listening to whatever your child has to tell you. It may not always be related to the death. Indeed, sometimes she may be testing to see if you love her enough to listen to the minutiae of her life. But we can promise you this: If you don't listen to your child talk about the small things, then she may never talk to you about the big ones.

Pick a place to talk that's physically comfortable for your child. With young children, it may help to sit on the floor. Likewise, many preteens and teenagers seem to talk most freely on long drives or during family vacations, when for some reason they feel safe enough to let down their guard.

Many children end up sleeping with parents after someone in the family dies. Often parents struggle with whether or not this is appropriate and/or helpful. Clearly, Mom's or Dad's presence helps kids feel safe at night, a time that can be scary. And in some cultures, it's common practice for families to sleep together, regardless of whether someone has died. So what's the problem?

Over the short term, with young children, there is none. Over the long term, their fear may interfere with their ability to participate in activities such as sleepovers with friends or campouts with Scouts. And this sleeping arrangement may not be the best for you. Many parents find it tough to get a good night's sleep with a child in the bed. Further, at some point you may wish to get away by yourself or with a friend for a night or two. If your child sleeps with you on a regular basis, she may find it more difficult to sleep peacefully without you. And if you're widowed, you may eventually remarry. Having a child in bed may add stress to your new relationship; changing the pattern when a *new* spouse enters the picture sets *him* up as the bad guy.

What can you do if your child insists on sleeping with you? First of all, talk to your child about his night fears, why he wants to sleep with you. Don't judge his reasons or try to change his mind. Just listen. Often simply naming fears helps to resolve them. You might suggest solutions (nightlights or sharing a room with a brother or sister), but if he is not interested, don't push him. Give him a chance to work it out on his own. Often children return to their own beds on their own once the rest of their world feels back in control.

If your child continues to want to sleep with you over time, you may choose to help him confront his fear, one ministep at a time. Start by asking him to sleep on a mattress or sleeping bag right next to your bed so that you can sleep better. After a while, suggest moving it out into the hallway but at an angle so that he can still see you in the bed. For the first few nights back in his own room, you may find it helps if you sleep on a mattress next to his bed—at least for part of the evening. Be sure to tell him you may return to your own bed later at night. Finally, it may help to buy him an inexpensive walkie-talkie or baby's intercom system: that way he can feel connected to you and at the same time be "cool"—and in his own room.

DEALING WITH BAD DREAMS

---

1. Create the conditions that nurture sound, peaceful sleep:
    *   Watch your child's food intake: no caffeine and a limited amount of food.
    *   Avoid mental stimulation. Discourage watching horror movies or reading exciting books.
    *   Maintain a regular bedtime ritual as well as consistent times for retiring and waking.
    *   Encourage your child to get his worries out during the day so that they're not lurking in his mind at night.

2. Create an environment for your child that feels cozy and safe:
    *   Use a nightlight.
    *   Play soft, comforting music.
    *   Tuck favorite stuffed animals around your child. Use favorite blankets and pajamas.

3. If your child dreams of the person who died, don't assume that's scary for her. Many grievers — children and adults — dream about their dead loved ones and find it comforting. Discuss the dream with your child. What happened? How did it make her feel? If the dream was troublesome in a certain way, explore why she might be experiencing those emotions. Help her think about whether her conclusions are realistic.

4. Use the Dream Catcher ritual. Explain how Native Americans believe that a dream catcher lets good dreams through the spaces in its web while capturing bad dreams. Suggest that you try it together to see if it works for your child. Sometimes this ritual enables a child to believe bad dreams won't happen, and his belief can help to create the reality!

5. Ask your child to tell his dreams to somebody. Sometimes talking about a dream can make it less real and less scary. Suggest to your child that he envision a better ending for his bad dreams, an ending in which he is powerful and conquers the bad guy or situation. Encourage your child to go over the good ending repeatedly.

DEAL WITH YOUR CHILD'S HEALTH CONCERNS

According to the Child Bereavement Study, over 60 percent of grieving children worry that surviving parents will die, and almost 20 percent worry that they themselves will die.

Sometimes this happens because a child, depending on her age, doesn't really understand death. As we discussed in Chapter 2, some children think death is contagious. Or they may not understand what caused the specific death. When Tamara's father died of a heart attack, she heard her mother tell someone that it broke Tamara's heart. Tamara then became fearful that she, too, was going to die, and she refused to leave her mother's side, even to go to kindergarten. When Tamara's mom realized what had happened, she called the pediatrician and set up an appointment. The pediatrician explained to Tamara what a heart attack really was, and together she and Tamara made a tape recording and "took a picture" (an EKG) of Tamara's heartbeats. By "seeing" and hearing her own healthy heartbeats, Tamara was reassured of her own health.

Of course, if your loved one died from a genetically based condition, your child, as he matures, will benefit from talking to his health care team about the risk that he might contract the illness. You'll also want him to know what self-care strategies he can employ to maintain his health in the face of those risks.

Getting a checkup yourself may help alleviate your child's fears. Your nurse or physician, if skilled in talking to young children at their own developmental level, could tell your younger child that you're healthy. (If you're unsure of how "kid friendly" a health professional is, ask her how she would explain the death. Then judge for yourself: Would your child understand such an explanation? If not, find someone else.)

For preadolescents and teens, who may not want to *talk* about their fears but who worry nonetheless, you could ask your doctor to write a summary of your health status. If this summary is understandable and carries no cause for alarm, you could leave it lying around for your older children to read. Alternatively, stage a conversation with another adult, a conversation your child is certain to overhear, during which you tell your friend the results of your health exam.

Of course, don't distort the truth. If you have a serious health concern, tell your child about it. Explain what's wrong and what you're doing to stay as healthy as you can. If you can honestly say that most people with your condition live a full life span, tell your child that. If you are likely to die before your child reaches maturity, explain to your child that it may happen and what provisions you've made for her care.

Regardless of your current health status, your children may be comforted to know what would happen to them if you died. After Mary Ann entered our family, for example, she formally adopted Jim's kids. They understood that if Jim died, she would take care of them. She was able to say that the family would stay together, in the same house, in the same school, with the same friends—at least until they all went off to college.

Later, when Jim's brother and sister-in-law died together in a helicopter crash, our kids realized that we could both die. What would happen to them then? We explained who would take over the parenting role in that case as well. As painful as it was to discuss, the kids appreciated knowing that someone would be there to keep them safe. They knew they couldn't make it on their own. It helped to know that plans were already in place.

HELP YOUR CHILDREN BELIEVE IN THEIR ABILITY TO BE POWERFUL IN THEIR OWN LIVES

Part of what's scary when someone dies is the feeling that life is out of our control. Adults as well as children can end up feeling like victims. As a result, they may live in constant anxiety and even feel hopeless at times. Needless to say, their self-esteem can plummet.

For your children, you can help reverse this tendency in concrete ways. First, always validate their experience. When adults use phrases like "You can't *really* believe that" and "It's silly to feel that way," we're telling children not to trust their own experience, not to trust themselves. Instead of downplaying your child's experience, acknowledge his right to have those thoughts or feelings. Set limits to his behavior if necessary, but never teach your child to distrust himself.

Next, encourage your child to develop new skills. Help your daughter learn to cut the lawn, take out the trash, do the grocery shopping. Help your son learn to cook meals and do the laundry. While it's never a good idea to give children parental responsibilities, it can boost their self-confidence to know that they can take care of many of their own needs.

For some children, learning a martial art like tae kwon do can prove particularly empowering. It can provide a channel for releasing aggression while also making your child feel he is master of his fate, not its victim. Make sure to choose a program and instructor whose focus is self-protection, self-control, and personal growth as opposed to aggression. Watch a class to gauge how comfortable you are with the program.

If the death in your family was violent or sudden, your child may feel more confident if she knows how to call 911 or administer CPR or mouth-to-mouth resuscitation. These techniques can give her some real power in certain life-threatening situations.

Next, give your older child choices in many areas of her life. Not only will she learn that she can influence outcomes, she'll also learn to trust herself. Giving her choices shows her that *you* believe in her. *You* trust her to make these choices.

Younger children benefit from making choices in smaller matters: what to wear, what to eat for lunch or dinner, which video to watch, and so on. Remember that a young child may not be able to sift through a number of alternatives; it usually works better if you offer just two or three options. You might say, "Would you rather watch *The Little Mermaid* or *The Lion King* tonight?" Or you might ask whether he prefers pork chops or spaghetti for dinner. As your child matures, he can competently handle more significant decisions and a broader range of options.

Additionally, help your child learn techniques for soothing himself when he is upset. Help him identify what makes him feel better. Teach him to ask for a hug or to be held when disturbed, to talk to someone who listens, to rock in a chair or swing in a swing, to cuddle up with a favorite stuffed animal, to curl up in blankets and draw or color, to go for a long walk or run.

TACKLING TEASING

A neighbor or classmate teases your child about a dead parent or sibling. He feels powerless to stop it. How can you help him find his own strength in the midst of teasing?

1. Teach him to ignore it. Help him understand how frustrating it is for the teaser when he doesn't respond.

2. Practice potential responses with your child beforehand. Help him learn to:
   • Walk away with a disgusted look on his face.
   • Ask the teaser how he would feel if his parent died.
   • Pretend that he doesn't hear them and keep asking "What?" or "I beg your pardon?" The combination of not getting a rise out of the child and having to repeat themselves over and over again can be embarrassing for the teaser.

3. Remind your child that friends or other adults can help by telling the teaser to cut it out.

4. Suggest that just because someone teases someone that doesn't make his remarks true.

5. Help him realize that teasing usually stops as kids get older. (It's a very immature thing to do.)

6. Remind him not to fight or let teasers provoke him into trouble — or else they've really won!

Adapted with permission from handout of Fernside: A Center for Grieving Children in Cincinnati, Ohio

---

Finally, teach your child to use her imagination to feel more powerful. Like an athlete whose performance improves with visualization or a salesperson who continually perfects her sales calls in her mind, your child can gain confidence by imagining herself over and over again as competent and strong. Encourage her to play jungle, acting out the role of a powerful animal. Help her imagine herself as a superhero conquering the bad guys. Make up stories together in which she solves the problem and saves the day.

UNDERSTANDING THE DEATH

As we explain in Chapters 2 and 6, the younger your child is, the more she'll struggle with understanding the concept of death, its finality, and the fact that everyone eventually dies. So the more you'll have to help her understand what happened. These are some ways to work with her.

First, be courageous enough to provide accurate, concrete information. Answer the questions your child asks, but don't overload him with information. Know that he'll ask the question again and again and, over time, in deeper and more significant ways. (For help with explaining various causes of death—cancer, heart attack, suicide, murder, and so on—see Chapter 14.)

We strongly suggest inviting your child to attend a support group for grieving children, where she can learn from others in a similar situation. (We discuss this important resource in Chapter 7.)

You can also read books together, or watch videos and television programs together, that enhance your child's understanding of death. (We suggest some books in Appendix A.) As you encounter new books or videos, review them first yourself to make sure that they are accurate about death and dying as well as the grief process. Some videos, for example, show a death scene immediately followed by a scene in which everyone is happy and carefree again! Such videos teach children that grief is a short-term phenomenon, and that if you're in pain for very long, then something must be wrong with you.

Beyond a mental understanding of death and grief, your child also needs to grasp that "gone-ness" in his heart. We all do, when someone dies. As Karen said after her seventeen-year-old daughter died, "I just can't get it into my head that she's dead. I find myself making mental notes about what I'm going to tell her when she gets home. I expect her to pop in the door any minute. I pass a sweater in the store and wonder if I should buy it for her for Christmas. I know in my head that she's gone. I just don't know in my heart."

Realizing that someone is never coming back takes a very long time. It's as if you need to perform a million little experiments every day to discover whether it's real. Will he come home *this* time? Could it be her on the phone? Will he answer if I call into the other room? Will he come back to bed—is he only in the bathroom? Only after many, many such moments do you really, *really* know (at least most of the time) that the person you love is not coming back. It's as if there are levels of "realness." Over time, the death becomes more and more real in more and more ways.

However you think about it, this increasing sense of reality is not a process that you can speed up, either for yourself or for your child. It takes whatever time it takes. All you can do is help her face the reality as it begins to sink in. But how?

Help her give voice to her loss. Help her verbalize her increasing understanding of what happened and why. And use the *name* of the person who died when you talk about him. Encourage others to do the same.

Whatever you do, don't try to distract your child from her loss with activities. She needs to experience her loss in order to heal. Avoiding it now will postpone her grief, and postponed grief accumulates, becoming more difficult later on.

Finally, don't try to wipe out the loss by replacing the person who died with a new stepparent or child. It just won't work. Your child doesn't really want another dad. She wants *her* dad, the one who smelled of a certain shampoo and teased her in a particular manner and comforted her just so. Against those expectations, a stepparent is bound to fail.

And as wonderful as a new baby can be, his birth will not diminish the loss or the grief that your child feels. In fact, in her immaturity, she may feel cheated: *This new brother was supposed to make me feel better, but he doesn't. And to top it all off, now Mom and Dad have even less time for me.*

MOURNING THE DEATH

Watching a child mourn is perhaps the most heartwrenching experience for any adult. You may feel powerless, but there are concrete steps you can take to help your child mourn the death.

One of the best ways to support your child is to act as his "emotional coach." When you're teaching him to hit a baseball, for instance, you not only talk him through how to do it, you also take the bat in your own hands and show him. The same is true of grieving. As important as it is to talk about feelings, talking alone isn't enough. If you say it's okay to be sad but you never let your child see your sadness, how believable are your words? If you say it's normal to be angry but always deny you're feeling anger (even when your tone of voice betrays you and your face is turning red), your child will learn that there's something wrong with anger.

As in every other field, coaching is a tough balancing act. On one hand, you need to show your child that tears are normal. On the other, if you're a sobbing blob on the floor, this can be scary for your child. Sobbing blobs usually can't take care of their children very well, and their children know it.

Likewise, you need to be careful what you demonstrate. Scared parents create scared children. But parents who admit to a concern and actively problem-solve it in the face of difficulty teach their children to tackle their problems head-on. They coach their children in resilience.

When you yourself are grieving, of course, all of this is easier said than done. It takes tremendous energy to figure out what behavior to model and how to be an emotional coach. Sometimes you won't have the inner resources to do it. But each time you do, you'll empower your child to heal more fully.

You can also help your child grieve by playing with him, drawing pictures together, or creating games with him. One father played Feelings Football periodically with his eleven-year-old son. Each time he or his son threw the football, he had to name a feeling (sad, mad, stupid, lonely, jealous) that a person might feel if someone they loved died. If the person throwing the football thought a griever might feel a lot of that feeling, then he would throw the football high into the air. If he thought the feeling would be present in only a small way, then he would throw it close to the ground.

This wise father used an activity his son already enjoyed, football (especially played with Dad). It gave Dad the opportunity to expand his son's horizons about what normal feelings of grief are, but importantly, he didn't press his son to say how he himself was feeling. Instead, by letting his son say what he thought *other* people would feel, he helped him to express himself without the possibility of embarrassment or what an eleven-year-old boy might see as too much mushiness.

Other families engage in mutual storytelling, in which the developing story passes from one person to the next. A child might begin a story by saying, "Once upon a time there was a rabbit with two sisters. They played together and had fun. *Pass.*" When it's your turn to continue the story, you can develop it in a way that teaches your child something about feelings or grief. To teach your child about mixed emotions, for example, you might continue, "Most of the time, this bunny liked having his sisters around. But sometimes he liked it when they went away to spend a night at a friend's house."

If a story ends in a way you feel is not helpful, you can say, "I wonder if we can come up with a different ending to the story, one in which there's a reason to be a little sad but mostly happy at the end."

If your child likes to bake, make cookies together and use icing to create faces expressing the feelings people sometimes feel when someone dies. If your child likes to play make-believe, act out "hospital" or "funeral" or other scenes that she might have feelings about. The options are limitless. Simply think of ways to use your child's natural interests to express what's inside her.

At times, your child may wish to express her feelings alone. She may like to keep a diary of her thoughts, to write poetry or songs, to beat drums or bang out a song on the piano or guitar, or to create artwork. You can help her by providing special books to write in, colorful markers or paints and paper, percussion instruments, and clay to pound and to mold.

Despite the fact that many grieving children feel anger (at the person who died, at the medical personnel who didn't heal the person, at the surviving parent, at God), anger remains a very difficult emotion to express. It may help to explain that anger is simply your body's way of getting ready for a fight when you feel attacked. It's a buildup of chemicals inside that generates a lot of energy for your body to use in response to a threat. For that reason, kids (and adults) need ways to vent that "angry energy."

A popular feature of many children's grief support programs is a room for getting out "big" energy like anger. Sometimes these rooms are named after natural disasters: a "hurricane," "volcano," or "tornado" room. You can create such a space easily in your basement or garage. Just stock it with expressive materials:

- telephone books or magazines to rip apart

- bubble wrap to stomp on

- foam bats to hit the wall with

- a punching bag with gloves

- pillows or duffel bags filled with clean rags to wrestle with

- large paper cups to smash loudly with angry feet

- clay to throw against the wall

- a tape recorder to yell into

- pillows to kick

- paper bags to blow up and pop

- golf tees to hammer into thick styrofoam

And post a few rules. Common rules include: Don't go in unless someone else is home; always tell someone where you'll be; and clean up after yourself. Allow only one person in the room at a time so that no one gets hurt. Then, when the tension is building, invite your child to visit the hurricane room.

Other extracurriculars that can help manage anger include martial arts, distance running, building (such as Habitat for Humanity), wrestling, drumming, gardening, weight lifting, bread baking, and practicing clay-based arts.

Finally, you can help your child mourn by letting her create or participate in various rituals, such as visiting the cemetery.

STAYING CONNECTED WITH THE PERSON WHO DIED

When Kevin turned seven, he and his dad started building a tree fort with materials left over from the remodeling of the kitchen, which was occurring at the same time. When his dad died a few months later, Kevin often returned to the fort for some quiet time. Eventually, he convinced the kitchen subcontractors to help him finish the fort. From a few simple boards, it grew to have a tile floor, windows, and wallpaper. His mom finally capped the project when Kevin told her, "Mom, if you decide we have to move, don't worry about me. I'm going to get electricity and water in the fort, so I can just stay there and I'll be fine."

It's hard to know whether to laugh or cry at Kevin's remark. What's clear is that Kevin, like most other grieving kids, longed to stay connected with his dad. In the Child Bereavement Study, more than 80 percent of grieving kids said they felt that the person who died was watching them. Roughly 60 percent said they spoke to their loved one. Grieving kids—again 60 percent of them—dream of the person who died. These kinds of experiences are common—for adults as well as for children. If you are spiritually oriented, you can explain to your child that spirits survive even though bodies die. But aside from that, you don't need to do anything about such experiences. They're just ways of staying connected.

Staying connected to a loved one who has died helps kids, providing comfort as well as provoking healthy emotional expression. Your child will love to hear stories about the person who died. He'll enjoy looking at pictures and cherish photos of himself with the person. Over time he may pick up a sport or hobby that his loved one enjoyed. He may be comforted by wearing their clothes—not only the hand-me-downs of an older brother or sister but also the T-shirt or socks of a parent who died. Even infants may find it soothing to be wrapped in a sweater that still carries the smell of a parent who died.

Often caring friends and relatives question grievers' attempts to maintain ongoing connections. If a child's wall is covered with pictures of the person who died or if the room of a child who died remains unchanged, they wonder, "Isn't it time to move on? Is it healthy to keep a shrine for someone dead?"

But as a society, we do it all the time. When a famous person dies, we read their biographies for wisdom. We encase their letters in glass, display their shaving kits, their baby shoes, their bifocals, their rocking chairs. We buy the home they grew up in and make it a national historic treasure. We thank the person who envisioned creating the museum, and we praise their efforts to preserve a piece of our history. So why do we struggle so much when a family wants to preserve *its* history with someone who died? Why do we think it's unhealthy somehow?

Therese Rando, an international expert on grief and grief gone wrong, discusses two criteria for judging the healthiness of a griever's mourning. First, does the person believe that the person is dead? Second, is the griever's behavior supporting her in healing and reentering the normal flow and functions of life?[1]

For example, if a child of eight or older (old enough to know what *dead* means) keeps setting a place at the dinner table for a father who died six months ago, that's a concern. She needs extra help. Likewise, if she's suddenly so wrapped up in a hobby cherished by her dead parent or sibling that she has little time for the kinds of friends and social activities that are normal for her age, then seek expert advice.

Short of those criteria, enjoy watching your child stay in touch with the person who died. It's one way your loved one is still with you.

In addition to everyday activities, life's turning points offer opportunities for encouraging ongoing connections. Confirmations, changing schools, graduations, sports events, engagements, weddings—all of these are times to remember, to tell stories, and to reinforce the bonds of love with people who have died. Our Kate's mother spent a lifetime in love with the theater. Mary had the lead role in her high school play, studied theater in college, and as an adult, worked for a professional theater company. So the night Kate readied herself for her first high school performance, it represented more than just another fun, extracurricular activity. It was a connection to her mom, who had died six years earlier. To mark the occasion, Jim gave Kate a ring that Mary had received during a high school performance. Made of the tragedy/comedy masks that have symbolized theater for centuries, it was a way for Jim to say, "Your mom is with you onstage tonight, Kate, and she's very proud of you."

RESUMING CHILDHOOD AGAIN

When all is said and done—after all the tears and fears and anger and exhaustion—your grieving child is still a kid. Sometimes that's hard to remember. Because he's been through so much already, you may feel you need to make sure his life is close to perfect, regardless of the fact that kids need to make mistakes in order to learn that their behavior has consequences. Or you may want your child to be more responsible after a death: you just don't have the energy to cope with his lapses in responsible behavior, lapses that, although aggravating, are common for his age. And while he may need to play with you, you may shy away from it: after all, how can you be lighthearted when your heart itself is broken?

One night, after a daughter of our friends died, we baby-sat for the remaining kids, taking them for a meal at a local diner. While we were waiting, Jim began to make crazy jokes and silly faces. Everyone at the table erupted in giggles, which continued for some time. What a relief it was to hear them laugh! It said to us that the children were not completely soured on life because their sister died.

Of course, they will revisit the first four challenges again and again. They'll need reassurance about their own safety. They'll rework their understanding of how their sister died and why. They'll feel overwhelming feelings at times. They'll look for ways to stay connected. But for now, the giggles showed that underneath all the pain and anguish, they were still just kids.

Don't let your child lose the only childhood she'll ever have. Celebrate her birthdays and holidays as well as you can. Find ways to play with her. Learn to tolerate both her need to be near you and her need to be apart. Help her to meet, head-on, the normal challenges that life hands out, to grow and mature. Plan something that she can look forward to: a picnic, vacation, or other outing planned with no purpose other than the sheer fun of it. Sing songs together. Shoot hoops. Build sand castles. Guide her, without envisioning her childish blunders as lifelong character flaws. Be silly sometimes. Laugh. Give her the chance to see that life, as rotten as it feels some days, can also be good again.

HOW TO COMMUNICATE WITH

A GRIEVING CHILD

When my wife suffered a serious heart attack, she was kept alive by life
support systems for three days. I had to make the wrenching decision to
discontinue it. My eight-year-old daughter was angry about her mother's
death for months. She wouldn't even talk to me, but I didn't know why.
One night, out of the blue, she screamed at me: "Why did you have to
kill Mommy?!" I still don't know how to explain "life support" to an
eight-year-old.

— Mark, 32 years old

PETER'S PARENTS DIVORCED WHEN HE WAS TWO YEARS OLD.
When he was eleven, his mother died suddenly of a stroke. The
night before she died, Peter argued with her. He wanted to go to a rock
concert with his friends, but she said he was too young. Furious, Peter
fought with her for half an hour. Exasperated, she sent him to his room
to cool off. On his way upstairs, he yelled at her, "Drop dead!"

When Peter awoke the next morning, he found his mother on the
kitchen floor unconscious. He raced over to her to see what was wrong
and immediately called 911. Help arrived too late to revive her. Then
Peter remembered with horror the last words he spoke to her.

Peter's adolescent years with his father were turbulent. He was often
in trouble with the law and performed poorly in school. He partied
every weekend, getting drunk, or high on pot. After high school, he
took a job in the shipping department of a large corporation. He
worked hard, but he was absent often and in danger of being fired for

missing too much work. The employee assistance program at the corporation referred Peter to a counselor, who worked with him over several months. Peter made a major breakthrough, both in therapy and in his life, when he identified and worked on the guilt he carried from childhood about causing his mother's death. Peter was twenty-four years old when he first talked about it.

Communicating with grieving children about death, dying, grief, and loss is critical to the way they process their thoughts and feelings. In fact, the quality of that communication can determine how they will ultimately heal from their experience. Children who do not communicate what they are thinking and how they are feeling can be affected adversely for years to come.

Many parents, however, find it difficult to talk to their children about grief and death. But in most cases, you don't need a specialist or a therapist to get your children to talk about their grief. It is a simple process that you can do with the knowledge of a few basics.

WHY IT'S CRITICAL TO COMMUNICATE

If you want your child to heal from her experience of loss, nothing is more important than to communicate with her about what happened and why.

INFORMATION TAMES FEARS

When a family member dies, children are often terrified. From the time they were born, your children could count on being fed, changed, held, nurtured, and cared for. They felt safe and secure in your presence, and they felt safe and secure in the world. But after the death, the assumptions they made about their world are shattered. Children assume, for instance, that only very old people die, that parents will always be around for their children, and that hospitals fix people and make them better. After a death, they know these assumptions to be false.

Children are like boats that are securely anchored by their parents. When one "anchor" is taken away, either because the parent dies or is depressed from grief, children begin to drift on a sea that appears dark and cold. Death itself is not necessarily frightening to children, but the loss of safety and security undoubtedly is. By communicating with their children about the death and about their grief, surviving parents or guardians can recreate a secure place from which children can learn to trust the world once again. Grieving children need to be "re-anchored," reassured that the world continues to be safe, that they are going to be okay, and that you will be there for them.

INFORMATION GIVES KIDS A SENSE OF CONTROL

When children feel "anchored" by their parents, they feel in control. Within that structure they can become confident, competent human beings. They can test their independence for a while, then retreat to their parents when things get scary. But when a parent dies, they often feel out of control. They feel confused and besieged by unfamiliar emotions. Talking and communicating with grieving children helps them regain a sense of control in their lives. And when they maintain a healthy sense of control, they are less likely to lash out at others or engage in delinquent behavior.

COMMUNICATING GIVES KIDS PERMISSION TO EXPRESS THEIR FEELINGS

Children need to have opportunities and permission to talk openly about death and dying, knowing that you will be receptive. They should be able to come to you at any time and talk about the strange emotions they may be experiencing. As we've seen, kids don't grieve on cue. Feelings of sadness, anger, guilt, and fear can and will erupt at any time and subside just as suddenly. Knowing that they can come to you whenever that happens can be very comforting. Good communication is like a pair of open arms that conveys the message "I'm here for you whenever you want to talk."

GRIEVING KIDS DESPERATELY WANT TO COMMUNICATE

Children want to know. They are insatiable learners. They possess an amazing curiosity about life. And since death is a part of life, they are curious about death, too.

Grieving children want to know what happened to their parent who died, where that parent is now, and what will happen to that parent.

Children are generally very comfortable with death education. Those who are afraid of the concept of death have learned from someone or something that it is taboo, a mystery of life that should not be discussed. Talking about death with children makes it less forbidden and mysterious and more like the natural part of life that it is.

IF YOU DON'T TALK TO THEM, KIDS FILL IN THE BLANKS THEMSELVES

In the months and years ahead, your grieving kids may have hundreds of questions. If you don't answer them, they will seek the answers from their peers or, worse, fill in the blanks by themselves. When the facts of life—either sex or death—are left up to friends or the imagination, children may hear and believe a variety of misconceptions, half-truths, and rumors that they may live with uncomfortably for years.

GOOD COMMUNICATION CAN HELP PREPARE KIDS FOR FUTURE LOSSES

Children who learn that death is a part of life realize that all living things eventually die. Understanding this concept can prepare them for future losses. Over the years, they come to realize that all possessions and relationships are temporary; thus, all of life is precious. Through an understanding of death, they will learn a new appreciation of life and all that it offers each and every day.

Future losses, both large and small, will continue to be painful. Children will still *feel* the sting of separation and the loss of relationship. But at least they will *know* what happened. They will understand that all living things die. It will not come as a total surprise, as it would to children who are sheltered to believe that the world is a perfect place and that people live forever.

WHY PARENTS AVOID COMMUNICATING

In our work with grieving families, we watch parents awkwardly trying to talk to their children about death. Before we help them with their communication skills, we try to identify the cause of their discomfort with the topic. We've observed five general reasons for difficulties in discussing death.

"MY PARENTS NEVER TALKED ABOUT IT"

We often parent the way we were parented. And our parents rarely communicated with us about death or dying. When a loved one died, our parents often protected us from learning much about it. We are continuously surprised at the number of adults who come into our office having just learned of a sibling who died at a young age. Their parents never told them. It simply became a family secret.

In order to shelter their children even more from death, many parents in the past also did not allow their children to attend a relative's wake or funeral. And if a relative had a terminal illness, children were often forbidden to visit him in the hospital or to witness the dying process. Parents often claimed that they would rather have the children remember the dying person as he was when he was healthy and well. Consequently, the child had no opportunity to say good-bye to a person close to him.

Children who are not told about the death of a loved one, or are told in simplistic or dismissive ways, often grow up filled with misconceptions, anxiety, and bitterness. When Russell Baker was five years old, he watched his father go to the hospital for diabetes treatment. His mother told Russell that his father went to the hospital "so he can get better." The next morning, Russell was playing outside when two of his cousins came down the road. Seven-year-old Kenneth broke the news. "Your father's dead," he announced to Russell. "They want you to come home right away."[1] As we have seen, Russell initially denied that it could be true.

When he arrived home, his mother was still at the hospital. Women from the neighborhood had gathered in his house to do the cleaning and cooking. Too busy to take care of a hysterical five-year-old, they sent him across town to Bessie Scott's house. Bessie listened to Russell as he cried and questioned God's motives for making his father die. Bessie told him "about the peace of Heaven and the joy of being among the angels and the happiness of my father who was already there." She reassured Russell that he would understand someday. But the effects of his father's sudden death—and the mushy explanations he heard—lasted a long time.

"After that I never cried again with any real conviction, nor expected much of anyone's God except indifference, nor loved deeply without fear that it would cost me dearly in pain. At the age of five, I had become a skeptic and began to sense that any happiness that came my way might be the prelude to some grim cosmic joke," Russell writes in *Growing Up*. In their efforts to protect Russell from harsh realities, the adults in his world actually set him up for a poor integration of his father's death.

"I DON'T WANT TO REMIND THE KIDS OF THEIR LOSS"

The death of a parent or sibling is such a staggering event for a child that it stays with her on some level all the time. It's not something she forgets—not now, not ever. So to avoid talking about it for fear of causing her more pain is unrealistic.

An insurance agent who worked with widows settling their life insurance claims asked us this question. "When I meet with a widow," he said, "I never talk about the loss of her husband because I don't want to cause her more pain by bringing it up. Is that the right thing to do?" We informed him that the pain of grief is probably the worst pain most people experience in their lives. During the first few months of bereavement, a widow's pain pulls at her constantly, as she thinks about the loss of her husband all the time. The pain is so overwhelming, in fact, that bringing up her loss could not add to it. Most widows actually find comfort in talking about their husbands, we said. Unfortunately, so many people avoid the topic that we thought he could provide a great service to his clients by acknowledging their losses and giving them opportunities to talk about their husbands and the life they shared together.

The same is true with a child who has lost a parent or sibling. Bringing up the subject would not add to her pain, but *not* bringing it up might make the loss seem mysterious or scary and cause her to wonder why you refuse to talk about it.

"I DON'T KNOW HOW"

For many people, grief is a new experience. They are entering uncharted territory, and they feel very uncertain about their responses. Even the most competent and confident parents, who have been raising bright, articulate children with high self-esteem and strong values, fall apart when trying to communicate with their kids about the death of a loved one. They stumble and fumble and aren't sure about what to say or how to say it. They're afraid they'll say the wrong thing and make matters worse. They can talk to their kids about topics ranging from sex to drugs to AIDS, but when it comes to the topic of death, they remain tongue-tied.

Without any training in death education, parents don't know how to talk to their kids about the facts and the feelings. It's just not something you prepare to discuss before it happens. Afraid to say the *wrong* thing, parents often say *nothing*.

"I MIGHT BREAK DOWN"

Some parents fear they'll cry or become emotional in front of their children. Then again, some parents are afraid of showing emotions in front of *anyone*. Men whose wives have died may think it's a sign of weakness to cry in front of their children. And a surprising number of women whose husbands have died refrain from crying in front of their kids in order to be strong for them.

By hiding their emotions, such parents are once again trying to protect their children from more pain. One of the things we hear over and over again is "Whenever I cry, it upsets the children. They start crying too." But pain is a major part of grief, and crying is a major release of pain. Crying is good.

When you cry in front of the children, it gives them permission to let go and let it out. If they never see you cry or show emotion, they will imitate that behavior and suppress the feelings that they yearn to express.

William Kroen, in *Helping Children Cope with the Loss of a Loved One: A Guide for Grownups,* states:

> Young children are confused by stoic behavior. They might wonder, "Why does Mommy seem normal when I feel so sad?"

"Doesn't Daddy care what happened?" "If I cry, that will only upset Mom, so I'd better not cry." Children are much more perceptive than we generally give them credit for. They know how we feel and can see beneath the mask. Sharing your grief lessens the burden for everyone.[2]

"IT MIGHT BE HARMFUL"

Death education and sex education are similar. Both suffer from the misconception that the more kids know, the more they'll experience. Some parents are afraid that if their children learn about sex, they will try to put their knowledge into action and become promiscuous. Likewise, some parents believe death education to be morbid and unpleasant and that it will result in sadness or depression.

Generally, the opposite is true. Good, solid explanations about death, dying, and grief actually comfort children. Knowledge is power, and understanding how death happens helps rather than harms. It can take away fears and misconceptions and answer a multitude of confusing questions.

The key is to provide "good, solid explanations." Some explanations that parents give can cause greater confusion or worsen fears. Later in this chapter, we suggest the best ways to communicate with your child and how to answer his questions about death with confidence.

HOW TO GET KIDS TO TALK ABOUT THEIR FEELINGS

Before you can talk to your child, you need to start a conversation. There are some simple ways to initiate a talk, particularly if your child expresses feelings about her loss, or when she is upset or confused about the many everyday "crises" in her life. We hope these suggestions will help you become a better listener and communicator, and help you develop a stronger relationship with your child.

LISTEN WITH EMPATHY

When your child comes to you with a problem or in distress, give him your full attention. Stop whatever you are doing, sit down with him, and look him in the eye. By doing so, you're setting the tone of good communication. You're saying, "I respect you enough to stop what I'm doing and listen to your problem." The child immediately feels accepted and esteemed.

Next, be empathic. Put yourself in your child's shoes. If you are about to listen to your six-year-old, remember how important a teacher's approval was at that age, how devastating a parent's rebuke was, and how you could spend a good part of the morning watching a frog swim in a pond. If you are about to listen to a fourteen-year-old, consider how important a *yes* was when asking someone out on a date, what a huge loss it was to get cut from the team, and how just a few emerging pimples could make you hide in your room for an entire weekend. Things that we perceive, as adults, to be silly or inconsequential seem critically important to children.

Putting yourself in your child's shoes will prepare you for the next guideline—perhaps the most difficult suggestion for parents to follow.

DON'T INTERRUPT

Here's where we suggest what *not* to do. Not interrupting is an exercise in self-control and restraint; it often goes against every natural inclination that a parent feels. We often interrupt our children's explanations with advice, criticism, warnings, solutions, judgments, suggestions, or other responses that we think are appropriate or helpful. But as soon as we interrupt with a response, we start to shut down the communication process. The control of the conversation shifts from the child to the parent, who has more power and authority. To get a child to open up and talk about her feelings, it is crucial that the parent hold back from imposing immediate solutions or reactions.

Be aware of and practice not interrupting. In ordinary conversations with your child, notice how often you interrupt. Sometimes there is nothing wrong with it; but if the conversation is about feelings or a problem, interrupting may shut it down before your child is able to communicate what is at stake for her.

KEEP IT OPEN

Keep focus on the child by acknowledging her feelings with a word or simple gesture, such as "Oh," "Mm-hmmm," or "Really," or by nodding your head. Use what Thomas Gordon, the author of *Parent Effectiveness Training,* calls a "door-opener" or an "invitation to say more."[3] These are phrases or statements that invite your child to further express her feelings or ideas, such as:

"I see."
"Is that so?"
"Tell me about it."
"Tell me more."
"Tell me the whole story."

Consider a child who has been reprimanded by the principal at his school. The child starts telling the parent about it, but before he gets very far, the parent interrupts, saying, "What did you do that caused him to scold you?" From the child's perspective, that response is very harsh, implying the judgment that the child did something wrong when perhaps he was innocent of any wrongdoing. And besides, what the child is really trying to express to you is what happened and how he feels about it. "Tell me about it" and "Tell me more" are responses that encourage him to do so.

ACKNOWLEDGE THE FEELING

This final step is to figure out what your child is feeling and name the feeling for her. By doing so, you acknowledge her feelings. You also convey that you respect her feelings, and she, in turn, learns to trust them. It then becomes easier for her to identify her own feelings and to share them with others.

Instead of analyzing the content of your child's conversation, look for the feeling he is trying to express. For example, the parent whose child was yelled at by the principal might respond with one of the following statements:

"You sound angry about that."

"You must have been really embarrassed."

"It seems like you were afraid."

If your attempts to name the feeling don't connect with what your child is experiencing, he'll let you know, and you can talk some more until you can identify the actual feeling. This may take a little work, because children don't always have the inclination or the skills to express their feelings. But naming the feeling is worth the effort. It is something a child in crisis desires badly.

In summary, if you want to help your child express his feelings, try these guidelines: Give your child your total attention, be empathic, resist the temptation to jump in with advice, use "door-opening" statements, and identify the feeling. It's a simple process, but not an easy one. Most of us are used to communicating in a more direct way, and it is hard to break old habits. But with practice, awareness, and focus, you can help your child name his feelings, trust them, and share them. It is one of the best gifts you can offer, both for your child and for your relationship with him. As Gordon points out, "When parents say something to a child, they often say something *about* him. That is why communication to a child has such an impact on him as a person and ultimately upon the relationship between you and him."[4]

FIVE TIPS ON TALKING TO A GRIEVING CHILD

As important as it is to talk to your child about her feelings, it is just as necessary to communicate with her about the death of her parent or sibling and why it happened. Talking about it now, with her and as a family, may alleviate years of anxiety and pain over "unresolved issues" of childhood loss. Here's how to do it.

BE HONEST

No matter the age of your child, it is very important to explain death honestly. In the past, as we have seen, one approach to communicating with grieving children was to protect them from knowing all the details. The fact that Russell Baker's family was less than honest about his father's death resulted in lifelong scars of mistrust and skepticism.

If your wife killed herself, explain that to your child. If your husband died of AIDS, say so. If the cause of death was a heart attack or cancer, tell your child what happened. If your child's baby sister died of SIDS, explain to your child that SIDS was the reason she died. (We discuss how to explain specific types of death in Chapter 14.)

As we've said before, a child who has lost a parent is very scared that the surviving parent may die, leaving him all alone. Inevitably, he will ask you directly or indirectly if you are going to die too. How do you answer that question honestly while reassuring your child that he will be safe and secure? Some people recommend that you tell the child that you will be fine, live a long life, and not die until you are very old.

We recommend that you be honest. Tell your child that, as far as you know, you are very healthy and you don't expect to die for a long, long, long, long time (with young children, be sure to stress how very long it is likely to be: to a three-year-old, five minutes can feel like an age). If something should happen to you, make sure he knows that his uncle and aunt (or grandmother or whoever) will be right there to take care of him.

Your child is developing a perception of reality, struggling to make the death a part of his world map. By trying to protect or shield children from illness and death, parents only confuse them. What they tell their children is often contradictory to what the children perceive.

As psychologist Maxine Harris states:

> A child grows up needing to believe that what he or she sees and hears is true and real. In order to make accurate judgments, in order to learn from his or her experience, a child must trust that the experience is an accurate reflection of the reality in the world. When well-meaning relatives deny or lie about the circumstances surrounding a parent's death, they shatter a child's belief in his or her accurate perception of reality.[5]

BE AS FACTUAL AS THE AGE REQUIRES

When you explain death to young children, be factual and answer their questions directly. Most experts who work with children suggest explaining death as the absence of life or familiar life functions. People who are dead no longer eat or breathe or talk. They don't feel any feelings, and they don't think anymore. Dogs don't bark, run, or play. Plants don't grow or blossom.

If a young child asks you, "What is dead? Why did Daddy die?" you might respond like this: "Sometimes a body is really, really, really sick—not just a little sick, like when you have a cold or the flu, but so sick that the body can't make itself better. Usually, it happens when a person is very, very old—not just old like your mom or dad or teachers, but really, really old. Dad's body was so sick that it stopped working. That's what it means to be dead: the body doesn't work anymore. The body doesn't feel anything, it doesn't need air, or food, or water."

If Mark wanted to explain life support systems to his eight-year-old daughter, he could first explain what it means to be dead. Then he could say that hospital machines can sometimes keep the heart beating and the lungs breathing, but the brain can't think any thoughts. The person can never get up again or speak again or eat again. The body has stopped working and can no longer work by itself.

You can ask the child if you've been clear, if she understands what you said, and if she has any other questions. If she does not, leave it at that. Your brief explanation is probably enough for now. But expect further clarifying questions in the future. In fact, encourage her by saying something like, "If you have any questions about what it means to be dead, you can always come to me and ask. I'll try to answer your questions as best as I can. I'm really glad you're curious about stuff like this."

In order to explain death and grief to a child, it is helpful to have an understanding of how much she can comprehend at her level of intellectual development. (If necessary, please review our descriptions of these levels in Chapter 2.) Consider what your child is thinking, and tailor your conversation to his level of understanding.

How do you respond with a factual explanation when your child asks a religious or spiritual question? People often ask us what they should tell their children about what happens to people after they die. They want to know if they should tell their child that "Mommy is in Heaven now" or "Daddy is with God and is very happy."

There are no established rules about sharing religious beliefs with children. It's your call. Religious beliefs are a family affair. Share whatever beliefs your religious tradition holds about death and the afterlife, keeping in mind your child's cognitive abilities.

However, it is probably not a good idea to say "God took Daddy because he wanted him to be with Him" or "God took Mommy because she was so good," because these kinds of phrases imply to a young child that God is a "taker," someone who swoops down and takes you away from your family.

But it *is* all right to say, if it is your belief, that "Mommy died because she had a rare illness. When people die, their heart stops beating and they don't breathe any longer. They can't feel or see or eat. Their bodies don't work anymore. But we believe that people have a soul, an invisible part of them. We believe that, when people die, the soul goes to heaven and lives forever in peace and happiness." Because concepts like *soul* and *heaven* are very abstract for young children, prepare yourself for many follow-up questions.

And it is also acceptable to say that you're not sure what happens after death. You can explain that some people believe there's a heaven and some people don't. Phyllis Silverman, who has studied children and death extensively, stated in a *Parents* magazine article: "When my son was five, he asked what happens after people die. I told him that I really didn't know, that some people believe that nothing happens—the body returns to nature and nourishes the soil and we live on in people's memories. Some people believe we go to heaven, and they see heaven in a very concrete way. And others simply believe that in some way the spirit lives on. My son thought for a while, then said, 'I think I believe that somehow your soul lives on.' And that was the end of it. That was all he needed to hear."[6]

Share what you believe honestly in a way that children can understand. Don't use God or religion as a pacifier to make grieving children feel better. It probably won't work. Do not explain death as a punishment or a reward from God. Children will not be endeared to any God who takes their parent or sibling away for any reason. As always, be there when they ask questions about God, religion, afterlife, the soul, and other concepts, knowing that it is always okay to say, "I don't know."

BE PATIENT

Young children have a peculiar communication style, one that can drive parents nuts. They often ask the same question over and over in a different way, or they respond to every answer you give them with "Why?" They do that because that's how a developing brain functions. It's how they cognitively digest difficult concepts. You are probably answering with responses that are too abstract for them to comprehend. So they will whittle down your responses until they can be comfortable with them. When children go into repetitious or clarifying questions, you should respond to each one with a concrete answer and as much patience as you can muster.

Dan Schaefer, author of *How Do We Tell the Children?*, offers an example of this type of questioning and how to respond:

- "Will Grandpa ever move again?" (No, his body has stopped working.)
- "Why can't they fix him?" (Once the body stops working, it can't start again.)
- "Why is he cold?" (The body only stays warm when it's working.)
- "Why isn't he moving?" (He can't move because his body isn't working anymore.)
- "When will he come back?" (He won't. People who die don't come back.)
- "Is he sleeping?" (No. When we sleep, our body is still working, just resting.)
- "Can he hear me?" (No. He could only hear you if his body was working.)
- "Can he eat after he's buried?" (No, a person eats only when his body is working.)[7]

When you have answered your child's questions, he may be satisfied for the time being. But a few days later, he may return with a new set of questions. Be patient. As he churns this new information in his mind, each new answer may present a new question. Welcome the new questions, and realize that the process of your communication together is as important as the content of the answers. Create a welcoming environment for your child's curiosity, and you will be helping him accommodate the loss and make some sense of it over time. If you become impatient with him and tell him you've answered that question a million times before, you will be shutting down the possibility of future conversations. In that case, he must rely on his own resources for the answers, and that could be dangerous.

As T. Berry Brazelton says,

Children need to be reassured over and over that they are loved, and were loved by the absent parent. Children need to hear repeatedly that they hadn't any responsibility for the death of the parent. They need to know that they can be "bad" without losing the surviving parent.[8]

WATCH YOUR LANGUAGE

The concrete thinking of younger children and parents' desire to protect them can be a dangerous combination. A parent may try to soften her language when explaining death to her child; but by doing so, she may plant ideas in his head that weren't there before and that may be frightening or harmful. For example, a child who thinks very concretely may misinterpret these statements:

• "We *lost* your grandfather last night." (If grandpa is lost, he can be found and come back to us.)

• "Your mom got *sick* and died." (The next time your child gets a cold, she may think she's going to die.)

• "Uncle Bob *went to sleep* forever." (Your child may think that she will die when she goes to sleep at night.)

If your child is very young, avoid phrases like *passed away, passed on,* or *moved on.* Your child may interpret them to mean that your loved one is taking a trip and may return. Avoid the word *expire.* That's something that happens to a driver's license or a credit card, not to people.

One little boy who was told that his grandmother had expired and that he would never see her again was afraid to go out and play because he might "sweat too much and disappear."

As we've suggested before, be factual in the words that you choose. Use *dead, death,* and *died.* Explain what *dead* means at your child's level of comprehension, and you will do just fine.

REVISIT AND RECOMMUNICATE

By now, you realize that we are strong believers that grief has long-term effects on individuals and on families. It is a chronic condition that you never "get over." You learn to live with your loss and integrate that experience into your life. Children also learn to live with their loss and create a new life. But there is a difference here between adults and children. Especially for younger children, working through the loss of a parent or sibling involves revisiting the loss as they grow older. This is one of the most difficult aspects of childhood grief for parents to understand. Once they have explained the death to a young child, answered her questions over and over, and paid close attention to all of the feelings that she expressed for months after the death, they think that they have finished their job. But in fact, they have finished only for now, at that particular level of the child's development.

In order for your child to work through the loss, she will have to revisit her comprehension of that loss at various points of her development, until she reaches adulthood. If you don't revisit and recommunicate the loss with her, her thoughts and feelings may well remain at the same level as when you first explained it to her.

A six-year-old may be told that Daddy's body doesn't work anymore because he got very, very, very sick. But when that child is ten, she may want to know what the cause of death was and whether it was preventable. And when she's sixteen, she may wonder what her father was like as a person and whether he's still alive in another mode of existence.

It's amazing how many teenagers have inaccurate information about parents who died when they were young children. They never knew the actual cause of death because they relied on the explanation they were given as young children. And even though that explanation may have been honest and factual, as children they were unable to understand the cause of death on an abstract level. Never revisited and recommunicated as they grew, their knowledge did not grow with their capacity.

Get ready to answer questions about death and grief for a long time. It takes years, sometimes even decades, for a child to comprehend a difficult concept that occurred at a very traumatic moment. Clarify and reclarify the facts and feelings over time, and your child's misconceptions surrounding the death of the parent or sibling will be minimal.

"BUT MY CHILD NEVER TALKS ABOUT IT"

Just because a child shows no outward expressions of grief does not mean that he is not grieving. Children grieve on their own time line and in their own way. The hurt may be too much right now, and he may not want to face it. He may feel too raw and vulnerable to deal with it. He may not feel that he is enough in control. He may postpone grief until he's ready for it. But rest assured that grief *will* come. No one can bury grief. You can suppress it for a while, but it will emerge eventually.

As a parent, the important thing for you to do when that happens is *be there*. Be present and available when he is ready to grieve. Be open and responsive when he is ready to talk, even if it is months or years after his loved one died.

If your child never talks about the death of his parent or sibling, it may be for one of four reasons: He may desire to protect you; he may be frustrated by "closed-ended" conversations; he may be unable to express verbally; or he may be sharing his grief elsewhere.

Protecting you As we noted previously, your child is very sensitive to you and to your reactions to your loss. He loves you and doesn't want to hurt you. He learns quickly that talking about the loved one who died generates deep emotional reactions and may cause you to break down and cry. So he avoids bringing up the subject to protect you from further pain.

Tell your child over and over that you cry because you miss the person who died, but that it's okay to cry. In fact, it helps to cry at those times, and everyone feels better afterward. Assure him that he can talk about his parent or sibling anytime, and that you can both share a good cry together.

"Closed-ended" conversations If your child once talked about her grief but has ceased to do so, you might consider your communication techniques. If you jump into a conversation to give advice or express your reactions, you may close down the communication. After a while, kids simply stop trying to communicate because they can't get across what they would like. If that's the case, you might want to try more open-ended discussions (as explained earlier in this chapter).

Inability to verbalize Young children do not always have the skills to put into words what they are feeling or thinking. If your child doesn't have the capacity to express his feelings or thoughts verbally, look at his behavior. He may be communicating by doing. And there are ways you can channel his behavior to "get out" his grief through play and activities. (See Chapter 4.)

Sharing elsewhere Finally, if your child is not talking to you about his grief and loss, he may be talking to others. This is especially true for preteens and adolescents, who tend to talk less to their parents anyway. We were both concerned that our teenage son was keeping his feelings about his mother's death inside and not sharing them with anyone. When we went to a parent-teacher conference at school, however, we learned that he was quite open about his loss, talking about it with teachers and even bringing it up in class. It is not unusual for grieving children to talk about their feelings and thoughts with teachers, principals, guidance counselors, school nurses, coaches, Scout leaders, ministers, rabbis, neighbors, or friends. There may be a great deal of communication going on that you are not aware of.

The best way to get grieving children to talk about their grief is to join a support program for grieving children. If there is a program in your area, we strongly encourage you to attend it. (See Chapter 7).

Communicating with grieving children can reassure them that they will be safe. It offers them hope that they will regain a sense of security and control in their lives. It gives them permission to talk about their feelings and to ask a multitude of questions about the mysteries of life. It can diminish their fears and prepare them for future losses, while building a new sense of appreciation for what they have.

Talking to children about death will not harm their development. It will only help. There is nothing dangerous or harmful about discussing death, dying, or grief. But *not* talking about those topics could be detrimental to a grieving child for a long time, as Peter, whom we met at the beginning of this chapter, could tell you.

HOLDING COMMUNITIES:

CREATING AND USING THEM

I've never felt so alone before. My parents retired to Florida just before
my wife died. My friends have their own lives to lead. And I'm not sure
I can do this by myself. I know I can make a *living* for my kids, but can
I make a *life* for them?

—Mike, 42 years old

YOUR HUSBAND DIES, OR YOUR WIFE. YOU PROMISED TO "TAKE
care of the kids." That's what you remember. That's what haunts
you. In your heart, you want to fulfill that promise. But now you wonder: Do you have enough to give? Can you, all alone and by yourself,
fill the gaps in your child's life?

Or your child dies, and you realize that, without support, your surviving kids could carry serious emotional scars throughout their lives.
They, too, could end up as victims—albeit living ones—of the illness
or accident that took the life of one child. There's only one problem: You
don't know how to crawl out of your own grief enough to help them.

These worries are realistic ones, not only because of your own grief
and your own human limitations, but because of the very nature of children's grief. Unfortunately, as important as you are as a parent, you alone
cannot fully meet the needs of your grieving child. You need a community of others to help.

OTHER CARING ADULTS ARE CRUCIAL FOR YOUR GRIEVING CHILD

You already know that it's unpredictable what will trigger a grief "spasm" for your child. It could be the sight of a family together at the mall, a holiday happening at school, or something else that makes them sad, mad, or scared and thereby brings up grief feelings. This unpredictability means that your child may well "fall into" her grief outside the home, with nonfamily members for company. And try as you might you just can't be available to help your kids twenty-four hours each day, seven days each week. Sometimes meeting the needs of one child (by attending sporting events or parent-teacher conferences, for example) forces you to spend time away from the others. Work, school, your child's extracurricular activities—all of these ordinary elements of daily life separate family members on a regular basis.

What's also important to realize is that your grieving child has many different kinds of needs requiring many different kinds of support. Therese Rando, an internationally renowned expert in grief who lost both parents before the age of eighteen, identifies seven different types of support that are helpful after a death.[1] All these types of support can be provided by nonfamily adults.

Support for social activities Parents of grieving kids often say that after a death, recreational activities are the first to go. Newly single parents feel stretched just to accomplish the necessary tasks of daily living—there's no time left over to "waste" on fun. And parents who have lost a child often have little playfulness to share with the rest of the kids in the family.

Adults outside the immediate family can help fill this gap by offering grieving kids moments of fun, a helpful break from their grief. They can watch a funny movie together, or play basketball. They can include him in a group going ice skating or to the beach. Other adults can give her a periodic distraction from the pain she's feeling inside.

Instrumental or practical support When Jim's wife Mary died, a good friend helped our kids by taking them shopping for school clothes. She took Kate for haircuts. For certain tasks, our kids knew they could depend on Dottie to help. Such support helps both the child and, indirectly, the parent as well.

Informational support Nonparents may be in a unique position to help grieving kids understand the facts of the death or the circumstances surrounding it. Why? First, those with backgrounds in health or emergency services may be able to explain it more fully than you can. Second, your child can ask others those questions that they fear may upset you. They may not feel the same need to protect neighbors or teachers or relatives that they feel about you.

Sheer presence Children take comfort from hanging out with adults whom they know to be safe and loving. It doesn't matter what activity your child does with his grandfather, aunt, teacher, or dad's best friend: chores, watching television, even performing separate activities in the same room can maintain a supportive bond. Cuddling and lap time console younger children, even when no words are said.

Validational support Simply identifying and acknowledging the feelings of a grieving child gives her a sense that her feelings are acceptable, and it affirms her experience. "You seem sad today," your neighbor might say. "Some days I feel sad too." Sometimes nothing more needs to be said. Just that basic stamp of approval teaches grieving kids a lot about normal grief.

Relational support Grieving kids are still kids, and they need someone to listen to the normal tugs and pulls involved with growing up. They benefit from adults who help them learn problem-solving skills. They enjoy the gentle joking and fooling around that only bosom buddies can provide. This kind of support maintains the close relationships that make these activities possible.

Emotional support It's this last type of support that first comes to mind when you think of grieving children. But as you can see, your child craves support of many kinds. No wonder you can't do it all!

Finally, you may need the help of others in raising your grieving child because, as we've noted before, many children actively avoid talking about some aspects of the grief experience with others in the immediate family. Hope Edelman, in her book *Motherless Daughters,* illustrates how this occurred in her family. At seventeen, Hope lost her mother to cancer. One night her father, overwhelmed with single parenting and angry at the kids, packed his bags and threatened to leave. "In the end, he didn't go anywhere that night," Hope reports, "but my siblings and I quickly learned how to tiptoe through the minefield in this new landscape we all shared, careful not to tread too hard on any topic that might make our father explode."

She elaborates:

Because the children in my family were too young—and too afraid—to risk total abandonment, we chose silence. The times our father did show emotion and let us see his pain, we deliberately forced him back into the safety of suppression. To us, his tears signified the first stage of what we assumed would end in complete collapse, undermining the only security we had left.[2]

Despite the hesitancy of many grieving children to express themselves within the family, most *do* yearn to talk about it. In the Child Bereavement Study, researchers found that over half of the children interviewed wanted to talk to peers about their grief. Fortunately, most of these young grievers found their friends willing to listen and talk. Similarly, one-third of the children wanted to talk to teachers about their grief, and for the most part, teachers responded in warm, caring ways. Every one of us, at whatever age we grieve, longs for someone to hold us in our pain.

HOW TO FILL THE GAPS: A HOLDING COMMUNITY

When three-year-old Jason, whose father committed suicide a year earlier, visited the new Wal-Mart in town for the first time, his eyes grew wide with wonder. His mom, Sara, was also overwhelmed by the aisles and aisles of stock and murmured, "This place must have everything you could ever need. What should we look for first?"

"I need a new daddy," Jason whispered hopefully. "Where do they keep those?"

Jason's poignant response expresses the most fervent wish of grieving kids. *If my mom* (or dad or brother or sister) *can't become alive again,* they wonder, *how can I get a new one?*

No studies reveal how children try to fill all the gaping holes left when a loved one dies. But if Hope Edelman's study of motherless daughters can be extended to grieving kids in general, many young grievers never find even a partial substitute for the person who died. In Edelman's study, 37 percent of the women who lost their mothers between infancy and young adulthood never enjoyed the presence of a surrogate mother.

Of the motherless daughters who *did* find one or more substitutes, most found a family member: 33 percent, an aunt; 30 percent, a grandmother; 13 percent, a sister. Young grievers identified a mix of parent substitutes outside the family as well, with 13 percent naming a teacher; 12 percent, a friend; 10 percent, a coworker; and at lower levels, neighbors, friends' mothers, stepmothers, and cousins. Later in life, mothers-in-law, husbands, and lovers also filled part of the gap.[3] Maxine Harris, who studied men and women who had lost parents in childhood, notes examples of men who looked to coaches, bosses, and mentors as parental substitutes.

In our experience, most grieving children find at least some adults or older friends to fill parts of the gap. The bad news is that it can take them years to do so. In the meantime, many of their emotional and psychological needs go unattended.

That's why it's so important for you to consciously develop other adult resources for your children—adults who stand ready to "catch" them when they "fall" into their grief; adults who can invite your kids to think about what's happened and to feel whatever feelings they have; adults who can help them keep memories alive.

We call such groups of adults *holding communities.* They hold your grieving kids close even when you're not around.

CHARACTERISTICS OF IDEAL HOLDING COMMUNITIES

Although few holding communities enjoy all of the following characteristics, here are some elements to look for in the group of adults you gather for your child. An ideal holding community:

• *Offers many different types of support*—recreational, emotional, informational, and so on.

• *Is ongoing.* Since children grieve over the course of many years, the ideal holding community will be made up of people who will be there for your child throughout his childhood. For this reason, extended families are often ideal.

• *Is committed to learning about children's grief and how to help.* Without educating ourselves, we don't know what it's like and how to help. Generally, helping grieving children is not complicated, but it does require understanding. Good holding communities spend the time necessary to read up on the subject.

• *Is made up of folks who are able to make commitments and keep them.* Grieving kids already have suffered the profound disappointment of someone who was there one moment and gone the next. They don't need any more unpredictability in their lives.

• *Contains adults who are sensitive to the child's needs.* Even if an adult provides mostly social support and is unable to listen to the child's emotional unloading, ideally he'll be able to discern when the child needs emotional succor. And he'll know how to find that help for the child.

• *Includes at least some adults who can listen to the more difficult aspects of a child's grief.* Not every adult can tolerate expressions of rage or tearful outbursts. But since these are likely a part of your child's grief experience, it helps when at least some adults in his world can let them happen without panic or a need to shut them down or fix them.

• *Enjoys kids!* In the best holding communities, adults just like kids. They find them fun to be around. They love their perspectives and their struggles.

Holding communities take various forms. Some are totally ad hoc and informal, which was the case for Jim's children when Mary died. As we've said, many friends helped in practical ways: taking the kids shopping, for haircuts, even on vacation. Some teachers became friends, taking the kids on outings; others kept an eye out for signs that the kids might not be grieving in constructive ways.

Mary's family kept her memory alive by telling stories and by sharing pictures and possessions that Mary had held dear. A great-aunt cleaned Mary's wedding dress and tucked it away, in case Kate wants to wear it someday. And Mary's sister Maggie phoned Kate from Atlanta every Monday night at 8 P.M. Some nights they read a story together. Other nights they simply chatted. For five years, every Monday night, Maggie provided Kate with important support in her grief and a vital link to her mother.

Letters and e-mail are relatively inexpensive alternatives to long-distance phone calls for supporting a grieving child. For some kids, they're even better than in-person support. Standard mail is less immediate and less personal than face-to-face (or even phone-to-phone) communication. That makes it more comfortable for private people (many adolescents, for example, or children who learned early on to repress their grief for fear of being "weak" or "emotional"). One grandmother maintained an ongoing e-mail correspondence with her grieving granddaughter. "Her fingers are permanently glued to the keyboard anyway," she said, laughing. "She might as well hear from me as from the friends she sees every day at school!"

Such informal holding communities are perhaps the most common healing experience for grieving families. They certainly work for kids. The parent should solicit each individual's help, educate them all about the child's needs, and keep them all informed.

Other holding communities are formal groups such as Concerns of Police Survivors (COPS), a nationwide network of police officers dedicated to ongoing support for the families of officers killed in the line of duty. When Patty's husband was shot, COPS stepped in to help immediately. "I don't know what I would have done without them," she says. "Aside from helping with all the practical stuff, they helped me realize we're not alone and that we're going to make it. We've attended the national conference and the summer camp, and each time, I come home saying to myself, 'If everybody else can get through this, so can I.' "

SUPPORT GROUPS FOR GRIEVING CHILDREN

Children's grief support programs are also formal holding communities for children. When six-year-old Malcolm first showed up at The Cove's support group for grieving kids, seven-year-old Tyrone ran up to greet him. He gushed out in twenty seconds flat, "Hi! I'm Tyrone. My dad died from a heart attack, and I was there. The firemen came and tried to keep him alive but they couldn't. I saw it all. Then we had a wake and a funeral, and now it's just my mom and me. Who died in your family?" Unfazed by Tyrone's outburst, Malcolm told his story too.

Such experiences are typical of support groups and illustrate why grieving kids like them so much. At Fernside, a grief support program in Cincinnati for children and adolescents, kids listed the top ten good things about support groups. Here's what they said:[4]

- "When you are part of the group, you feel less alone."

- "A group can be a good place to tell your story to people who will listen really well because they understand a lot."

- "A group can be a comfortable place to get your feelings out in safe, fun ways."

- "A group can give you good ideas for adjusting to all the changes in your life."

- "A group can help you preserve and cherish your memories because you get lots of chances to remember all the good things."

- "A group can be really fun. Even though there are sad moments, there are lots of laughs, too."

- "Going to a support group can be a good way to make sure the grown-ups in your family get some support for themselves because they can talk to other caring adults."

- "At Fernside, the groups enjoy a great LaRosa's pizza dinner before each group meeting. No cooking those nights!"

- "Groups can help you relax."

- "A group can make you believe that you will 'make it' because there are others who are starting to feel better."

In a typical children's grief support group, the meeting opens by inviting each person to say his name and who died. Saying who died in the introduction serves three purposes. First, it reminds children that others have had similar experiences. Second, it helps to make the death more real over time—a sad but necessary part of healing. Third, it reaffirms that the group is a safe place where participants can freely talk about death and the experience of grief.

Next, the children participate in age-appropriate activities designed to help them express what the grief experience has been like so far. Older children and teens may mostly talk about their thoughts and feelings. But because younger children tend to communicate their grief in behavior more than in words, their groups use activities like arts and crafts, music and games to prompt the kids to share their stories and their feelings.

Preschoolers, for example, might have a pretend conversation with the person who died on a disconnected phone. They might listen to stories and draw pictures. They might put on a puppet show or play dress-up, perhaps acting out a wake or a funeral. They might take an imaginary trip to a place that was special for the person who died.

Kids of elementary school age might make a video or write a letter about how it feels when a person dies. They might make "feelings masks" or, for Valentine's Day, create a "hearts mobile" full of the names or pictures of people who love them. They might use clay or yarn to create worry dolls, giving them an opportunity to talk about their concerns. They might draw pictures of themselves before and after the death, which gives them a chance to talk about changes in their lives.

Whatever the activity, all the groups typically close with a brief ceremony that symbolizes the end of the evening. Often groups offer food either before or after the program. At some support programs, while the children's support groups are in session, the parents gather informally and discuss their own grief.

In a few programs around the country, like The Cove, entire families are the focus. In addition to the children's groups, we have a formal parent meeting to discuss children's grief, as well as a family activity time, during which the family as a whole works on a project designed to foster communication about the death and its repercussions.

IS THIS SUPPORT GROUP RIGHT FOR YOUR CHILD?

Before signing your child up for a support group, you may naturally have some anxieties. After all, you may not know much about the program or its leaders. To help determine whether a particular support group is right for your child, ask the following questions:

1. Are there enough commonalities between your child and the others who would be in her group? In an ideal world, your child's support group would be filled with other kids of her same age and culture, kids who experienced the death of the same family member (father, mother, sister, brother) from the same cause (cancer, accident, and so on). Unfortunately, that's rarely possible. On the other hand, if your child is the only five-year-old whose sibling killed himself in a group of children over ten years of age, all of whom lost a parent to cancer, the group is unlikely to be of much help to him. There should be enough points of connection between himself and the others for him to feel that he's one of the group.

2. Do the program leaders know about kids and grieving? Often children's support groups are led by community volunteers trained in how to help grieving kids. And since people in grief generally need support, not therapy, that's fine. On the other hand, you'll want to know that they've been trained by experts in the field and that someone is available to evaluate whether group members need extra help.

3. What is the philosophy of the program? Does it treat grief as a mental health problem to be fixed or as a life experience to be integrated and learned from? Are the staff members open about the program, its goals, and the planned activities? Support groups work, in part, because children know what they say will be held in private and not shared with parents (unless the child's safety is at risk). But a strong program should help you understand how they are trying to help your child and why.

4. After a few meetings, does your child want to go back for more? Often grieving kids resist going to a support group because they can't

predict what it will be like. It feels scary to try something new. Especially with an older child, you may need to contract with her to attend three or four sessions, after which it will be her choice whether to continue. Usually after the first meeting (and certainly after several), kids love the experience.

If your child still balks at returning, talk with her. Perhaps there are too few kids she connects with. In that case, another group might prove more helpful. On the other hand, she may simply not be ready to work on her grief at this time. In that case, don't force her to go. It won't help, and it may just sour her on the idea of support groups in the future. This group simply may not be appropriate for your child right now.

5. If your child is already working with a mental health professional, does he or she agree that attending a support group makes sense for your child? Usually, mental health workers appreciate the value of support groups for grieving children and encourage parents to take them to groups. But if your child's social worker or counselor thinks the timing is off for some reason, trust that judgment. He knows your child's mental health status best.

However the support group is structured, it's important to realize that it is not a therapy group. Support groups are intended for kids with otherwise normal backgrounds who have endured an overwhelming experience, the death of a loved one. If your child seems to be having an unusually difficult time with his grief, support groups will refer you to a qualified grief specialist in your area.

How can you find a children's support group near you? Your local hospice or pediatric hospital can often supply you with the phone numbers. Our Web site (www.neclt.org) lists all the programs across the country of which we are aware.

CREATING A HOLDING COMMUNITY

"You cannot keep the birds of fortune from flying overhead," says an old Chinese proverb, "but you can keep them from nesting in your hair." So, too, you can't undo the death of your husband or wife or child.

You can't prevent your child's grief. You can't force people to care. But you can create communities to hold your children in their grief, thereby showering them with healing attention. It takes just a few simple actions to start the ball rolling.

EDUCATE THE ADULTS IN YOUR CHILD'S NATURAL COMMUNITIES (EXTENDED FAMILY MEMBERS, SCOUT LEADERS, COACHES, AND THE LIKE) ABOUT CHILDREN'S GRIEF AND HOW THEY CAN HELP

Dealing with grief terrifies many adults. They don't know what to do, and they fear making a mistake. When they see a child's natural playfulness and joy return in public settings, they want to believe the child is "over it."

When Jim's brother and sister-in-law died in a helicopter crash, we were determined that their children would be well supported. So we took the initiative. We collected articles about grief in young grievers and how to support them, and we sent them to key people (including peers) in our nephews' and niece's natural communities. We bought copies of books we thought were particularly helpful and shared them with family members who were especially close. Appendix A of this book lists many of these resources. Your local hospital, hospice, or children's grief support center can also provide rich materials on these topics.

Many adults in your child's life may want to help but don't know how to start a conversation. You can offer some simple suggestions:

Share memories. "Remember when . . . ?" is a great conversation starter. Adults can open up touchier topics by sharing tough memories of their own: a time when they were angry at the person who died; something they regret about their relationship with the person who died, or what they liked least about him or her.

Share stories of which the child may be unaware. Grieving kids especially appreciate stories about childhood (their own or that of the person who died), what happened the day they were born, what they were like as little ones, what trouble they got into, what it was like growing up, how they handled problems, funny incidents, and the like.

Encourage others to use starter phrases like "I remember when . . ." or "Something I bet you didn't know about your sister/father/mother . . ."

Share personal thoughts and feelings. Great conversation starters include:

• "Sometimes, I feel/think . . . I wonder if other people who have had somebody die feel/think that way? What do you think?"

• "I miss . . . What do you miss?"

• "Something that surprised me was . . ."

• "When my own mom died, I remember worrying about . . . Do you think other kids worry? What about?"

Remember to temper the sharing so that the kids continue to feel safe. Some topics, such as your own fears, or memories of wild college partying, may be scary or inappropriate to share with a grieving child.

For those adults who can't commit to significant involvement with your child, propose indirect ways that they can support the family. Encourage them to spearhead efforts to bring a speaker on children's grief to your PTA or to a teacher in-service day. Suggest that they supply this book to key community members, like ministers, school personnel, and pediatricians. Advise them to donate time or money to a local grief support program for children.

Finally, make sure the school personnel and health care professionals who care for your child are well informed. Share with them the information in Appendix B.

BE A MODEL FOR OTHER ADULTS ABOUT HOW TO COMMUNICATE WITH CHILDREN IN AN HONEST WAY THAT CHILDREN CAN UNDERSTAND

If you whisper to other adults about the death or your family's grief; if you always pretend that everything's fine; if you hush your child or change the subject when he brings up a death-related topic in public— then you encourage other adults to do the same. They take their cues from you. You need to teach the adults in your child's world, by your words and by your actions, how you would like them to behave with your child.

TEACH YOUR CHILD TO ASK FOR WHAT HE NEEDS

With two- or three-dozen students per classroom, your child's teacher may not realize when your child is struggling, especially if your child rotates teachers throughout the day. Your child may be too young to say he needs to vent his anger. He may be too old to willingly admit that he's on the verge of tears. Still, he can learn to ask permission to visit the school nurse, guidance counselor, or social worker when he isn't feeling up to facing the day.

Often he may simply need to know that such visits are possible whenever he requires them. Your child may crave your approval for taking advantage of the supports that are available; he may need to know that you don't consider it a sign of weakness or laziness to ask for help. Sadly, many kids believe they're expected to tough it out on their own.

ASK OTHER ADULTS TO HELP YOUR CHILD WITH WHAT SHE NEEDS

When Kit turned thirteen, her father recognized that she needed an adult woman in her life. She needed someone with whom to process her emotions, but he wasn't the best choice, not only because he was the parent from whom she was trying to break away, but also because he was such an emotionally private person. Kit obviously hungered for a female role model; her father hoped she would settle on a mature, kind, competent woman.

Instead of leaving it to chance (or to Kit's own whims), Kit's dad took action. Kit had expressed interest in the peer helper group at school, a program run by a woman he deeply respected. He called the director and related his story, his daughter's interest, and his own respect for the director. He asked her to personally invite Kit into the group. Flattered by his regard, the director took a special interest in Kit. The relationship flourished for two years, until Kit moved on to the high school.

Most adults care. They'll jump if you give them specific ways to help. You just have to ask.

REINFORCE HELPFUL BEHAVIORS IN CARING ADULTS

Adults thirst for affirmation every bit as much as children. When they receive it, they're more likely to repeat the actions that bred the approval.

Use this pattern to your advantage. Catch adults in the act of supporting your child well. Compliment them. Tell them, in front of others if possible, how much you appreciate their help. Write a note. Explain what a difference they've made in your child's life.

ADVOCATE FOR YOUR CHILD OVER THE YEARS

Perhaps you can rely on family over time, but the rest of your child's holding community will change with the years. Kids graduate to other schools. Coaches change from year to year. Scout masters and church leaders take on new responsibilities, leaving the old ones behind. You're the only constant advocate for your child. That means you periodically need to reeducate your child's holding community members.

Unfortunately, the details of your child's challenges will probably not follow her as she changes schools or even grade levels. New teachers and new schools will not know that your child is grieving unless you tell them. And since they may not know that grief recurs throughout childhood, they may think that a death that occurred a few years ago is irrelevant.

For this reason, we encourage parents to talk with their child's teachers about his grief at parent-teacher conferences each year. And don't stop informing them after the first year or two. Every year for the past nine years, we've visited our kids' teachers and let them know that their mother died suddenly several years ago. We've asked them to call us if they notice any weird behavior coming from them in their classroom.

If your child had a physical condition that challenged him on a regular basis, you'd keep the teachers constantly aware. Don't let the invisibility of your child's grief hold you back from talking about its reality.

Chapter 8

DEALING WITH HOLIDAYS
AND OTHER SPECIAL DAYS

Next week it'll be one year since Doug died. I don't think the kids even realize it, but I'm drowning in it. I don't know how I'll get through the day, let alone help the kids. All I know is that Doug is supposed to be here, and he's not.

—Beth, 34 years old

H OW WILL WE EVER GET THROUGH THIS?" MARCIA ASKED AT THE beginning of November. Her husband, Jules, had died suddenly in July, and she still couldn't fully believe that he was gone, much less that he wouldn't be around to celebrate the holidays with her and their four young children. In a few weeks, they would be expected at the annual family Thanksgiving; then would come Christmas; and January 15 would be Jules's birthday. She dreaded all of it.

Marcia's kids, on the other hand, seemed to look forward to the holidays. They asked who would be attending Thanksgiving dinner, and they'd already made Christmas lists. Marcia didn't want to spoil her children's excitement, but she couldn't get in a festive mood. "In fact," she told us, "I wish I could run away and escape the next two months altogether."

Coping with holidays, birthdays, and anniversaries is difficult for any adult grieving the loss of a loved one. But when you have children to take into consideration during those special times of the year, the situation can become even more confusing and emotional. In this chapter, we discuss why the holidays are so difficult for grievers and suggest methods of getting through them with as little discomfort as possible. We hope these ways to deal with special days will not only help your family cope but will also help heal the wounds of separation and maintain connections to your loved one. Through the use of rituals, you and your child can get through the holidays and regain some control.

WHY THE HOLIDAYS ARE DIFFICULT

Most grieving people say that anticipating a holiday is worse than the day itself. That's because the pain often has very little to do with the holidays; instead, it stems from feelings of separation and transition. As painful as separation and transition may be, they are the only way to get through grief and form a new life. The pain teaches you that your loved one is gone and that your life will never be the same. Knowing this can make a difference in coping. It won't necessarily make it easier for you or take away the pain, but you may feel less blindsided by it.

Usually you can take a break from your grief process, but the holidays make that more difficult. During this time of "celebration," your sense of loss may increase when you see the perfect gift you'd like to buy for him or when you receive a greeting card addressed to both of you. Normal levels of anger may turn to rage as you see other couples walking together or families with all of their children still alive. The sense of unfairness may become exaggerated and seem to mock you during the season of good cheer.

Your sadness and depression may intensify as you attend holiday parties and observe the laughter, gaiety, and singing. You may also feel guilty because you think you're pulling everyone else down and ruining their holiday celebration. And if you are struggling with issues of meaning, their number may increase at the holidays. You may not feel very thankful at Thanksgiving; you may struggle with the search for joy at Chanukah or Christmas; and you may resist making resolutions at New Year's.

If you feel more stressed than usual during the holiday season, it's probably a magnification of your normal grief reactions. The intensity of those feelings will pass as the holidays conclude and the rest of the world doesn't contrast with your world so much.

Another reason grievers feel so low at the holidays is that everyone else seems so high. Most grieving people idealize the season. They look back at previous holidays with nostalgia, remembering the good moments but not the bad.

Grieving people also idealize their deceased loved ones. They remember the perfect holiday with the perfect spouse or the perfect child. If only he were still alive, they think, life would be perfect once again. Obviously, that's not true—every spouse and every child has imperfections and peculiarities. It's helpful to keep that perspective.

In other words, don't beat yourself up over the fact that life is no longer the paradise it once seemed to be. The holidays can make you feel that everyone else is enjoying the perfect life, but it's just not true. Realistically, your loved one was as human as everyone else, and your holidays in the past were likely filled with as much stress as joy. Realizing that everyone idealizes the holidays can make them just a little less difficult at a time when you don't need to add to your pain.

WHY BIRTHDAYS AND ANNIVERSARIES ARE DIFFICULT

Birthdays When your loved one's birthday approaches, you may once again remember the loss and feel the pain of separation. In the past, you thought about what special gift to buy, what card to select, and what special meal to prepare. You might have helped your child pick out a gift or create one. Now, as the day approaches, there's an eerie emptiness. You and your child know that a birthday celebration always took place on that day, but the person for whom you shopped, prepared a meal, and sang "Happy Birthday" is gone.

Birthdays resemble holidays in that both remind you that your loved one is gone and life will never be the same. But birthdays are different because your total environment is not all tinsel and glitter. It's an invisible "holiday," a day you mark and remember as a family, but most other people don't realize the day's significance. This can be difficult in its own right, though, since no one knows to support you at this time.

Celebrations Life-cycle celebrations can trigger more emotional ups and downs. When the family gathers for christenings, bar mitzvahs, graduations, and weddings, you may feel the absence of your loved one more acutely. Typically, people celebrate life at such events, but now you struggle with the effects of death.

Grieving families experience pain more intensely at those events when they occur within a few months of the death of their loved one. During the early months of mourning, life-cycle celebrations become lessons in separation and transition. But you and your child will probably find that those celebrations bring on twinges of pain years and even decades after your loved one has died. Even if a child's mother died when she was four, that child may break down the day she gets married, wishing her mother were still alive to share in her special day. And if she bears a child of her own one day, the excitement of that miraculous event may be tempered by a feeling of sadness.

Allison's father died in a motorcycle accident when she was twelve. Six years later, Allison, a bright, energetic senior, was graduating from high school and looking forward to college. She had worked hard for the past four years and was ranked in the top 10 percent of her class. On graduation day, Allison received her diploma and graduated with high honors. When she returned home after the ceremony, she was greeted by her mom, sister, brother, and countless relatives and friends. Joy and happiness filled the house as everyone congratulated Allison and showered her with gifts and cards. Allison tried to smile and laugh, but she couldn't shake her melancholy—the nagging reminder that her father was not there to celebrate and share in her accomplishment. All she could think about was how proud of her he would have been.

The Anniversary of the Death The anniversary of the death may also stir up strange feelings. Not only will it remind you of your separation and new life, it may also bring back a flood of memories about the death itself. You may recall in graphic detail that day that changed your life forever, and many of the old, intense feelings of anger, resentment, and sadness may briefly rise again.

Older children who remember the anniversary of the death may become more sullen, quiet, or removed as the day approaches. Younger children probably won't have a clue about the actual date unless you tell them or they pick up that something's wrong with the general family mood. But they may associate a season or a particular part of the year with the death, like Stacy, whose sister died just after school let out. Even though Stacy doesn't remember the specific date of her sister's death, the ending of each school year reminds her it's coming close.

Since most children will not remember the date of a loved one's death, you may want to remind them and ask if there is a way that they would like to observe the anniversary. If they wish to participate somehow, that's great. If not, that's okay. Don't force them to participate. They may want to observe the day in their own way. It doesn't mean that they've forgotten or that they're not sensitive to the loss. You can observe the day in your own way as well.

GETTING THROUGH THE SPECIAL DAYS

Knowing why the holidays, birthdays, and anniversaries are so difficult for grieving people can help you gain some control over the situation. But for most parents and caregivers of grieving children, that's not enough. You want to know what to do as the holidays, birthdays, and anniversaries approach. You want to know whether to celebrate or not to celebrate, whether to acknowledge them or not acknowledge them, and what's best for your child. It's confusing enough for you at holiday time; helping your child get through the holidays as well can be overwhelming. Here are some strategies other families have found helpful.

HELPING YOURSELF

Let's deal with you first. If you are falling apart during the special days, you will not be of much help to your child. So here are some suggestions for getting yourself through holidays, birthdays, and death or wedding anniversaries.

• *Exercise.* Even though you may not feel like it, push yourself to get some exercise each day. Walk, jog, do aerobics, or do whatever you can to get the heart pumping. Exercise reduces stress, and that makes you feel more in control.

• *Slow down on gift-giving.* You're grieving and you're entitled to cut back on gift-giving for a year. Other than the kids, you can decide who gets a gift and who doesn't. If you do buy gifts, consider mail-order catalogs, gift certificates, or food gifts. Shopping is an extra stress that you don't need and that you can legitimately curtail for a year.

• *Accept help.* Remember all of those people who said, "Please let me know if there's anything I can do to help"? Now is the time to take them up on it. If people offer to help around the holidays, by all means accept. You sure can use it, and it will make them feel as though they are contributing. They can write cards for you, buy gifts, or bring supper to your house to ease the burden.

• *Don't be afraid to cry.* By now, you know that special days can bring up many memories and make you feel pretty low. If you feel the tears coming on, let them flow. And if they come on in front of others, it's okay. It will not ruin the day for you or them. Get it out and continue, over and over if necessary. The tears you do *not* release are the ones that will hurt in the end.

• *Have fun when you can.* If you are in an activity or setting where you are having fun, go for it! There is nothing wrong with feeling good and enjoying yourself. It is not a betrayal of your loved one or your grief. Give yourself permission to have joy when you can and permission to mourn when you must.

• *Watch what you eat and drink.* Parties feature lots of sweets, but sugar gives you a quick lift, followed by a rapid decline. Eat meals that are well balanced and nutritious. Drink plenty of water. Stay away from alcohol and caffeine; they increase stress and can depress you.

• *Be selective about parties and dinners.* Holiday time is party time. When you are invited to a party or dinner, accept the invitation if you wish, but politely decline if you don't feel up to it. If you do accept, ask permission to be tentative. Tell the host that you're in mourning and some days are better than others. Tell him you would enjoy attending, but you're not sure how you'll feel on the day of the party. Ask if it would be all right to decline at the last moment if you are not feeling well. If you do go and you feel uncomfortable, simply say, "It's a great party, but I'm a little overwhelmed by grief right now." You *can* be in control of parties and dinners during the holidays.

• *Plan a January celebration.* Promise yourself a reward for getting through the holidays. Buy tickets to a play, go to a friend's house, invite a friend to your house, or plan a trip. Congratulate yourself for making it through a difficult period.

• *Most of all, feel the feelings and express them.* Whether you are sad, angry, guilty, depressed, or afraid, get it out. Write in your journal or talk to a good friend. Acknowledge that this year will be different. If others don't like it, that's too bad. It's your grief, not theirs, and you're entitled.

WHAT ABOUT THE KIDS?

If this book focused primarily on the grief of adults without children, our advice about coping with special days would go something like this: *There are no right or wrong approaches to holidays, birthdays, and anniversaries this year. Keep traditions the way they were, change them, or ignore them altogether. Stay at home for the day, go to a friend's house, or just take a vacation. Do what you feel like doing, and avoid what you don't feel like doing.*

But when you must take a grieving child into consideration, the advice changes. If you focus on your child's needs, you can no longer do whatever you want to do at special times. Such days may not mean so much to you, but they are magical times for your child. They're part of the rhythm and wonder of his life. For you to avoid them or run away from them would represent another loss for him. All of the other children are thinking about special dinners, the gathering of relatives, and the exchange of gifts. To dismiss special days now would make him feel even more different from his peers.

How a grieving child approaches a special occasion depends in large part upon her age. A young child may appear almost callous, thinking more about celebrating, decorating, and gift-giving than about the absence of her loved one. But remember that she is in an egocentric stage of development and is concerned about what the day means for *her* world. Further, special celebrations offer her a break from her grief. Her joy at such times does not mean she doesn't love her parent or sibling who died or doesn't miss him. Young children have a wonderful capacity for compartmentalizing life, and she is simply separating the pain of grief from the joy of celebrating with people who love her.

Older children may feel more inner conflict. They, too, want to participate in observances, but they likely feel the loss at the same time. Their celebrations are often bittersweet, although most would still prefer to observe the occasion rather than ignore it. Whether your child is young or old, recognize that the day will be awkward and that you cannot make it the same as it was, no matter how hard you try.

Special days can actually be helpful for a grieving child. You can turn painful periods into healing opportunities for your child. Consider them in light of the five challenges of grieving children (Chapter 5).

Observing special occasions helps *reestablish a sense of safety in the world.* It proclaims that although a terrible tragedy occurred in your family, life will continue with a sense of rhythm and dependability. Just as it is important to make a grieving child feel safe and secure by not moving or changing schools right away, recognizing special days adds a sense of stability for a child whose world has been shaken.

Special occasions can help your child *understand the death* by confirming that his loved one is gone and will not return. A young child, for example, may hold on to the magical wish that his loved one will come back for the holidays. When that doesn't happen, he understands a little more deeply that death is irreversible and forever.

Special occasions can help a grieving child *mourn the death.* For instance, it is impossible to celebrate special days without bringing up memories of the person who died. Sharing the feelings associated with such memories can help heal the pain of separation and transition.

Memories can also *maintain connections* with a loved one. A child may talk to the person who died or bring a favorite holiday memento of her loved one to her room. Decorating the tree "like Daddy used to" or baking cookies "that Mom really loved" are ways of maintaining connection. Also, mementos (Dad's jewelry, a framed picture of Mom and the child together, Dad's baseball mitt) make great gifts that also heal.

Finally, a grieving child can *reenter the normal developmental processes of childhood* at special occasions. They're times when kids can just be kids. They can laugh and have fun with other relatives. They can get away from their grief for a while and revel in the delight of childhood.

Keeping in mind the challenges of grieving children, here are some suggestions for celebrating as a family:

• *You have choices about how to spend the day.* There's no single "right" way, except the way that works for you and your family. While it's helpful to keep many traditions, you don't need to keep them all. But it's important to talk about it beforehand. Make sure everyone is heard and accommodated as well as they can be.

• *Whatever choices you make this year, you can change them next year.* Experiment with new ways of celebrating the holidays and special days. If they don't work, you're not locked into keeping them. You can always return to your familiar traditions next year. One family who experienced the loss of a child decided to chuck tradition and get away for Christmas. They went to the beach for three days, dressed warmly, flew kites, and read stories. The next year they put up a tree, decorated the house, and lit a candle on Christmas Eve in memory of their child.

• *Do something that honors your loved one.* Observe the day by supporting a cause that your loved one perceived as important. Before Bonnie's husband, Terry, died, he was a very active member of the town library board. Each year after his death, on Terry's birthday, Bonnie and her four children bought and donated books to the library in his memory.

In our own family, all of us dreaded the first Mother's Day as it approached. While the other kids in class were making Mother's Day cards, our kids would be dismissed to the school library. So when Mother's Day came, we recalled how much their mother loved the theater and went to see a Broadway play. This enjoyable day honored the mother we loved in a way she would have loved.

• *Return to the true meaning of the holiday or special day.* In the midst of a stressful, commercial culture, it can be refreshing to focus not on gifts and parties but on the people who are important in your life. You have a great excuse to pull back from outward celebrations when a loved one dies. Take advantage of it by spending time with those you love.

• *Have a backup plan.* Since you don't know exactly how you'll feel or how much energy all of you will have, be flexible. If you plan to visit family or friends, discuss the possibility of leaving early and going home. Or if you choose to stay home, figure out where you might go to have a lighter moment, if it proves just too painful.

• *Plan some way to acknowledge the pain of the day.* Everyone will feel it to some extent. Pretending to ignore it simply adds the pain of isolation to the pain of grief.

RITUALS

There is perhaps no better way of observing holidays, birthdays, and anniversaries than celebrating a ritual. A ritual is an external action that symbolically expresses how you feel. You can avoid much of the awkwardness of the special day—wondering how everyone will respond and not knowing what to say or do—if you plan a ritual in which the family can participate.

Evan Imber-Black, a well-known marriage and family therapist, states that rituals can express contradictory feelings and processes at the same time. "Ritual," she says,

> heals because it connects people with something larger than themselves and it has the capacity to hold contradictions like continuity and change. Through ritual, you can have a sense of both at the same time. And I don't know of anything else in life that does that in quite as powerful a way.[1]

Rituals can also express contradictions such as mourning and celebration, grieving and moving on, sadness and joy, contradictions that grieving people feel as they mourn their loss. For a grieving child, rituals provide a safe way of expressing these mixed emotions. First, rituals use action, a means of expression that is much more familiar and comfortable for kids than words. Second, good rituals enable a child to participate as much or as little as she wishes. That sense of control—of a personal, emotional "safety valve"—helps a child touch more intense parts of her experience because she knows she can stop at any time. Third, because rituals have a beginning and an end, a child knows she will only be confronting her pain for a short time. And fourth, rituals that are repeated feel safe to a child because she knows what to expect.

A ritual is also a communal way to acknowledge the day and the person who died, providing an outlet for much of the tension and anxiety that family members are feeling. When you create a ritual, involve all of the family members in planning it. Accept the child's suggestions, whenever possible, and leave some aspects unplanned to allow for spontaneity.

The first December after their mom died, our children wanted to decorate a wreath and bring it to the cemetery. They picked out the wreath and scoured our home looking for items that represented their mother. She enjoyed sewing, so they placed spools of thread on the wreath. She loved the theater, so they found some playbills and taped them to the wreath. They took the wreath to the cemetery and placed it with pride on her grave. Few words were spoken, but the gentle tears that fell said it all.

Make the rituals your own—here are some suggestions to get you started.

Holidays

• Wrap a favorite keepsake or a framed picture of your loved one, and give it as a gift to a relative or friend. Let your child help choose the gift and wrap it.

• Tell the stories behind the ornaments on the Christmas tree and the role your loved one played in making those memories.

• Help your child choose or create a special ornament labeled with the name of your loved one and hang it on the tree.

• Decorate a candle and light it at mealtime in memory of your loved one. If you celebrate Chanukah, recall a special memory on each of the eight nights that you light the menorah. Rotate the lighting and storytelling among family members.

• Purchase a holiday book—perhaps a favorite of your loved one or of your child—and donate it to your local library or school. Ask your librarian to place a label in the front cover, inscribed, "In memory of (your loved one's name)."

• Encourage your child to draw pictures and create gifts inspired by her memories of her loved one to give to other family members. Create a cut-out star, with your family's hopes and dreams for the future written on its points, and hang it in your home. Thinking about tomorrow is part of your healing.

• If you celebrate Christmas, consider a twist on the stocking tradition. Instead of not hanging (or not filling) your loved one's stocking, ask each person to place inside a written or drawn memory of the person who died. Then before or after stockings are explored, draw out the memories one by one and share them.

• Together watch your loved one's favorite holiday movie. Share his favorite movie snack or dessert.

Birthdays and Anniversaries

• Make a book of pictures and memorabilia about your loved one to give or simply to share with one another.

• Make a donation to a favorite charity in your loved one's name. Create a scholarship to keep his memory alive, and announce it at a gathering of family and friends. Involve your child in the process.

• Work with your child to prepare your loved one's favorite food. Bring it to share at a special dinner or at a soup kitchen. Mention her name in the blessing over the food, or propose a toast to her memory.

• Share anecdotes and favorite stories about the person who died. Sometimes others need permission to talk about the deceased. Let them know you would rather keep the memory of your loved one alive than pretend nothing has changed.

• On the anniversary of the death, your family may want to create a picture collage to place at the grave. Or you can use a tree branch to create a mobile filled with favorite items of the person who died: an empty ice cream box, an album or video cover, a favorite cap or team insignia, and so on.

• Engage your kids in planting a tree or flowers at home or at a special place that was meaningful to your loved one, such as a place of employment, church, synagogue, or ballfield.

• Participate as a family in a favorite activity of the person who died. Go to a ballgame, the beach, the theater, or a favorite restaurant; take a hike; or go fishing.

• Bake a cake on your loved one's birthday to celebrate the fact that she was part of your lives.

Finally, remember that it's not important that the ritual be perfectly executed or elaborate. What *is* important is that it expresses what needs to be said at the time and that each person participates as much or as little as she wishes.

However you decide to cope with special days—with old traditions or with new ones, with or without rituals—remember: The emotions that arise on special days need to be acknowledged. Expressing these feelings, even in small and private ways, is better than attempting to hold them in.

TEENS AND GRIEF

Grief or adolescence? Adolescence or grief? I can't figure out what Todd's silence and anger are all about, so how can I know what to do? Do I step in more because he's grieving? Or do I back off because he needs to become his own person?

—Jane, 45 years old

B EN, A WIDOWED FATHER, CALLED OUR OFFICE ONE DAY, HIS voice filled with pain and distress. His wife, Rachel, had died of breast cancer nine months ago. He and Rachel had three children, ages eight, eleven, and sixteen. He told us he was "at his wit's end." Ever since her death, he had been trying to keep things together for his family. He spent less time at the office and more time at home. He attended as many school functions and parent meetings as he could. He talked to the kids about their mother and tried to get them to talk about her as well.

Each of his children seemed to be dealing with the loss in a different way. The eight-year-old brought up her mother in normal conversation or when she was feeling sad, talked about her, and then returned to playing. The eleven-year-old was the opposite: He never talked about his mother at home and changed the subject when anyone else in the family did so. But his teacher said he talked about his mother in class, and that his behavior was fine and his grades were as high as they were before she died. So his father was not too concerned about him.

The reason Ben called us was his sixteen-year-old, Aaron. The teenager had been particularly close to his mother. Aaron talked with her in depth about school, his friends, his feelings, and even about the girls he liked. But since his mother's death, Ben worried that Aaron seemed a "lost soul." "After his mother died," Ben told us, "Aaron's attitude changed dramatically. He is sad at times, but mostly angry. He gets angry at me, at his brother and sister, at teachers, and at some of the kids at school. He's watching a lot more TV, doing a lot less homework, and he's talking about quitting sports. But what bothers me the most is the group of kids he's hanging around with. I don't like them at all. And the other day, I found a half-pint of vodka in his drawer. When I asked him about it, he told me it was no big deal."

Ben told us that Aaron had always felt closer to his mother than to him and that he was having a hard time reaching his son. Aaron wouldn't spend more than a few minutes with Ben and barely spoke to him at all. "Is this normal?" Ben asked. "Or should I start looking for a grief therapist?"

In an "intact" family, raising an adolescent challenges most parents. In a bereaved family, it typically presents even more confusion, questions, and concerns about "whether my child will be okay." The statement we hear most often from parents of grieving teens is "I don't know if his behavior is normal teenage development or related to his grief."

If you are raising a grieving adolescent and find yourself, like Ben, at your wit's end, you are not alone. There may be no more difficult period of life during which to lose a loved one than adolescence. It can wreak havoc within the teen himself and within the family. Confusion reigns as the teen struggles to deal with his grief and the rest of the family struggles to deal with the teen. This chapter will examine the stages of development for adolescents, what the death of a parent or sibling can do to a teen's development, and what adolescents need in order to work through their grief. Then we will offer some practical suggestions on how to help your grieving teen, making your life and the life of your family more peaceful.

IS IT ADOLESCENCE OR IS IT GRIEF?

Let's address the big question first. Since adolescence is such a turbulent life phase, most parents of grieving teens wrestle with the reasons for their child's actions and attitudes. In our own family, as our children progressed through the adolescent years, we often found ourselves asking whether sudden verbal attacks, periods of sullenness, radical mood swings, smoking cigarettes, loss of interest in school, changes of friendship, lack of communication, fights with siblings, or other reactions were due to normal adolescent development or to grief. Having observed scores of teenagers (both bereaved and nonbereaved) and having raised three adolescents, we've concluded the following: *Adolescence itself is a stage of life filled with losses. Therefore, to a greater or lesser extent, all teens are dealing with grief, and adolescence itself is a period of mourning.*

What does a child "lose" during adolescence? Physically, she enters puberty and experiences radical changes in her body. Mentally, her magical thinking and concrete reasoning give way to an ability to think abstractly. Emotionally, she loses her dependence on her parents as she separates from them to begin to define herself. That little child who believed in fairy tales and thought you were the most important person in the world loses her innocence and begins to let go of your ideals and advice in order to become her own person.

Every physical, mental, and emotional change is a loss to be mourned and causes familiar grief reactions: denial, sullenness, depression, anger, guilt, and fear. Every C on a test, every cut from team tryouts, every failure to get a part in the play, every breakup with a boyfriend, every fight with a best friend, every curfew that's imposed triggers a grief response. Adolescence spills over with these—so perhaps it is no surprise that the fashion color of choice for so many teens is black.

If your adolescent experienced a radical transformation from the human being you used to know, fear not. If he lashes out at you, slams his door, sits in silence, picks on his siblings, and brings home Godzilla as his new girlfriend, remain calm. If you're not sure whether his behavior and actions are typical of adolescent development or of grief, rest assured that they are both. Since typical adolescent development is a grief process, your teenager would probably be acting a little funny even if his loved one had not died. As Anna Freud once said, "To be normal during the adolescent period is by itself abnormal."

Lloyd D. Noppe and Ilene C. Noppe, professors of human development at the University of Wisconsin, observe: "Separation from one's parents is a necessary component of the process, but it is a loss that may be construed by an adolescent as a form of death. . . . In a sense, adolescence represents a period of mourning for the loss of that parent-child attachment relationship."[1]

So in a sense, it doesn't matter whether a particular behavior is related to development or to grief. All adolescents are grieving. Of course, for your child, the death of a parent or sibling compounds the normal losses of adolescence. Now, if her sibling died, she's lost a person with whom she shared memories, dreams, frustrations with peers and parents, and strategies for overcoming life's obstacles. If her sibling was relatively close to her in age, she may have lost one of the key people who would have companioned her through all the other losses of adolescence.

If her parent died, she mourns the loss of her touchstone, her guide, her source of wisdom and comfort, and so much more.

Under any circumstances, adolescence is a painful series of losses, but with an "intact" family, at least it's a gradual process, and a child has the company of his peers. He knows that what's happening, as painful as it may be, is part of growing up. And he can see that at the end of this turbulent period, he'll be in a better place: more free, more independent, more confident.

With the death of a parent or sibling, however, all of a sudden he's walking into a whole new world, a world with seemingly overwhelming challenges and far fewer resources. He may be the only one he knows on this journey of grief. And there's no light at the end of the tunnel: Mom or Dad is gone, and gone for good.

Just as a teen must mourn each loss of adolescence individually, he must mourn and process the death, too, over time.

GRIEF AND ADOLESCENT DEVELOPMENT

So to ask whether a grieving teen's behavior is due to the death of a loved one or to normal adolescence is to ask the wrong question. The more accurate question for parents of grieving adolescents to ask is this: How will the death of the parent or sibling affect my child's *development*?

THE THREE PHASES OF ADOLESCENCE

Adolescence in today's world is the time of life between childhood and adulthood; more precise definitions vary. Some experts say it begins at thirteen and ends at nineteen. Others suggest that it begins earlier because puberty often begins earlier; still others say it lasts longer because young people these days postpone adult commitments. We find it useful to think about adolescence the way a growing number of human development experts do: as falling into early, middle, and late phases. The phase of adolescence in which a child experiences a death may affect the developmental issues peculiar to that phase.

Early adolescence generally falls between the ages of eleven and fourteen, a time when your child first begins the long search for an identity he can call his own. He moves away from identifying with you and toward identifying with his peers. Your role as the hero in his life shrinks as he relates to new heroes in sports, music, and movies. During this phase, he becomes interested—awkwardly and with shyness—in members of the opposite sex. You might know this initial stage well, as you wonder *What happened to the child I knew so well?* and *Why is he so embarrassed to walk with me in the mall?*

Middle adolescence from ages fourteen to seventeen, generally coincides with the high school years. At this time, the teen's quest for self-identity grows stronger. Where he used to separate simply by ignoring you or avoiding your presence, now he actively pushes you away. During this phase, nothing you do is right. You don't wear the right clothes, your hair looks "geeky," you talk funny, your values are too conservative, and everything you do is boring. Your child rejects most of who you are and what you stand for, in order to find out who he is and what he stands for. It can be a very difficult time for a family, filled with stress and altercation. It's normal and it's healthy, but it's not easy.

Your child is also becoming much more independent as she masters new skills: learning to drive; getting her first "real" job; figuring out banking accounts; and taking on responsibilities in sports or clubs.

Late adolescence, ages seventeen to twenty-one, is the period when your adolescent completes her separation from you and connects with others, developing intimate, mature relationships. That turbulent stage during high school gives way to a quieter, more stable one. By going off to college or getting a full-time job, your child gains skills and competence that can boost self-esteem and sense of worth. Late adolescents tend to "come around," treating their parents as viable members of the human race once again. Feeling better about themselves and their own place in the world, they can safely let you into their lives and respect you as a trusted adult and a worthwhile friend. Parents of late adolescents often advise parents reeling from rejection by their middle adolescents, "Be patient and don't worry. They *do* come back."

You play a critical role during the phases and transitions of adolescence—*being there.* You provide that anchor with which your child can moor her "emotional boat," sail away for a little bit, then come back to anchor again. It's a passive job and an extremely vulnerable one: You need to be there so you can be rejected!

Since you are the primary attachment figure in your child's life, she counts on you for safety and security as she completes her tasks of separation and reconnection. Your child trusts you and knows that you love her unconditionally. So she feels safe when she rejects you and ridicules you, knowing that dinner will still be on the table when she comes home.

You also provide her with a sense of direction to help her make life choices. By encouraging her to participate in new experiences and to learn new skills, you help her achieve a sense of mastery and competence. By modeling behavior and values, you offer her choices about shaping her life. You are an example that she may imitate or reject but that she cannot ignore.

But what happens when a parent dies or is not there? Or what happens if a parent is so absorbed in his own grief that he is emotionally unavailable to his teen? Will the grieving teen be okay?

WHEN A LOVED ONE DIES

Adolescence is the period of life *between* childhood and adulthood— but it's not adulthood, not yet. It's often difficult for parents to remember that their teenager—particularly those ages fourteen to seventeen—are still *children.* Although they surround themselves with a pseudosophistication that resembles adulthood, they remain children at heart.

When your family member died, your adolescent may have appeared to respond in an adult way. He understands death intellectually as you do, although he does not have the same needs. We often hear parents say that a teen is "handling his father's death well," which usually means he is controlling himself and responding "like an adult."

Do not be fooled. It's easy to think your teen is reacting to the death with the mature resources of an adult, but that is rarely the case. On the inside, your adolescent is grieving like a child, with many of the same needs that children have.

But teens no longer have the same childlike attachment and dependence on a parent that younger children do. Adolescents are breaking away from their parents, but they also need them to be there in order to break away from them. As William Van Ornum and John B. Mordock write:

> Adolescents first develop their own ideas by resisting the ideas of others. Through rebellion they discover who they are. When a parent dies, the process of resisting, developing independent ideas, and then rediscovering the parent's viewpoint has not been allowed to come full circle. Death of a parent can throw an adolescent into a tailspin.[2]

If a child is in early adolescence when a parent dies, she may experience difficulty separating from her family in appropriate ways. She may struggle with the process by staying connected to her family and, instead, rebelling against other adults or by getting angry in the wrong places with the wrong people. In fact, she may become even more enmeshed in the family, taking on parental roles. She may fear separating from the family: after all, how could she willingly move away when she knows how scary and lonely it can be without just one family member?

Alternatively, she may back away from the family as a whole while remaining fiercely loyal to the person who died. Or she may distance herself from the family's painful expressions of grief as a way of protecting herself or as a way to stay connected to her peers. In effect, she may be saying, "Yeah, my family's grieving, but I'm not. I'm still like everyone else."

She may also wrestle with her peer connections. On the one hand, out of desperate loneliness, she may jump into friendships quickly and indiscriminately. On the other, she may struggle profoundly with giving her heart to another. After all, she was "abandoned" once by someone who was always supposed to be there—how can she trust this person now? The persistent chip on her shoulder may be a form of self-protection. *Maybe,* she may unconsciously think, *it's easier to reject everybody else before they reject me.*

If the child is in middle adolescence when the loved one dies, his growing sense of competence may come to a screeching halt. Missing vital support from his parent, he may find it difficult to reach out and acquire the real-life skills (early job skills, social skills, and the like) that normally develop in these years.

Consider Aaron. When his mother died, he lost his coach and cheerleader. Without her encouragement and communication, he began to lose self-confidence. He stopped trying out for musical groups. He no longer believed he could lead the technical crew for the spring play, a longtime dream of his. Even though he'd applied for full-time summer work before his mom died, he continued doing lawn work in the neighborhood. His world shrank—just at the time when it should have been expanding.

The late adolescent who experiences a death in the family may wrestle with developing intimacy skills and making commitments. Like the early adolescent who stuggles with trusting enough to form deep friendships, the late adolescent may grapple with giving her heart to one particular other. Why put yourself in a position to be hurt yet again?

Yet some older teens may rely on romantic relationships to fill the emotional void left by a death. Early sexual experiences often come out of that void. That sense of oneness (not to mention the sheer pleasure) that comes from physical intimacy can provide a moment of life when, inside, a grieving adolescent himself feels particularly dead.

Late adolescence continues to be a time of skill-building, ultimately leading to lifestyle and vocational choices that fit the teen's unique temperament and capabilities. But if development of an independent identity and talents is thwarted, choosing a career might be put on hold.

The early research on adolescence and grief indicated that following the death of a parent, teens experience a drop in grades, lower self-esteem, and more behavioral difficulties. But more recent studies claim that teens who lose a parent keep their grades up and behave as well as their nongrieving peers. Researchers have discovered that self-esteem not only holds its own after the death of a parent; in many cases, it rises. Many grieving teens experience a boost in self-worth and a higher level of maturity than nonbereaved adolescents. "More recent empirical investigations regarding self-esteem and adolescent bereavement have contradicted earlier findings by suggesting that adolescents may experience either no shift or in some specific areas may report both an increase in feelings of self-worth . . . as well as a sense of increased personal maturity . . . following the death of a loved one."[3]

Why is there such a gulf between the earlier research and the more recent studies? Which is right? Probably both. It is our experience that an adolescent who loses a family member travels on one of two paths. Either she has difficulty resolving the loss and continuing with her normal developmental process, or she develops greater maturity and growth. Which path your child takes rests, in part, on *you*. Parents who understand the process of adolescent development, how grief affects that development, and what grieving teens need can help produce a better emotional outcome for their child.

Of course, parental knowledge and responses are not the only influences of the outcome of adolescent grief. Personality, genetics, peer groups, and coping skills are also important factors. But it's not *all* left to fate, and there are things you can know and do to help your grieving teen avoid emotional complications and grow from the experience.

WHAT GRIEVING TEENS NEED

Molly was sitting on top of the world. At fifteen, she'd just landed a starting position on the girls' basketball team. She was doing much better in school this year, and she liked all of her teachers. The captain of the football team asked her out a few months ago, and since then dated steadily. For the first time in a while, things seemed to be going well. After several tumultuous years, she finally began to feel that she fit in. Things were even settling down a little at home, and she was beginning to communicate with her parents without major blowups or shouting matches.

Then one day in the middle of school, she was summoned to the office. The principal and school social worker informed her that her father had suffered a heart attack. The social worker drove her to the hospital and accompanied her to the coronary care unit, where her mother and three younger sisters were huddled together in a corner, crying. A priest sat next to them. Molly's mother, with tears streaming down her face, told Molly, "He's gone."

In the months that followed, Molly's world crumbled. Her mother fell apart, refusing to see visitors or answer phone calls. She gave away all of her husband's clothes and possessions. If Molly mentioned her father's name or brought up a memory about him, her mother changed the subject. Molly stepped in to take care of her three younger sisters, getting them off to school in the morning and helping them with their homework at night. She took on many chores that her father used to do: cutting the grass, shoveling the snow, paying the bills. With no time for her own homework, her grades slipped. With no time for practice, she quit the basketball team. With no time for her boyfriend, he stopped coming around.

After a while, Molly started getting into trouble. She fought with her teachers and ended up in detention on a regular basis. She stayed out late at night, sometimes until three or four in the morning, hanging out with older boys and drinking beer. She was sexually active with a couple of the boys and, at times, would spend the night with them. Molly thought that her mother was upset only because she was not home to take care of her sisters.

Molly felt trapped. She knew she was spiraling downward but didn't know how to stop. Her future looked bleak, and she lost all sense of direction. When an English teacher assigned a paper with the instructions "Explain where you will be five years from now," Molly wrote in bold letters across the page, "I may be dead five years from now."

Molly's grief turned bad. Grief, of course, is a natural response to loss, as there is nothing pathological about grief in and of itself. But the circumstances surrounding a loss or the family environment or the child's personality can turn a normal reaction into something problematic. In Molly's case, her mother functioned so poorly that she was unable to meet Molly's needs.

What were those needs? We've observed six particularly important needs for grieving adolescents. Here they are, along with our suggestions of how to help:

SECURITY

Teens need security and safety. No matter how much an adolescent knows in his mind that both his parents love him and care for him, it is normal for him, in his heart, to feel abandoned when a parent dies. What a teenager knows and what he feels may be two different things. That's one reason parents often feel frustrated with their teens. A parent may see a situation very rationally and feel baffled that her teen doesn't get it. The adolescent, on the other hand, may actually understand the situation as rationally as his parent but operate for the time being out of his feelings. For example, a classmate dies in a car crash, and you observe your son speeding down the street the following week. Rationally he *knows* that speeding can kill, but he *feels* immortal, that death happens to other people.

Your adolescent's pseudosophistication often cloaks a need for security. He appears more mature than he really is, and parents of grieving adolescents must see through the mask and pay attention to the little boy or girl huddled in fear on the inside.

Calm the fears of your grieving adolescent by letting him know that everything is going to be okay. Share with him, as appropriate, your strategies and plans for tackling the challenges resulting from the death. Adolescents are mature enough to anticipate specific problems; taking specific approaches to resolving those problems will resolve their fears more fully than a general "It'll all be fine." Even if things don't look okay to you at the moment and your world seems to be falling apart, let your child know that you're all going to make it through this.

Being there provides safety and security for your teen as well. If you can be physically present after school, at sports events, at the play he's in, or in other settings, you'll provide emotional shelter for your child. If you are working or out of town, call home often and make sure he has a way of reaching you whenever possible. Our kids used to call in the middle of a business meeting to ask where a particular shirt was. The call actually had nothing to do with a shirt; they wanted to know where their *dad* was. Simply being there for your grieving teen is one of the most basic things you can do to help, and it will provide him with an important resource from which he can build a new life.

INTIMACY

Closely related to security is the need for intimacy. When a parent dies, a child loses 50 percent of her most intimate relationships, and if a sibling dies, she may feel she's lost 100 percent as her parents focus on the child who died and on their own grief. In the past, no one loved her more closely, more compassionately, and more unconditionally than her parents. Now, one (or both) of the people she counted on to hold her and hug her, in good times and in bad, is gone.

Yet because she is pushing away from you, your teen may appear to be "in control," to not need the tender loving care that a child does. But when one of the most important people in her life is gone, she still needs to feel loved and cared for.

Find ways to be close to your teen. First and foremost is the hug. We cannot say enough positive things about hugging teens, even if yours is taller than you are or she grunts out "Ugh!" when you do it. Hugging your child seems like such a little thing, but it can make a big difference. This nonverbal connection between you and her is very useful at a time when verbal expressions are at a minimum. Hug her, and hug her often.

Making time to listen also deepens intimacy. "Wasting time" listening to the details of her life shows that you care and that you consider her to be an important person. It can make or break a sense of self-esteem following a parent's death.

Molly's mother ignored her after her father died, never letting her know she was still loved and appreciated. So when Molly couldn't find intimacy at home, she looked for it elsewhere and became sexually active with older boys.

CONNECTION

Not long ago, mental health professionals believed that resolving grief involved breaking the bonds between the griever and the deceased. They thought grieving people could not "move on" with their lives until they did so. Many still use the language reflecting this philosophy, counseling, "It's time to let go."

Today we know that grievers never "let go" of a loved one completely and never "get over" the death fully. In fact, most mental health professionals knowledgeable about grief suggest that it's unhealthy to try to detach completely from your loved one. It's important to stay connected in some ways and to maintain a healthy attachment with the person who died. People stay connected by going to the cemetery and talking to their loved one, wearing a piece of jewelry that he used to wear, or bringing out the family photo album and reminiscing.

Your adolescent, too, needs to stay connected to his loved one who died. Don't worry if he doesn't seem to be "letting go" or "moving on." It may be critical to his emotional well-being that he remain attached until he can move away on his own. If he is in the process of separating, he may hold on to the memory of the dead parent so that he can break away from him and continue the developmental process. The parent may die, but the anchor remains.

Last year, as birthday gifts, we gave our three children a video containing a compilation of old home movies. It showed them with their mother when they were very young. Hopefully, over the years, it will keep her alive in their hearts.

Many teens (and adults) fear that if they let go of their grief, they will lose the person for whom they are grieving. They're afraid they'll forget the person. But by providing connections to a family member who has died, you help your child keep that parent's memory alive and allow her to remain attached in a healthy way.

There is a balance to the practice: the key word is *healthy*. It is not helpful to sanctify a parent who died or to remain so connected that the child refuses to believe she is dead. Obsessively keeping the deceased's room exactly as it was when another child needs the space, turning a corner of a house into a shrine for a dead child while the mementos of surviving children are filed away—these are not healthy means of maintaining connection. Simple symbols and rituals (as described in Chapter 8) are more appropriate.

Molly's mother gave away all of her husband's clothes and possessions after he died. Consequently, she had nothing to give to Molly as a symbolic connection. And when Molly tried to talk about her dad or bring up memories, her mother changed the subject, making Molly feel even more lonely and abandoned. Any connections and any memories that Molly hoped to have of her father would have to come from Molly herself.

Provide connections for your teen. Think of ways that he can maintain a healthy attachment to his loved one. Go to the cemetery, bring out the photo album, talk to relatives together—do whatever it takes to keep the memory alive.

SHARING FEELINGS

As part of the separation process, adolescents shut down and clam up. That little child of yours who used to run into the house eagerly, proudly show you her latest artwork from school, and hurriedly tell you about her day in great detail, suddenly is gone. When you ask her a question or try to start a conversation, you often get a one-word answer. The classic parent-teen caricature of exchange has become:

"Where'd you go?"
"Out."
"What did you do?"
"Nothing."

And when you directly ask a teen how he feels, you are likely to get nothing more than a blank stare. But that doesn't mean he has no feelings to share. They're in there, in abundance. When a teen starts talking about his feelings, they flow like a river. Sometimes they have been pent up so long that they come uncorked like a geyser.

How can you help him get out the anger, fear, guilt, confusion, and sadness inside? The same communication skills we described in Chapter 6 will work with your teen. Develop empathy, listen well, and use mirroring phrases with your child—all can help him name and express his feelings periodically. If that doesn't work or he doesn't allow you in because he's in the process of pushing away from you, find others who can help him get it out.

Talk to everyone you know who may influence your child. Teachers and counselors at school are a logical beginning. You'd be amazed at how many teachers connect with children who have lost a parent. They often get a student to talk about things she would never talk about at home.

And there are other listening sources as well, especially members of the holding community: aunts and uncles, grandparents, coaches, Scout leaders, employers, clergy, relatives, and others who connect with your child. Find someone that your teen trusts and talks to, and ask that person to engage him in conversation about the person who died. It doesn't matter too much whom he talks to; it does matter that he talks and gets out the feelings.

If you can find a support group for grieving adolescents, sign him up. If you can't find a support group for grieving teens, why not start one? You don't have to run it, just get the idea rolling. In our opinion, the best support groups for teens take place in school, where they know the other kids, the facilitator, and the setting. It takes less time to build trust, and they get into the issues sooner. Contact your school social worker, guidance counselor, or nurse, and see if the school can begin a program.

RELIEF FROM PAIN

Related to the need to share feelings is the need to find relief from the emotional pain. A death in the family pummels the adolescent emotionally, mentally, and physically. When others fail to understand her needs and do something about them, her pain grows.

Child psychologist David Elkind says adolescents build a "personal fable," a series of assumptions about the world from which they operate. When a parent dies, the personal fable is shattered and the world she knew is destroyed. It will take a long time for the grieving adolescent to rebuild and enter a world that can be trusted once again.[4]

The grieving adolescent, like the grieving adult and child, is in anguish. Unlike the adult, he often cannot talk about his feelings easily or find a supportive group in which to release the pain. Unlike the child, he cannot blurt out his feelings without feeling foolish, and he cannot find relief in play.

But getting out the feelings will help relieve the pain dramatically. If it is not relieved in a healthy way, most teens will find ways of self-medicating. In our experience, nearly every teenager who abuses alcohol or drugs or engages in violent acts of aggression is trying to relieve the pain caused by some kind of loss (such as a death, abuse, abandonment, or divorce of parents).

REGAINING NORMAL DEVELOPMENT

When a loved one dies, teens need to get back on track in the normal course of their development. They must do so without some of the resources they've previously relied on, and they must do so in their own time. The grieving adolescent not only has the ability to regain normal development, she also has the opportunity to grow in ways she never thought possible.

To keep a grieving adolescent on the path of healthy development, you should continue to be a good parent. She needs you to be a solid anchor. Clearly, be sensitive to your child after a death, but remember it's no time to be permissive and open to anything. Expect her to do homework and behave well in school. Expect her to continue to do her chores and even pick up a few more to help you out. Expect her to abide by her curfew and accept responsibility for any failure to do so. She needs, and wants, direction and guidance from you.

On the other hand, a grieving adolescent should not be expected to assume the responsibilities of the parent who died. Taking on a few extra chores to help out is one thing; becoming the new "man of the house" is another. Your child is breaking out of childhood. He's not an adult. Be careful of placing too many responsibilities on his shoulders.

When we speak to parents of grieving teens, one particular feeling comes up over and over: helplessness. A parent or caregiver who is raising a grieving adolescent often feels as though there is nothing he can do to help. When he tries to ask questions about feelings or reactions, the teen turns away or refuses to respond. Frustrated by the teen's unwillingness to talk, the parent suggests that the teen see a professional. Most grieving teens do not accept the suggestion with enthusiasm. So the parent throws up his hands and says, "I don't know what to do. He won't talk about his mother with me, and he won't see a therapist. I feel helpless."

As helpless as the situation appears, there are ways to help. Perhaps the best thing you can do for your grieving teen is to be patient. Remember that it takes a long time to go through early, middle, and late adolescence. Even though he may seem like an alien to you right now, he will come back. Remember that you will all get through this in time.

If you do all you can to actively help your child by providing security, intimacy, connection, and a way to share feelings and relieve the pain, and by being firm, fair, and patient, rest assured that you have done all you can to help. You have given him the best opportunity possible to come through this with a greater sense of self-worth, compassion, competence, and meaning. There are no guarantees that that will happen, but you will have done your part to ensure that your grieving adolescent will be okay.

Chapter 10

WHEN GRIEF GOES WRONG

Sandy was always such a social kid. But since her mom died, I'm worried about her. Every day after school, she goes in her room, closes the drapes, and listens to music. She wants to paint her walls black. I look at her face, and it doesn't seem sad. It just seems like there's nobody behind it.

—Patrick, 41 years old

HOW DO YOU KNOW IF THE BEHAVIOR YOU'RE SEEING IN YOUR son or daughter is typical for grieving kids or cause for concern? If you're like most parents of grieving children, this question haunts you—and for good reason.

The Child Bereavement Study indicated that, within the first two years after a death, 36 percent of grieving kids show symptoms troubling enough to warrant seeking professional mental health care. In some way, theirs is grief gone wrong: normal grief that's distorted or broken down. Experts call this type of grieving *complicated mourning*.

Unfortunately, no single clue (short of total ecstasy after the death of someone close, or suicidal behavior) indicates complicated mourning. Mental health professionals consider a wide range of behaviors to be normal. Rather than a one-time incident, it's the persistence of symptoms or their interference with everyday functioning that indicates a more complicated mourning pattern.

Sometimes grieving adults and children behave in unusual ways. As unsettling as that can be, it's still no reason to panic. For a child under ten who behaves "strangely," there's rarely any short-term danger to waiting a few weeks while you watch to see what's up. Even for a pre-teen and adolescent, you have time to look, listen, and consult with others about the situation (unless you suspect he may harm himself or others).

If you think your child is suffering from a more complicated mourning pattern, try to take it easy. Even though it may take some work with a mental health professional, complicated mourning can usually be resolved without severe long-term consequences.

RISK FACTORS FOR COMPLICATED MOURNING

Although many children can slip into a complicated mourning pattern, some children run a much greater risk. If your circumstances are listed below, you'll want to be especially sensitive to signs that your child may need extra help.

THE DEATH OR THE CIRCUMSTANCES SURROUNDING IT WERE TRAUMATIC

Understandably, a child who witnesses a murder, suicide, fatal crash, natural disaster, or other traumatic event may have more difficulty coping with the death. Even experiencing just a piece of the event (for example, hearing but not seeing the gunshot, smelling a burning building) can prove traumatizing for children and adults alike.

Moreover, a death can traumatize a child if he hears a significant amount of gory detail all at once (especially without an ongoing safe, supportive environment).

That's not to say that children can't process an amazing amount of emotionally difficult information, such as the details of a suicide. But children who cope well with such information are those who learn the facts over time, in bits and pieces, and in an environment characterized by open communication and the continuing presence of caring adults. Such adults are sensitive to the child's moment-to-moment capacity to take in and understand information; they recognize the signs that he has heard all he can tolerate for the time being, signs like restlessness, changing the subject, leaving the room, asking if he can go play, and so on.

Likewise, receiving no information can prove traumatizing for a child. She may conclude that the truth is too horrible to talk about or, as we've mentioned, use her imagination to supply the missing "facts," which may be even more terrifying than the reality.

Fir… stances can be traumatiz… wn died from sudden i… ere both distraught as po… ed their house for days. … year-old son, Ryan. Not… ut he now worried abou… to jail, Mommy?" he as…

Li… uscitate a dying person… electric paddles to reviv… l.

Fi… s can be traumatizing a… ap child." So when her… some relatives, she cont… to bed. One night, after the cancer had spread to his brain, she was on his lap when his brain suddenly threw him into seizure. Unable to control his movements, his hand hit Cini in the chest. After the seizure stopped, Cini's mom found her huddled in her closet sobbing. "Why did Daddy hit me like that?" she asked between sobs. Thereafter she was terrified to go near her dad.

YOU, THE SURVIVING CARETAKER, ARE NOT FUNCTIONING WELL ON AN ONGOING BASIS

Everyone who is raising a child functions better on some days than on others. Grief intensifies those swings. But if your grieving child misses solid physical or emotional support from you or other close adults over time, then she herself may cope in less healthy ways.

Help your child by helping yourself. See Chapter 13 for ways to take care of yourself so that you'll more competently care for your grieving child.

YOUR CHILD HAD A LOVE-HATE RELATIONSHIP WITH THE PERSON WHO DIED

Unfortunately, families are not perfect, and relationships within them can be harmful as well as helpful. Many families are afflicted with alcoholism, drug abuse, incest, or severe physical, emotional, or verbal abuse. Even the more common family conflicts (like bitter divorce battles or the normal struggles with teens) can leave grieving children to grapple with very mixed emotions: love *and* hate; missing the person who died *and* feeling relief; anger at the death *and* pleasurable fantasies of revenge.

Holding communities sometimes compound the problem by expecting grievers to hold only warm, loving feelings toward the person who died. It's a lucky child who can say "I hate my mommy" while a supportive adult listens without judgment!

YOUR CHILD'S ENVIRONMENT REMAINS CHAOTIC, WITHOUT CONSISTENT DISCIPLINE

Like all his grieving relatives, your grieving child is struggling to figure out what he can count on in his newly altered world. But if his world keeps shifting because of moves, ongoing changes in caregivers, variations in rules, and the like, he's likely to worry even more about where he stands and how safe he is. Of course, some change is inevitable after a death, but if your child's world is chaotic, he's more at risk for complicated mourning.

THERE IS LITTLE OR NO SUPPORT FOR NORMAL MOURNING IN YOUR CHILD'S WORLD

As in years past, some adults still believe that children don't understand enough to grieve, or that if they do grieve, it's only a temporary phenomenon. Other adults believe that grief is such a private affair that it belongs only in the home, not in schools or community activities.

Such beliefs encourage kids to stuff their emotions, to push them down inside. That's like trying to put a lid on a volcano. All that energy has to go somewhere. If you don't let it come out naturally, it will "blow" in some unknown, potentially risky way—either now or in the future.

YOUR CHILD HAS SUFFERED SEVERAL SIGNIFICANT LOSSES

Multiple losses (such as from divorce, a series of deaths, moving, a serious illness) plague children in particularly difficult ways. First, because children process a loss over and over again as they pass through various stages of development, a series of losses can set a child on an unrelenting grief journey.

Second, multiple losses can skew a child's view of how the world works and encourage unhealthy ways of coping. Kathleen, for example, turned four a few months after her older brother died in a bicycle collision with a car. Six months later, her younger brother died of meningitis.

After three years of grieving, her parents decided to have another child. They worried about how Kathleen would react but were relieved that she continued her life as normal after the baby was born. A few months later, however, they noticed that Kathleen hardly played with the baby at all. She never talked to the child and helped only when specifically asked. "Why should I bother?" she later asked a therapist. "He's just going to die anyway."

THE PERSON WHO DIED WAS ILL FOR A LONG TIME (OVER SIX MONTHS)

As strange as it sounds, there seems to be an optimal timetable for dying—at least from the perspective of a family trying to cope. Sam's family is a good example. When his wife, Laura, was dying, she defied the odds. While her doctors predicted she'd never make it to summer, she pulled through the fall and into the holidays. By Christmas, she lay in a coma. Sam explained his dilemma this way: "All year long I've been saying, 'I'd better enjoy her while I can. This will be her last Easter or Mother's Day or vacation or wedding anniversary or whatever.' Except for work, I can hardly seem to tear myself away from her bedside. I know it's unfair to the kids. They need me too. But what am I supposed to do?"

An illness that goes on for too long wears down the family's coping resources. Parents tire out, having little emotional energy left for their grieving children, who now need their support more than ever. Without the care, support, and perspective of the surviving parent, kids are increasingly at risk for grief gone wrong.

YOUR CHILD HAS EXPERIENCED OTHER MENTAL HEALTH ISSUES

Does your child contend with depression, anxiety, ADD/ADHD, or another mental health issue? If so, then grief will complicate matters for her. The death may divert all of her internal coping resources to her grief, leaving none for her underlying struggles. At this stressful time, even if she has completed therapy for an ongoing mental health concern, she may well benefit from a "booster shot." Some extra work with a qualified therapist may provide additional external support just when her own internal resources are low.

SIGNS OF GRIEF GONE WRONG

Although no single clue definitively indicates complicated mourning, the following patterns can tip you off to a profound pain in your child that calls for professional help.

ONGOING RESTLESSNESS, HYPERACTIVITY, OR SUPERALERTNESS

Does your child seem to be waiting for the other shoe to drop? As we've said earlier, grieving kids tend to feel anxious. Your grieving child may well fear that you'll die, that he'll die, that his peers will reject him because of the death, or any of a number of other possibilities. He may be anxious this morning and fine this afternoon. For a spell of several weeks, he may be particularly hyper or restless.

What differentiates anxious children who need extra help from those who don't? In children with complicated mourning, their fear may be generalized in nature. Nothing in particular frightens them, but rather *everything* does. Even with a parent's help, they can't name what they're afraid of because no *single* possibility frightens them. It's a more basic fear, a general dread. They're *always* waiting for the other shoe—

whatever shoe it might be—to drop. That general, ongoing anxiety shows up as ongoing restlessness or hyperactivity.

Other grieving children who need extra help have specific fears—such as a fear of separation from you, of sleeping alone, of the death of someone else they love, and so on—that linger on and on. If you see such a persistent fear in your child, it may frustrate you enormously. You know what's bothering her, you've talked about it, and in your own adult mind, her fear may not even be reasonable. Yet it persists. In that case, it's time to call in professional help.

ONGOING AND SIGNIFICANT CHANGES IN YOUR CHILD'S PERFORMANCE AT SCHOOL, ON THE ATHLETIC FIELD, WITH FRIENDS, OR IN OTHER IMPORTANT AREAS

Contrary to popular myth, school grades among grieving kids typically dip only temporarily (if at all) after a death. The same holds true for athleticism: If it changes at all (either improving a great deal or getting significantly worse), it's normally a fleeting effect. Most grieving kids will have good days on the field or in the classroom interspersed with bad days.

But if your child's performance shifts and continues that way consistently for a couple of months without relief, even when you give your attention to the matter, it's a clue that your child is struggling in a more profound way than normal.

Pay attention to your child's social patterns as well. At the beginning of Ron's freshman year in high school, his eighteen-year-old sister, Natalie, died from cancer. In their mourning, Natalie's friends decided to take Ron under their wings. All of a sudden, Ron gained six "big sisters" and the attention of the entire senior class. Invitations to parties, concerts, and meals at the local diner poured in. In the space of six weeks, Ron's usually quiet social world turned from basketball with a gang of fourteen-year-old guys to hanging out with eighteen-year-old women.

Ron's mom reflected, "I wasn't sure what to think. I mean, I was bothered by the age difference: at eighteen, I'd expect girls to be into more advanced stuff than my son was at the time. On the other hand, I was thrilled that Ron was coming out of his shell a bit. I realize it's normal for boys to discover girls at some point. So although this discovery seemed sudden, maybe with Natalie's cancer, I had just been preoccupied and missed the signs that it was coming all along.

"It all came to a head, though, the night he came home high," she continued. "It became clear to me then that he was using the social whirl, and now marijuana, to avoid the pain of his sister's death."

Using social activity to shut down grief completely is a complicated mourning pattern, and social changes for the worse can also be calls for help. If your child becomes more quiet or withdrawn, shows less interest in social activities, hangs out a lot more at home on weekends, or receives a lot fewer phone calls, it may be a sign that something significant is happening. If it continues for a number of weeks without any letup, you may want to ask a professional for an evaluation. Especially in preteens and teens, social changes are often early signs of depression.

STRONG REACTIONS TO POTENTIAL SEPARATIONS THAT REGULARLY INTERFERE WITH YOUR CHILD'S (OR YOUR FAMILY'S) NORMAL LIFE RHYTHMS

After someone in a family dies, everyone will naturally fret more about each other's safety. Each of you knows only too well that you're not invulnerable to death. So hearing an ambulance siren in the distance, or seeing someone off on a plane, or realizing that someone is half an hour late may particularly trouble you or your child.

But if that level of worry starts seriously affecting how your family functions, then you need to think about getting extra help. After her husband died of a stroke while coming home from work on the bus, Cindy started working from nine to twelve each weekday at the local high school. Her five-year-old daughter, Leah, hated her mom's new job. Leah began to resist going to school, even though Cindy put her on the bus each morning and stood waiting for her when she got off in the afternoon. As Leah's resistance grew over the weeks, Cindy noticed that her daughter ate less and less and seemed especially tired. That's when she knew it was time to see someone, and she sought the help of a child-oriented social worker.

With the social worker, Cindy discovered that Leah linked her dad's working with his death. So when her mom started working, Leah feared that Cindy, too, would die, leaving her all alone. In her five-year-old mind, the connection seemed clear. Of course, that "logic" had escaped Cindy. It took the social worker, who was skilled in deciphering young minds, to uncover Leah's deepest fear.

Other activities that can trigger children's serious anxiety over potential loss are sleepovers, campouts, school trips, day camps, and support groups, as well as parents' business trips and even parents' night at school. If your child reacts in an extreme way to spending time away from you or from home, remember: The problem is not what you're doing, it's her fear about what might happen to you. That means that merely stopping the activity—staying with your child all the time, not separating—won't solve the problem. It will only postpone solving it.

Instead of yielding to her fear, you need to help her name and overcome it. She herself needs to realize that her fear is unlikely to be fulfilled. Naturally, you'll do your best to help her with those tasks, but if your efforts fail over time and fear of separation continues to interfere, get some extra help. Otherwise, you're simply letting her separation anxieties torture her.

REGRESSING TO THE BEHAVIOR OF A LESS MATURE CHILD ON AN ONGOING BASIS

Like a typical eighth grader, Shauna filled her life with boys, makeup, and socializing at the town's center. Then the grandmother who had raised her died of a stroke. Soon after, Shauna dropped her school friends and reverted to playing with the elementary school kids next door. Her grandfather did not think this behavior unusual, and lost in his own grief, he even felt relieved. He'd always believed that kids these days grow up too fast. And besides, he remembered playing ball and hide-and-seek with a whole neighborhood of kids, all of varying ages, when he was a boy.

But when Shauna's aunt came in town a few months later, she saw her niece's behavior differently. She worried about what the change meant and insisted that Shauna see the school psychologist. Shauna, it turned out, had decided that growing up meant growing old—and that growing old meant dying. So inside, she made up her mind to stay a child.

In a younger child, regression may show up as bed-wetting, thumb-sucking, clinginess, and an unwillingness to share—just when you thought he was past that stage! Older children may return to a rigid insistence on following rules or to playing by themselves rather than with a group of kids. Again, temporary behaviors are not cause for concern, but when they linger, it's time to consult someone with professional expertise.

Rather than actually regressing, a grieving child can get stuck at his current level of development and not progress socially, emotionally, or mentally. Duncan, for example, appeared to grieve his twin brother's death in a very normal way. But two years after the death, the summer Duncan turned sixteen, his unwillingness to look for a job began to bother his parents.

As the school year progressed, they noticed more signs of Duncan's stagnation. He put off getting his driver's license; in fact, he refused to sign up for driver's ed. Although he was very social, he did not start dating. He remained satisfied with the curfew set at the time of his brother's death. An evaluation by a professional counselor confirmed their suspicions: Duncan was emotionally frozen at age fourteen. It took six months or so for the counselor to get to the root of Duncan's issue: his guilt at surviving while his twin had died. Only after another six months of counseling was Duncan ready to reenter normal growth patterns for kids his own age.

ONGOING SYMPTOMS OF DEPRESSION

The death of Sasha's father when she was twelve years old prompted a series of drastic changes in her life. She moved, with her mom, into her grandma's house across town. That meant a new school and new friends, both tough adjustments for a junior high school student.

Still, both her grandmother and her mother thought Sasha was doing well enough. Sure, she seemed cranky a lot, but they chalked that up to the start of adolescence. She also seemed to get sick a lot—nothing major, just lots of sore throats, headaches, and stomach complaints. After a while, Sasha's grandmother took her to the pediatrician.

Her doctor saw nothing wrong but noted that Sasha hadn't gained weight since her last checkup a year ago. She ran tests that ruled out a physical cause, then began to suspect that Sasha was suffering from clinical depression.

At first, Sasha's mom felt frustrated with the diagnosis: after all, didn't Sasha have a right to be sad after everything that had happened? But soon she learned that clinical depression is more than just a lingering sadness. It's a highly treatable disease that affects a lot of people. In its more serious forms, it affects 4 to 8 percent of both adults and children. When milder forms of depression are counted, about 20 percent experience this disease at some point in their lives!

What might lead you to suspect depression in your child? The presence of several of the following symptoms for an extended period of time should be cause for concern:

• Sad mood or ongoing melancholy most of the time and almost every day. In your child, this could show up as an ongoing irritability as well.

• Significantly less interest or enjoyment of most activities, especially ones that he used to enjoy.

• Changes in his social life, especially withdrawing from friends and social activities.

• A pattern of physical complaints that, after consulting your pediatrician, prove to have no physical basis.

• Meaningful weight changes (gains or losses) without trying. As with Sasha, the absence of weight gain normal in a growing child can be a sign of depression as well.

• Noteworthy changes in sleep patterns: insomnia, waking up early, waking up a number of times in the middle of the night, or sleeping much more than normal.

• Changes in energy level: feeling restless or churned up most of the time or, in contrast, feeling tired or sapped of energy on an ongoing basis.

• Feeling guilty or, in adolescents, worthless or empty most of the time.

• In adolescents, a feeling of being physically slowed down. Some have described this feeling as living wrapped in cotton gauze or Jell-O.

• Recurring thoughts of suicide: how to do it, whether to do it, and so on.

REGULARLY TAKING ON PARENTAL OR ADULT ROLES WITH OTHER FAMILY MEMBERS OR FRIENDS

After her husband died, Elaine considered her fifteen-year-old daughter, Ellie, to be her best supporter. "I feel so lucky," she remarked. "She's really responsible, and I treasure our nightly cup of tea together. I can tell her what I'm feeling, and she listens. Not many mothers have that kind of relationship with their teenage daughters!"

Ellie, on the other hand, reflected, "I feel so frustrated. I want so much to help my mom, but she's just in so much pain! If my dad were here, he'd know what to do, but I don't. And sometimes I just want to run away from it all."

Like many grieving kids, Ellie assumed more chores after her dad died. But unlike others, she also became her mother's confidante and best friend, a role formerly filled by her dad. Elaine was right that not many mothers have that kind of relationship with their daughters, and there's a good reason for it: Assuming adult roles is not normal for children or teens. It's not developmentally appropriate, and it can take place only at the expense of the child involved. Teens normally try on various personality traits and behaviors at home, as a way of establishing their own identities, but for Ellie this process became a luxury she could not afford—her mother needed her to be a supportive listener. Ellie also had to put on hold her own normal, adolescent process of breaking away from the family.

Additionally, in order to be her mom's best friend, Ellie had to put aside her own grief in favor of soothing her mom's. In order to maintain a secure household, she had to shoulder responsibility for her mother's well-being at a time when the roles should have been reversed. As a result of her tending to Elaine's needs, Ellie's needs as a grieving child—for safety and expressing her grief—stayed unmet. Grieving children like Ellie, who are forced to postpone their own grief to take care of family responsibilities, often experience a more severe grief reaction later in life.

Parents who push children into responsible adult roles also unknowingly set up their children for potential failure and blows to their self-esteem. For example, no one could have relieved Elaine's pain over the death of her husband. But Ellie, at fifteen, had had too little life experience to understand that fact. From her perspective, her job was to alleviate her mom's grief, and she failed at it.

Finally, children who must assume adult roles are likely to feel a high level of resentment. According to the Child Bereavement Study, teenage girls who are forced to take on parenting roles in their families often develop behavior problems like chronic hostility or drug and alcohol use.

Yet sometimes taking responsibility for additional *specific* chores can improve a child's self-esteem, especially when they enable him to explore unknown areas of strength in himself or when they stretch him to master tasks that previously seemed beyond him. How do you tell the difference between a healthy and unhealthy increase in responsibility or expectation?

In two ways. First, healthy increases in responsibility and expectation require the child to stretch only in ways that are definitely within his reach and capabilities (perhaps with a bit of work). For example, an eight-year-old child might be able to supply food and tissues to a younger sibling who is sick with the flu. But expecting that eight-year-old to accurately monitor medicine intake and to comfort the sick child is asking too much. He is unlikely to have the discipline to give medication on schedule or the emotional capacity to empathize and soothe another person. Likewise, asking a college-age child to enforce the rules while baby-sitting is age appropriate. But expecting that same child to help a younger sibling choose a college is asking her to shoulder a parent's job.

Second, healthy increases in responsibility are those that in no way block normal behaviors and growth patterns for someone your child's age. Ideally, such increases complement and build on the developmental tasks that the child is already working on.

RISKY, POTENTIALLY SELF-DESTRUCTIVE ACTIONS OR BEHAVIORS

Watch for substance use and abuse, sexual promiscuity, high-risk sports, gang or cult activity, and the like. Krissy's pregnancy at fifteen surprised everyone—she had seemed to be thriving since her mom died two years before. Her grades soared. She won the election for class president. Socially, she flourished.

Only her boyfriend knew how physically needy she was. For Krissy, sex had become the way she made intimate connections, her method for dealing with a loneliness she could not even voice. She missed her mom ferociously, and she knew of no other way to fill that gaping hole inside.

Other kids may use drugs or alcohol to kill the pain, much as adults do. After a death, almost 30 percent of adult grievers use more alcohol or drugs than they did before.[1] How much more vulnerable teens must be to such behaviors after a death, given the peer pressure for even non-grieving adolescents to experiment!

For some kids, high-risk sports or risky driving may be a way to prove their own mastery over death, a kind of proof that they are invulnerable to it. Alternatively, it may be a subconscious death wish, a way to have death happen without actually killing themselves.

Finally, some grieving kids may be more vulnerable to gangs or cults. At a time when they're more likely to feel incredibly lonely, different, and therefore isolated from their peers, full of questions and regrets, cults may seem quite appealing. They may appear to offer just what a grieving child wants: easy answers and total acceptance.

CHRONIC ANGER AND/OR HOSTILITY

As we've mentioned a number of times, anger is a common reaction after the death of someone close. As such, it's generally no cause for alarm. But if it continues for months without letting up, it's time to see a mental health professional.

Hostility takes many forms: a silent withdrawal, a persistent "chip on the shoulder," destruction of property, overly aggressive driving, and other behaviors. Any of these, if they continue, should point you toward a professional.

ONGOING SIGNS OF TRAUMA

Trauma can persist over time in children and adults alike. Unfortunately, however, trauma can be difficult to recognize because over the course of months or years, its symptoms typically show up in alternating cycles of avoiding the trauma (or parts of it) and reliving it vividly.

During the avoidance phase, a traumatized child will dodge reminders of the person who died and of the death or the circumstances surrounding it. She may not even recall important aspects of the death or its aftermath. She may show signs of depression as well: lack of interest in previously enjoyable activities, a more limited range of emotions, or feelings of detachment from others.

In the second phase, the reliving phase, traumatized kids find themselves entirely unable to avoid the trauma. Despite their best efforts to avoid reminders of the deceased person, thoughts, images, and emotions intrude. It's as if the event were really happening all over again, in exquisite detail. Traumatized people see all the same sights. They hear all the same sounds. They feel all the same sensations. They experience all the same emotions. It's overwhelmingly frightening all over again. Older children and adolescents sometimes describe this reliving as a very lifelike daydream or as a movie reel or videotape that plays over and over inside their minds.

In younger children, reliving may show up as rigid, compulsive, and highly repetitive play. When Bubba was four, his father died in a collision between his car and a truck. Roughly six months after the death, Bubba's mom realized that her son was playing out the same scene over and over again with his cars and trucks: Each time a line of cars would be waiting, and a truck would sneak up and totally wreck the cars. The truck never missed. The cars always scattered. No one ever escaped the situation. Never did a police officer come to save the day. The script was always *exactly the same.* And when she tried to talk to Bubba in the middle of it, he was so totally absorbed that he seemed not even to hear her speak.

Therapists call this type of play *traumatic play,* a child's attempt to figure out what happened and perhaps to ward off the possibility of it ever happening again.

If you see your child playing this way, know that she can be helped, but she'll need someone trained in childhood trauma to work with her.

Finally, traumatized children and teens live in a perpetually aroused state. They are supercharged, overly restless. They seem always on edge. They're easily startled. They may have difficulty falling asleep or staying asleep. They may be cranky or have trouble concentrating.

One of our best early "teachers" about trauma was a sixth grader who we nicknamed the Pinball Wizard because, moment to moment, week after week, he bounced from one activity to another. Extremely bright and articulate, he nonetheless pushed his mother, Jeannine, to her wit's end. "He'd never been a problem before," she reported, "but ever since he found his dad dead at the bottom of the pool, he can't sit still. His teachers, his coach, his Sunday school instructors—everyone's noticed a difference, and none of us know what to do. I think the whole situation freaked him out, and he's just running on adrenaline overload all the time."

Jeannine analyzed the situation well. Some people have a physical reaction to trauma, a chronic persistent chemical "rush" that hangs on. In your child, that may show up as being on guard, easily startled, hyperactive, restless, or overly anxious.

A NARROWED RANGE OF EMOTIONS OR PERSONALITY TRAITS

For most adults and children, grief expands the number of emotions we feel. In addition to being happy and sometimes bored and periodically irritated, you may find yourself sad and lonely and anxious. Your child's experience is likely to be the same. But if your child's normal mix of emotions and traits narrows to only one or two, instead of expanding, or if an emotional response that's normal for your child is noticeably missing, then your child's grief is blocked or strangled in some way.

Ten-year-old Mack is a great example. He was notable for his demanding nature, for being determined, knowing his own mind— being stubborn, in fact. But after his older brother died, he lost his demanding nature. In fact, he became almost wishy-washy. Although he was easier for his mother to deal with, his change in personality made her uncomfortable.

Mack's teachers observed the change as well and referred him to the school psychologist, who eventually unearthed the reason for Mack's behavior. He viewed his brother's death, and death generally, as a punishment from God, one he wanted no part of. Knowing that his personality often grated on the adults around him, he chose to give himself up, to become submissive, in order to avoid such a severe punishment.

Over time, the psychologist helped Mack correct his view of death and God—and to find more agreeable ways to assert himself as well. Instead of pushing parts of his personality underground, Mack learned how to express his needs and wants while respecting the viewpoints of others. He learned how to negotiate. Now, instead of being either "stubborn" or "wishy-washy," Mack could be both assertive and flexible.

ONGOING PHYSICAL COMPLAINTS FOR WHICH YOUR PEDIATRICIAN CAN FIND NO CAUSE

Three years after her dad died, Libby developed severe migraine headaches. No one else in the family suffered from them. Her physician performed all the typical tests, found the results normal, and referred her to a neurologist. But the neurologist, too, was stumped. Clearly, Libby's pain was real, but the cause remained unknown.

Libby's experience is a common one, especially for girls. Whereas boys tend to get their emotions out in actions, girls (and preteen and teenage girls in particular) more often swallow them. Having nowhere else to go, girls' grief emotions may come out in physical symptoms.

So if you find yourself at the doctor's office or emergency room significantly more often, it may be time to examine whether something more complicated is happening with your child. If it continues, you may want to seek out a professional viewpoint.

SUICIDAL THOUGHTS OR GESTURES

Always take signs of suicide seriously. Let a mental health professional decide if the risk is real. That's his job—he's trained to do it, and you're not. Unlike other situations in which the consequences of being wrong are tolerable, the consequences of being wrong about suicide risk are too great.

Of course, the million-dollar question is, what signs might indicate your child is at risk for suicide? First of all, watch for the signs of clinical depression, discussed on pages 173–175. Usually, kids slip into clinical depression before they become suicidal. In adolescents, however, mere moodiness can mimic many symptoms of clinical depression, so you'll want to see if those symptoms continue for more than a couple weeks before taking action.

You'll also need to watch for more subtle signs. One young adolescent we know hung his childhood toy duck by a rope around its neck and put grotesque masks from art class on the wall of his room. When his parents first saw the decorations, they chalked it up to a typical young adolescent desire to shock them.

Then his parents noticed that his songwriting reflected a growing interest in being out of pain, he spent much more time in his room, and he began reading books on life after death. The overall pattern rightly disturbed his parents, who brought him for evaluation.

Second, your child is at greater risk for suicide if she has ever known someone who killed himself. When someone close models suicide, an already-depressed adolescent can reflect, "Hey, *he* saw it as an acceptable method for dealing with pain that seems inescapable. Maybe that's right for me."

She may identify so much with the person who killed himself that she wants to copy his behavior. This may explain, for example, the rash of suicidal gestures that followed the death of Kurt Cobain, the Nirvana rock star.

Some adolescents crave the outpouring of love that often accompanies funeral rites. They may see suicide as the only way to acquire that love for themselves.

Third, the risk of actually attempting suicide heightens when a child has thought about how he would kill himself and when he would have the means to put that plan into action. For example, a teenager who has thought about swallowing a bottle of his mother's pain pills and has access to those drugs is more at risk than one who thinks he might drive into a tree—except that he lives in New York City with no car at his disposal!

What can you, as a parent, do?

• Talk to your child about suicide. Tell him how much it would hurt you if he died. Ask if he considers suicide a real option. If so, ask him how he would do it. If he's thought about killing himself, and especially if he's got a plan, take it seriously. Get help now.

Some parents worry that talking about suicide will plant the idea in a child's mind, but that's not how it works. Kids consider suicide only when they're already in overwhelming pain and see no way out. By letting them talk about it and getting them help, you're actually offering an alternative they may not have known how to pursue.

• Talk to your child about how to handle problems. Let her know that you're there to help no matter what the problem is. Make sure she knows that although you may get mad at a certain behavior, your anger will be short-lived. Assure her that you will always love her and be there for her—no matter what—and that you'll work with her to conquer any problem that arises.

• Establish a rapport with other significant people in your child's life. Talk to them about depression and suicide. Encourage them to let you know if they ever think suicide is a concern for your child.

• Finally, if you've noticed the symptoms described above, discuss them with someone trained in mental health care.

CHOOSING A MENTAL HEALTH PROFESSIONAL FOR YOUR CHILD

By the time most parents of grieving children decide to look for professional help for their child, they're usually feeling scared and overwhelmed. After all, up until now, they, mostly by themselves, have coped pretty well with their child's ups and downs.

Now, though, life seems to be conspiring against them. They're grieving the death of someone they love. Single parenting and financial issues may be piling up. And on top of it all, serious consequences may be developing for the child.

If you're in this boat, you may be tempted to accept whatever mental health professional is recommended to you first. That's a mistake. As you know, different types of mental health professionals employ different methods and enjoy differing amounts of success with various problems.

Here's a quick run-through: *Psychiatrists* train as medical doctors. They're the best people to start with for a truly serious mental illness, and they are often involved in cases where a physical component is present. For example, an imbalance in brain chemicals often accompanies clinical depression. If your child requires medication, a psychiatrist or clinical nurse practitioner is the only professional who can prescribe it. Other therapists (social workers, counselors, and marriage and family therapists) work with specific psychiatrists if their clients need medication. Some, but not all, psychiatrists provide psychotherapy as well.

Psychologists' training involves a heavy component of psychological testing and evaluation as well as treatment. They tend to be called in to help diagnose complicated mental illnesses and to develop multi-pronged treatment approaches, one of which is usually therapy.

Because of their training, *marriage and family therapists* tend to look at the entire family system: how each person affects the others, how the group interacts, and so on. Often, they prefer to treat a couple together or the family as a whole.

Training for *social workers and counselors* varies greatly by state, depending on the local requirements for licensing. (*Licensing* simply means state regulation of the profession. Lawyers and dentists, for example, are licensed in all fifty states, but ministers are not. Many insurance companies will reimburse only licensed mental health professionals, regardless of the training an individual therapist has received.) Social workers and counselors tend to focus more exclusively on individual psychotherapy, pulling in a psychiatrist as necessary.

But even qualified mental health workers vary in how they understand mental health concerns and what they consider important in healing. That's why it's so important that you spend time making sure you're comfortable with your choice whatever their profession.

How do you get comfortable? First, ask around for the names of therapists with whom others have been satisfied. School social workers, guidance counselors, ministers, and other people in grief support groups often can recommend helpful professionals who specialize in grief and bereavement.

Second, shop around. Identify a few options, then call two or three for an initial consultation. Interview each therapist. After all, you and your child are the clients here, and you have a right to understand what you're getting for your involvement.

When you talk to the therapist, be prepared to ask whatever questions are important to you. For starters, ask how many clients of your child's age the therapist has worked with. Although most child-oriented therapists work with children and adolescents of all ages, some have more experience with preschoolers, school-age kids, or adolescents.

Additionally, ask about the therapist's experience with bereavement issues and children. Sometimes therapists who are inexperienced with bereavement will misdiagnose a child. It's important for them to possess a working knowledge of grief in kids or adolescents. Ask how many grieving kids he's worked with. Find out what training he's taken, and which books he's read on the subject.

Ask what the therapist thinks is important in helping a child to grieve. Compare her response to your own understanding.

Check out how she sees you involved in the process and how she expects to communicate with you. The older your child, the more careful a therapist will be to preserve your child's trust and confidentiality. Nevertheless, she can tell you how you will be kept informed of your child's progress.

Additionally, make sure your child feels relatively comfortable with the therapist. Naturally, your child may be a bit nervous about meeting a stranger, but if he truly dislikes the therapist for some reason, don't push it. Find someone else. Otherwise, the therapist may fight an uphill battle all the way, preventing her from helping your child to heal.

This is especially true for adolescents. As frustrating as it can be to check out three or four therapists, it's worth trying to find a person your child connects with (or at least doesn't profess to hate).

The gender of the therapist can also play a part in your choice. Younger children of both sexes work equally well with men and women. While older boys continue to work well with therapists of either gender, older girls prefer (and often work better with) female therapists.

Finally, make sure you yourself feel comfortable on a gut level with your choice. Your chosen therapist doesn't need to be your friend, but you should feel confident that he is competent. You should feel comfortable that you can work well together to help your child heal.

Chapter 11

LONG-TERM EFFECTS OF

CHILDHOOD GRIEF

The death of my mother was the defining event of my life, and it remains so. . . . I see all my memories through shattered glass.

— Rosie O'Donnell, comedienne[1]

WHENEVER WE EXPERIENCE A LOSS, IT CHANGES US," SAYS GRIEF expert Kenneth Doka. "We can't control that aspect of grief, but we do have some control over the *ways* in which we change."[2] Over time some children, like some adult grievers, change in positive ways, while others seem crippled by the experience.

What makes the difference? Two factors: your child's own built-in resilience, and his interpretation of what's happened.

NATURAL RESILIENCE

Each of us is born with a certain physical and biochemical makeup. While scientists are still learning how it all works, we do know that our body chemistry influences our personality and our temperament. So our own "formula" can make us more or less animated or more or less reactive to external stimuli. It can increase or decrease how sociable we are as well as how melancholy we tend to be.

Think of it this way. Each child's body chemistry lies somewhere on a continuum between almost complete inoculation against the tough times and complete defenselessness against them. Kids who enjoy a place on the "inoculated" side of the continuum seem more able to handle anything that life throws them: family problems, poverty, the death of a loved one. Sure, they get angry and sad and feel all the other emotions that swell up inside. But after a loss, their body chemistry strongly supports them in finding a way to rebalance themselves. They're naturally, chemically resilient.

On the other end of the continuum are kids whose bodies harbor a predisposition to depression, anxiety, impulsiveness, aggression, or substance abuse (much as some kids are more prone to diabetes or high cholesterol). Often it runs in their family, right along with height, eye color, and whether they have freckles! Over time it may not take much to push their biochemistry into a troubled state. Additionally, they may be more private and less verbal. The combination makes them more vulnerable.

Unfortunately, such kids can't lessen their vulnerability. That doesn't mean they're *sure* to become mentally ill. (In fact, no mental illness under any set of circumstances has been conclusively linked to childhood death of a parent or sibling. See Chapter 14.) But the combination of biology and grief seems to place some grieving kids at greater long-term risk.

Olivia, for example, stood on the risky end of the continuum. For years, her mom's mom had been depressed, cycling through many medications over time. Then, a week after Olivia's tenth birthday, her own mother slit her wrists and died. Throughout her adolescence and young adulthood, Olivia was moodier than her friends, and more melancholy. But she coped.

In her mid-twenties, after losing a job, Olivia found herself in a deep depression that just wouldn't go away. Fortunately, because of her family history, her internist suspected she suffered from a chemical imbalance and prescribed an antidepressant along with psychotherapy. After three months on medication, Olivia reported, "You know, I think I had always been kind of depressed, at least since after Mom died. The smallest thing could set me off. I just thought it was normal because it was normal for me. But when I lost that job—well, it was like everything came rushing back: Mom's death on top of the job loss. I felt like I was drowning. I just couldn't surface for air. I've been taking Zoloft and I have to tell you, I feel better than ever now."

Most kids stand somewhere in the middle of the resilience-to-risk chemistry continuum. Over the long term, they can thrive in the face of an amazing number of life challenges, especially when given the right support.

No matter where your child stands on the chemistry continuum, there are steps you can take to influence factors that enhance your child's resilience, such as her sociability, verbal skills, and problem-solving and coping abilities.

SOCIABILITY

Some children enjoy strong social skills from birth. By nature, they are relatively affectionate, outgoing, and good-natured, and as a result, they can easily "recruit" adults to help them in their time of need. But children who hold average or poor social skills do not have this advantage. Their parents can help in two ways. First, they can teach their children how to engage others in conversation and how to ask for what they need. Second, they can surround their children with adults who are honest, consistent, caring, and sensitive to the child's unspoken yet very real needs (as we suggest in Chapter 7).

VERBAL SKILLS

Research shows that children's verbal skills, especially as they develop through fourth grade, relate strongly to their resilience in the face of tough times.[3] Kids with strong verbal skills may more easily identify their feelings, express their needs, share their stories. They can also use books to figure out how to deal with some of life's difficulties. Sometimes verbal skills also correlate with greater social skills, leading to the same benefits. Finally, children with greater verbal skills are likely to perform better in school, improving their self-esteem.

Some children are born with a greater capacity for language than others, but verbal skills can also be developed in children. Whether they read mysteries or novels, magazine articles about sports stars or actresses, kids who read improve their verbal skills. So find out what your child enjoys, and supply him with those reading materials.

Likewise, parents who read to their children and who enjoy reading themselves encourage their children to read. Kids who write (in diaries, through songs or poetry, in e-mails or letters) tend to grow in verbal skills. And of course, reading teachers and specialists at school can often suggest ways to improve your child's verbal skills.

PROBLEM-SOLVING AND COPING ABILITIES

A child who gives up at the first roadblock or who is unable to focus on a problem long enough to solve it will naturally be less resilient after a death. Death arrives with problems in its suitcase. Likewise, a child who reacts to every problem, every frustration, by lashing out at others may drive away potential supporters.

In contrast, children who cope through humor or silliness enjoy a built-in emotional safety valve for their difficult feelings. Those with active imaginations often solve their problems through the trial and error of make-believe dramas.

But even children without built-in coping strengths can be taught skills that increase their ability to manage life's difficulties. You can teach your child how to analyze what's behind her emotions. You can teach her to identify what comforts her when she's sad, and how she can express her anger in constructive ways. You can teach him to think about which people in his world might be resources for him and to ask those resources for help. You can teach your children good problem-solving skills: separating valid emotions from the problem itself; focusing on the issue at hand; identifying potential solutions; evaluating the consequences of each solution; choosing a course of action; and making a backup plan.

THE INTERPRETATION OF THE DEATH

Over the past few years at The Cove, we've worked with quite a number of parents raising children who are grieving the suicide of a parent or sibling. In one situation, the parents refused to participate in our support program for grieving kids because they were afraid their surviving child would find out that her brother intentionally overdosed on drugs. Interpreting his death as a family failure, they didn't want anyone to know about it—not his sister, not other support group members, and not the community at large.

Another set of parents spoke openly about their adopted daughter's suicide by overdose. "Once Liz hit puberty, we knew we were in for a rough ride," said her mother. "She was depressed pretty consistently, and nothing the doctors did seemed to help for very long. We knew that most of the time, eventually, people with depression can be helped by drugs or other treatments. The only question in our minds was whether we'd find the right treatment in time. We didn't."

Liz's dad elaborated: "I always felt like Liz's condition was a ticking biological time bomb. Would we beat the clock or not? We feel we did everything we could, but the clock won."

In which of these two families would the surviving children fare better? To our minds, the second family's children are likely to end up in better shape. In the first family, by interpreting the death as their fault, the parents are leaving themselves and their daughter vulnerable to greater difficulties over the long term. And the daughter will find out— parents can rarely keep suicide a secret from other family members for long. Each person will wrestle with powerful questions: If I really loved this boy, why didn't I see his pain? If I saw his pain, why didn't I do something about it? If I tried to help but it didn't work, does that mean I'm powerless in life? Does this make me a bad person—or at least not good enough, not worthwhile?

DEATH AND OUR ASSUMPTIONS

Sometimes our interpretations of a death fit in neatly with our assumptions about life. During the fall that Allie went away to college, Allie's mom died after battling cancer for two years. Allie saw the death as an answer to her prayers. "Sure, I wish that she didn't have to die at all," she says. "But I wanted her to at least make it through my high school graduation. I used to pray that she could just hold on that long. Everybody prayed for that, and I guess God heard our prayers, because it happened." Death left Allie's assumptions intact: *God is good; I'm good; and I have the power to influence the outcome of events* (in this case, by praying).

At other times, interpretations of a death shatter all of our assumptions. One of our Cove kids explained his feelings about the death of his mom just days before his twelfth birthday. "Mom, why did you die?" he said. *"I had plans."*

The Child's History Of course, kids are not born with either assumptions or interpretations about death. And neither assumptions nor interpretations drop from the sky. They're the accumulation of everything that's happened to a child and every interpretation she's ever made or been handed by parents, teachers, and other significant people in her life.

So first, let's focus on a child's own history. Remember the classic poem "Children Learn What They Live"? That applies to grief as well. If a child grows up with parents always telling him what he's done wrong, he's more likely to doubt himself. Then, if a family member dies, he may be more likely to say, *It must be my fault that Mom died: it was because of something I did or didn't do. I'm bad.* Or he may feel that God "took" his mom as a punishment. He may believe that his mom "left" because he wasn't worth sticking around for. Any of these interpretations simply reinforce an already weak sense of self-esteem. And over the long term, self-esteem can affect everything from career performance to marital satisfaction.

Similarly, if a child has experienced multiple deaths in a short period of time (first a pet, then a favorite grandparent, then a parent), she may say to herself, *Everybody leaves me. Nobody can be trusted.* Clearly, such a belief will affect her capacity for loving relationships over time.

On the other hand, if a child's world has been positive—handing him mostly affirming and helpful experiences and interpretations— then with ongoing support, he'll be more able to see the death as an isolated incident. He'll certainly feel a great deal of pain and may even have some regrets, but he'll be less likely to blame himself. He's more likely to continue to see the world as a safe and loving place filled with people who continue to care for him. Those viewpoints will stand him in good stead over the years ahead.

Circumstances of the Death The circumstances of the death make a difference in how a child interprets it and therefore in the long-term consequences. For example, no matter how old you are, violent and mutilating deaths are difficult to interpret in a comfortable way. Both children and adults who have been raised in sufficiently positive environments tend to believe in the basic goodness of things:

- "I'm basically good—and so are most people around me."

- "God (or the world, the universe, the flow of life) is basically benevolent and fair. I'm safe."

- "The future holds good things for me and for the ones I love."

- "I have the power to control my life, to make life better for myself and the people I care about."

Most of us, when we hear about murders in the news, rationalize that we live in a safe neighborhood, live safely, lock our car doors at night, and so on. *Our* world is safe—even if some parts of the world are not. So when someone we love is brutally murdered, we're forced to reexamine our basic assumptions. It's not that our biology makes us more prone to melancholy interpretations. It's not that we fall on the risky side of the resilience continuum. It's not that we expect bad things to happen because we've had too many tough times in the past. *It's the type of death itself that causes us to reinterpret what we've always believed.*

Importantly, deaths that a child interprets as particularly preventable or random can totally shatter her assumptions about the world. Deaths that are seen as preventable (caused by human carelessness, for example) may lead to questions of fairness and blame. Apparently random deaths (for example, being struck by lightning on a golf course) force children and adults alike to doubt their assumptions regarding the safety of the universe and the reality of a supposedly powerful, loving God.

Parent's Interpretation How parents and other adults interpret the death and its aftermath strongly influences a child's understanding of the event. Some interpretations leave children more vulnerable to long-term difficulties, including mental illnesses like depression. Aaron Beck, the father of cognitive therapy (arguably the strongest nondrug therapy for clinical depression and anxiety disorders in adolescents and adults), talks about the cognitive triad involved in depressive disorders. According to his theory, depressed people tend to suffer from distorted, negative views of themselves, their world, and the future. As one young depressed woman told us, "After my dad died, I realized that he was right: I wasn't worth much, the world sucks, and my future—well, *what* future?"

CHOOSING INTERPRETATIONS

As a parent of grieving children, you need to consciously choose interpretations of the death, your grief, and your family's ability to cope, interpretations that will leave your kids with positive images of themselves, the world, and the future. You need to keep them focused on what's left as well as what's lost: their own strengths and resources, and all the many people who still love them as well as the person who died. You need to help them see themselves as survivors, not victims, and as individuals still empowered to lead happy, productive lives. If you're parenting grieving kids, you need to coach them in seeing that, despite its imperfections, the world has much to offer. Death cannot rob anyone of all of life's gifts.

Two young widows exemplify the contrast between more and less helpful interpretations. Both had several children in elementary school. Both young widows lost husbands to relatively sudden deaths: one to the late diagnosis of a particularly lethal cancer, the other to a heart attack.

Two years after the death of her husband from cancer, the first widow, Paula, remained focused on the loss, ranting to any friends and family who would listen, "I *told* him to get that pain checked out! But did he do it? No, of course not. He didn't care enough about us to do any of that. Now, I'm the one who has to figure out how the hell to survive with three kids!"

In contrast, Irene consistently stressed two things: how her other family members could keep their own hearts healthy, and how lucky they were as a family. One night these two widows were discussing their situations. Paula asked Irene, "Lucky! God, how can you say you're lucky?! I can't imagine a worse nightmare."

Irene explained, "Well, of course sometimes I don't feel so lucky. I mean, why did *my* husband have to die?

"But I don't want my kids to grow up angry or bitter," she continued. "I want them to remember how much their daddy loved them, that at least we had him for a few years. Some kids never know any daddy at all. And he left us able to take care of ourselves. We're not rich, but we have enough money to survive. Among the four of us, we know how to take care of most of the household stuff. And we have great memories.

"So, yeah," she finished up, "I wouldn't say we've had the perfect life, but we *are* lucky."

In the early weeks and months after a death, you and your child may well make many angry or blameful interpretations. But for the long term, choose your interpretation carefully. It will make a difference in how your child sees himself and the world around him.

EFFECTS OF INTERPRETATIONS

What specific differences can interpretations make for grieving kids? Researcher Maxine Harris, author of *The Loss That Is Forever*, examined adults who lost a parent at an early age and found effects in four primary areas: intimacy, trust, and loyalty; parenting; identity and meaning-making; and awareness of mortality.

Intimacy, Trust, and Loyalty For children, according to Harris, the biggest impact of an early loss is on relationships. When death snatches a vital person from a child, he questions the steadfastness of all his intimate connections. Trust and doubt battle for supremacy. "That's not to say that these people don't form trusting relationships," Harris explains, "but I do think they have to work harder for the rest of their lives to form them.

"There's a kind of anxiety about abandonment," she elaborates. "As a result, people seemed to go to one extreme end of the continuum or the other. Some people [in Harris's research] were relationship-phobic. As much as they tried, they could only get so close to another person without becoming overwhelmed by their own anxiety and imposing distance."[4]

Such individuals may take a very long time to enter relationships. They may cause conflict in order to postpone making a commitment. They may simply avoid getting close to anyone in the first place.

And once they have formed a relationship, they may leave their partner before they themselves are left. If the partner ends the relationship first, they may react more strongly, taking it as a personal rejection. Often they take longer to come back from rejection, and their ambivalence about relationships grows.

At the other end of the continuum are those who feel an ongoing sense of isolation and aloneness. Their insatiable need for intimacy, such as the intimacy they lost to death, may lead them to enter very quickly into long-term relationships.

Regardless of where on the continuum a childhood grief survivor falls, once they commit to a person, they're overwhelmingly faithful to that relationship. In fact, the low rate of divorce among survivors of childhood grief surprised Harris. "Part of the lesson they had learned is that no one *willingly* breaks up a home," Harris explains. "If you're lucky enough to find somebody, you're never foolish enough to end it, no matter what's going on." As Harris points out, that lesson and the fidelity it teaches can both help and hurt. To the extent that it encourages someone to work hard on the knots in a relationship, it helps. To the extent that it persuades someone to stay in an unhealthy or abusive relationship, it hurts.

Parenting For some adults who lost a parent in childhood, the question of whether to have children of their own looms large. "There is so much anxiety that history will repeat itself," Harris points out, "that they, in a very responsible way, do not have children. This is particularly true when the parent died of a genetically linked illness."

Other childhood grief survivors forgo parenting because they've already done enough caretaking. They may have been responsible for their younger brothers or sisters. Or their parents may have relied on them so much that they relish freedom from any form of dependence.

Those who do go on to have children of their own often feel inadequate as parents. They "assumed that others were confident, knowledgeable parents," Harris observes. "But they thought, 'I am insecure about what to do. I feel at a loss. I'm sure that someone who had two parents doesn't feel this same sense of uncertainty.' "

In fact, most first-time parents lack confidence. But many also rely on their own parents for advice, a resource lacking among those who lost a parent in childhood. Instead, parentally bereaved new parents must develop other sources of information—in-laws, brothers or sisters, other young parents, or professionals in children's health and development.

Identity and Meaning-making Speak with anyone who lost a parent as a child, and they'll tell you the experience contributed significantly to forming their identity. For adolescents and young adults, it may be the only self-definition they have. Noted writer Anna Quindlen has said, "My mother died when I was nineteen. For a long time, it was all you needed to know about me, a kind of vest-pocket description of my emotional complexion: 'Meet you in the lobby in ten minutes—I have long brown hair, am on the short side, have on a red coat, and my mother died when I was nineteen.' "[5]

After the death of a family member, grievers of all ages struggle to redefine themselves. Parents who lose an only child ask, "Am I still a parent?" Widows and widowers wonder who they are now that they're no longer husbands and wives, confidantes and caretakers. But at least mature grievers have more of their identities in place when someone they love dies. They've chosen professions. They know what they treasure. They've placed themselves somewhere in the world of community, church, and friends. So while the pain of grief may take over their identity for a time, so that they see themselves only as widows or widowers or bereaved parents, eventually grief becomes only one part of their life story instead of the sum total of it.

Like Quindlen, young adults must struggle more than mature adults to see themselves as separate and apart from their grief. This is not surprising since, under the best of circumstances, young adults wrestle with who they are.

On top of the normal struggle with identity, parentally bereaved young adults often feel they're missing out on important input from the mother or father who died. So, parentally bereaved young adults instead search outside the immediate family for role models. They piece together their identity from other adults: teachers, coaches, bosses, mentors, neighbors, in-laws. They search television shows, biographies, and novels for characters with whom they can identify. They mine the life story of the person who died for clues, hoarding stories told at family gatherings, reading letters and diaries, remembering what the person said to them, imagining what that person might do or say if he or she were still alive. They maintain an ongoing relationship with the person who died, even late in life. They look to him or her for inspiration.

Harris summarizes the experience of many parentally bereaved young adults this way: "They had to, as many people said, *invent* themselves. There was a kind of freedom that came with that, but also a kind of awesome responsibility. And when people felt they had done that [invented themselves], they had a sense of accomplishment, a sense of solid center that other people who have relied on external validation do not feel. But it was hard work to get there."

At first blush, youngsters grieving the death of a sibling, as opposed to a parent, would seem immune to such identity issues. But they struggle with it in other ways. First, some feel the burden of replacing the skills, roles, or personality traits of the sibling who died. They may feel they're expected to submerge their own identity and take on that of their dead sibling to lessen their parents' sense of loss.

Second, many grieving siblings avoid the normal process of identity formation because they fear that the process itself will hurt their parents. In early adolescence, normal kids begin developing their own identity by rejecting their parents. Their motto might be "I don't know who I am, but I know I'm *not you!*" Even nongrieving parents often experience this rejection as a loss. They cry, "Where's my little girl, who loved to go shopping with me, who thought I was a hero?" Grieving siblings intuitively sense how their parents might react to rejection and may choose to forgo this normal, healthy part of their own identity-formation process.

Third, grieving parents often are unable to be resources for teens in the later stages of identity formation. Normally, in late adolescence, young adults begin to take on at least some of their parents' values, personality traits, habits, motivations, and the like. That's why, for example, a child who at thirteen swore he would never be a plumber like his father may end up in technical school right after high school (whether or not it's the right job for him). But when both parents are consumed by grief, what is there for a young adult to identify with?

Later in life, both bereaved siblings and parentally bereaved adults may link their identities directly to the loss. Harris explains this phenomenon among her interviewees, all of whom lost a parent in childhood. "They take a look at who they have become," she says, "and realize that part of who they *are*, they are because a parent died. So some would feel, 'I'm very independent, and I love that about myself.' And then a lightbulb goes on and they say, 'You know, I'm only independent because I grew up without a mother.' It's a kind of coming to terms, where someone realizes that they have become a particular type of person, a person they *embrace,* because of adversity."

Writer Thornton Wilder tied his enthusiasm for life to his twin brother's death in childhood. In 1917 he wrote to his older brother Amos and said,

> I suppose that everyone feels that his nature cries out hourly for it knows not what, but I like to believe that mine raises an exceedingly great voice because I am a twin, and because by his death an outlet for my affection was closed—not affection alone, but energy, and in it I live and because of it I seem to see my life as more vivid, electric and marvelous than others so placidly do. I am continually surprised at people's lukewarmness; I am perpetually enthusiastic over some composition or book, some person or some friend.[6]

Other adults who lost family members early share how they were affected:

• "I've always been more mature than others. I think it has to do with really knowing what's important. BMWs are not important. What brand of jeans you wear is not important. I learned that early."

• "I think I see more deeply into people as a result of my mom's death. And it's because of that insight that I can write so well and that I *want* to write. I want to write about courage and hope and how we make it through."

• "I feel like my sister's death carved out this hole in me. Now I have space in myself to take somebody else's pain for a while, to kind of hold it for them."

• "If I can make it through both my parents dying when I was a kid, I can make it through anything! I have whatever it takes. I know that like I know my hand is attached to my arm."

Identifying such contributions often becomes part of a larger search for the meaning of the death. Harris reports, "Many of the letters from people in their sixties and seventies convinced me that this problem of making sense of the loss is a problem that an individual will work on at every stage of his or her life. If each of us is given some puzzle that we have to solve, this is the puzzle, the operative psychological dilemma for people who have had a loss [in childhood]. And they process it in successively deeper ways as they cross certain milestones."

While some adults search for the meaning *inherent* in the death, others work to *create* meaning out of what they see as an essentially meaningless event. A boy whose sister was murdered might become a police officer, detective, or prosecutor to gain justice for victims of violent crimes. Another might spend her life in search of a cure for the disease that killed her mother. Still another might devote all his emotional energy to his own children, attempting to ensure that they enjoy the parental love that he himself so sorely missed.

Awareness of Mortality Like other grievers, adults who grieved early deaths are more sensitive to their own death. Others fear the early death of others. In and of itself, these are natural consequences of loss at any age. But when some childhood grievers become parents themselves, fear of the death of others may be coupled with the need to be "perfect" parents, in order to conquer their own sense of parental inadequacy or to provide what they never received because of the death. Such parents can become overly involved in the lives of their children.

While the death of someone they love may cause some children to despair, others follow the adage *carpe diem*—"seize the day." They push to see it all, do it all, achieve it all early on. Who knows, they argue, whether we'll be around to do it later? Anna Quindlen remembers,

> When I was a young reporter—because I got to be a reporter when I was nineteen, and I went to the *New York Times* when I was twenty-four—people would say to me, 'Why are you in such a hurry? You've got the rest of your life.' And there was a part of me that just thought, 'Tell it to the marines, buster. The whole rest of my life could be five years, ten years.' I felt like everything was sort of speeded up.[7]

Psychologist Marvin Eisenstadt uncovered the same link in his study of 573 famous people. Among "eminent" or "historical" geniuses in the arts, humanities, and sciences, the rate of mother loss was as much as three times that of the general population.[8] Perhaps for some of these remarkable men and women, achievement represented a means to cheat death of anonymity: "You can kill my body, but you can't kill my accomplishments."

Finally, some who lose family members early in life seize the day by enjoying each moment. Hope Edelman explains that the death of her mother when she was seventeen affected her attitude toward everyday events:

> You can look at life and think, "My God. Every day that you have is so precious and so important." When somebody dies you realize that if they had to do it all over again they wouldn't want to win the Pulitzer Prize or make the best-seller list. If they had to do it all over again, they'd just want one more day at the beach, or to sit with their kids quietly on a blanket somewhere and talk about something one more time. I think the experience of my mother's death made me treasure those little things in a way I never would have before.[9]

STEPPARENTING A GRIEVING CHILD

No question about it . . . stepparenting a grieving family is the hardest thing I've ever done. I wanted to give so much but consistently felt like a failure. It's only now, after eight years, that I can see us really coming together as a family.

—Marie, 50 years old

WHEN WE—JIM AND MARY ANN—MARRIED, A FEW YEARS after Mary died, we threw a huge outdoor picnic. We invited more than six hundred people: Mary's family as well as Jim's; neighbors; friends from work and church and school; all those who cherished Mary Ann and who loved Jim and the kids. They came from thirteen states. They came to eat, dance, swim, laugh, and party. They came to celebrate the family's return to good times, the triumph of life over death, dawn over darkness.

Everyone at the picnic breathed a sigh of relief and gratitude. From the outside, we looked like a "whole" family again—two parents and three growing kids. *That* nightmare, the one that had started with Mary's death, was over at last.

Six months later, a neighbor voiced what everyone else was thinking. "Now that everything's back to normal," she said, "you can resume your old life." Because all the roles (mother, father, child) were filled, she thought we were a family. It's a common myth, one we all want to believe. Extended family, friends, and colleagues at work all long for happy endings. Finally, your "family" can be crossed off their worry list!

But Patricia Papernow, an expert on stepfamily formation, sees it differently. In *Becoming a Stepfamily,* she observes, "Remarrying couples often think of themselves as returning to the mainstream when they start their new family. In fact . . . the experience is more like being deposited in the middle of the rapids."[1] As parents, you may recognize that the new family is not flowing smoothly. It doesn't feel like any normal, biological family you've known. Unfortunately, you don't know why. All you can figure is that you've failed somehow, despite all your good intentions.

In truth, like many stepfamilies, you're comparing yourselves to the wrong standard. Consciously or not, you've bought into the myth that a stepfamily should develop, and rather quickly, the same level of love, cohesiveness, and comfort that a biological family enjoys. Judged against that criterion, your new family is destined to fail. Forming a new family together generates changes; changes bring more losses; the losses explode into yet another set of tumultuous feelings. As a result, although you may see yourselves as a poorly functioning first-time family, you're simply a group of individuals experiencing the normal stages of stepfamily development.

If first-time family closeness is unrealistic, what *can* you hope to achieve? A more reasonable goal is to create, over time, a web of safe, dependable, nourishing, and ultimately intimate relationships called a stepfamily. Do stepfamilies have rewarding relationships? Yes. Are they identical to first-time families? Unlikely.

Because the possibilities for stepfamilies are different from that of a first-time biological family, so is the path to getting there. That's why your stepfamily needs a different road map. You need to know the most "energy-efficient" way to travel. What will move you forward as a family? What will simply sidetrack you, wasting precious time and energy? What are the normal stages in the journey?

STAGES OF STEPFAMILY DEVELOPMENT

When Gloria married Arthur, a widower of eighteen months, she fully committed to his two grieving sons, ages twelve and fourteen. She moved herself and her eleven-year-old daughter into Arthur's home, quit her nursing job, and prepared herself to be the wife and mother that Arthur's first wife had never been—even before she contracted AIDS.

Imagine Gloria's shock when, six months after the honeymoon, Arthur's boys refused to speak to her except in four-letter words! She recalls her sense of isolation. "My own daughter wasn't happy because she was forced to move into a houseful of strangers," she says. "The boys only tolerated me because I was doing all the work. And Arthur was working like a fiend, as if nothing out of the ordinary were happening!

"I swallowed it all for about a year," she continues. "After all, these kids had had a rough life so far. And I reasoned that I was the adult, that I should be able to love them unconditionally, that enough love and consistent limits would turn the situation around. Finally, though, I had just had it. I confronted Arthur. I threatened to leave if he didn't start working with me on our new family."

As they began deciphering the situation, Gloria and Arthur realized they were in the normal turmoil of early stepfamily formation. They were experiencing what Papernow calls the "painful knots" that happen in young stepfamilies with "relentless regularity and frightening intensity."

According to Papernow, the progression in stepfamilies is predictable, advancing through seven stages: the early stages of fantasy, immersion, and awareness; the middle stages of mobilization and action; and the final stages of contact and resolution.

EARLY STAGES

Fantasy Jay and Angie agreed with all their friends: Despite their recent tragedies, they considered themselves lucky. They'd found each other. Sure, Jay and his eight-year-old daughter struggled after his first wife's death from a fall down a flight of steps, while Angie and her two daughters (ages seven and nine) still wrestled with her husband's death in a small plane crash. But after such horrific losses, they pondered, how often do you get a second chance at happiness?

It seemed miraculous. Jay and Angie had never imagined they could love again as strongly as they had loved the first time around. They knew they would make a great family together. Angie understood little girls from her own experience. And she already loved Jay's daughter, who, because of her age, could just slip right in with Angie's girls.

Jay watched Angie with her daughters and knew she was a great mother, something his own daughter sorely missed. Angie felt grateful that Jay was willing to parent her daughters: in fact, she knew he'd be an even better father than her first husband, who had traveled all the time on business.

When Jay and Angie married, without even knowing it, they jumped squarely into the first stage of stepfamily formation: fantasy. They succumbed to these common myths:

• that because they themselves loved each other, the kids (really mere acquaintances) would automatically love everybody as well

• that loving adults can fill the empty roles of mother or father for grieving children

• that a stepparent can take away the pain in the grieving family, "fix" it, and make the family "whole" again

• that new parents can do a better job than biological parents or, at the very least, lighten the load of single parenting

Children, too, engage in fantasy when a new stepfamily forms. Your child may believe that his new stepparent will replace his mom or dad and fill the emptiness in his heart and in the family. On a concrete level, he may also hope the new stepparent will fulfill more of his desires— play more baseball with him, allow him more sugar cereal, relax more rules—than his dead biological parent did. His fantasies may also be negative: he may remain fanatically "loyal" to the person who died, fantasizing that if he acts badly enough, he can drive the "intruder" (the new stepparent) away.

Sometimes grieving kids in new stepfamilies act like perfect children. Believing that their behavior somehow killed the person who died and destroyed the family once, they vow never again to act in a way that puts their family at risk. Usually, however, a mix of fear and anger is seething beneath that surface.

For a very young child still struggling with the notion that her dead parent will never return, a new "mom" or "dad" is particularly confusing. If you insist that she call her stepparent "Dad," what will she call her "old" dad when he comes back? Who sleeps with Mom when Dad is alive again?

Immersion In this stage of stepfamily development, reality sets in. You have a vague sense that this is not likely to be a "real" family anytime soon. If both of you brought children with you, you notice that everybody still lines up according to biological ties. The kids go to their "own" mom or dad for reassurance. They abide by their own family's rules. Most of the easy socializing happens among the blood relatives.

If you're the stepparent, you watch the interactions between the "real" parent and her kids, and you feel left out. You're subtly but consistently excluded.

Meanwhile, the "real" parent may not notice any problem. After all, nothing has changed from her standpoint. *She* still enjoys the same sense of closeness with her kids. *She's* not excluded. Often the biological parent may hear the stepparent's complaints and wonder if he's less committed to the new family. She wonders, *What's your problem?* And after a while, as a stepparent, you may find yourself wondering what's wrong with you too.

Awareness Over time, a stepparent will reach the firm conclusion that something's up with the entire family. It's not just her "problem." She gives up the fantasies of the first stage and begins to express her own feelings and her own needs. Eventually, she realizes she can't truly be part of the blood-based bonds and, instead, begins to focus on discovering the strangers with whom she shares a home.

The "real" parent, meanwhile, will start to understand the outsider position of the stepparent. She sees more clearly the distance and awkwardness, sometimes even the open hostility, between stepfamily members.

Now the pressure is on the biological parent. If you're in this role, you may be becoming aware that there's no easy formula for creating a family. Yet *you're* in the middle of it all! As the only person in the family who truly knows and loves everyone else (including the person who died), you're torn. You understand both sides of each conflict. You feel driven, but sometimes defeated, by the family's expectation that you will resolve them all.

In these three early stages, healthy, developing stepfamilies ultimately give up their fantasies and limit their expectations. They pare down their definition of success to two goals. First, they realize that simply maintaining hope in the midst of the confusion and growing pains is an accomplishment in itself. Second, they recognize that understanding each person's unique experience as a stepfamily member is the rock on which the family's future growth depends. Learning about each other is a valid challenge on which to focus energy.

MIDDLE STAGES

Mobilization Chaos and conflict characterize the mobilization stage. Now the differences are out in the open. If you're the stepparent, you'll speak out more as you fight to find your place in the home. No longer able to tolerate being excluded, you may lobby, loudly at times, for change.

As painful differences are exposed, stress may grow between you and your partner. The stepparent will likely argue for more discipline for the kids and more time alone as a couple. On the other hand, the biological parent will probably focus on the children: their loss, their grief, their ongoing need for stability and support from adults in their world.

Your children now give active voice to their complaints. Although the issues often seem small (whether dirty dishes belong in the sink or in the dishwasher, who brings in the trash barrels, and the like), they represent much larger concerns. One seventeen-year-old stated it this way: "Ever since Jenna married my dad," she said, "everything's changed. We never have pancakes for dinner anymore. We listen to classical music instead of jazz. Even the bedspreads are new. Forget the fact that my real mom died: it's like she never even existed in the first place!"

Loyalty, comfort, the need for time alone with the biological parent—all these may motivate the children to resist or resent changes initiated by the stepparent. Toward the end of this stage, every member of a healthily developing stepfamily realizes that there's no way everyone will get everything they want as individuals. They begin to listen to each other well enough to respect, if not agree with, each other's point of view. Eventually, each person chooses the few issues that really matter to him, the ones that, for whatever reason, he feels are worth standing up for. This sets the stage for the next leg of the journey: action.

Action In this stage, family members negotiate new agreements about the trouble spots. Anita and Kirk's stepfamily illustrates the change. "Two out of Kirk's three kids are just slobs," Anita says. "It really drives me nuts. For a while, I walked around after them and cleaned up. Then one day I got mad, flew off the handle, and said, 'Let the house be a pigsty! I'm not going to be a slave to your laziness!' Of course, they were more than happy to live in a mess. I was the one who couldn't stand it.

"Finally, we worked out an agreement," she continues. "They could leave the rec room downstairs in whatever condition they wanted, but the common areas upstairs (the kitchen, living room, family room) were to be picked up each night before they went to bed. I avoided going downstairs. I just closed the door. And they cleaned up the rec room every weekend."

Over time, Kirk's third child, the oldest, began to pick up the dishes in the rec room each night. "They get gross when they sit there for a whole week," he explained. Anita contained her surprise: she'd expressed the same thought so many times without feeling heard. Now she felt she had an ally in Kirk's oldest child, at least on this issue.

It often happens that way: New agreements, ones that better meet everyone's needs, allow new partnerships to form—this time including the stepparent. As family members see that compromise is possible, not every family activity blows up into a power struggle between "blood brothers" and "the invaders."

If you're in this stage, you increasingly find common ground with others in the family: shared interests, shared expectations of roles, shared assumptions about how the family "works," and so on. Finally there's reason to hope! And with hope, the pressure on you and your partner eases, enabling you to reclaim the energy you need to finish up the stepfamily-formation process.

LATE STAGES

Contact and Resolution After five distinct stages (and usually much pain), the honeymoon period comes at last. Now there's enough common ground for real relationships to form. Authentic intimacy begins to develop. Stepparents enjoy a clear, legitimate role. Often they are unable to name it—it's still not the role of the biological parent, but it's more than a friend or extended family member.

If you're the stepparent, you know you've made it into the family. You know you're an important guiding figure. In some cases, you may even find that you're a better confidante for your stepchild than her biological parent was. Together you may be able to talk about topics like grief, sex, and alcohol and drug use, topics that may be too uncomfortable for your stepchild to talk about with her biological parent.

Of course, there will always be issues, but now you know you'll make it through. Equally important, you'll know how to resolve them.

So congratulations! You've finished the hardest work. You're on the downhill side.

BUT YOU CAN'T HURRY LOVE

Just as it takes years to develop deep friendships, developing a stepfamily requires years of commitment. Based on her experience, Papernow estimates that the entire cycle, from earliest awareness to final resolution, requires four to twelve years.

On average, stepfamilies complete the process in roughly seven years. Four factors determine the speed with which a stepfamily completes its work. First, families that finish the formation process more quickly seem to start out with fewer fantasies. Sometimes the adults themselves grew up in a stepfamily and know firsthand the realities of the situation. Others have watched the process in the families of close friends or family members.

Second, families that enjoy lots of support early on tend to move through the process more quickly. They often possess at least one caring, knowledgeable person who understands stepfamily dynamics and validates the difficult feelings involved in launching a stepfamily. So even if such families *start* with strong fantasies, they more quickly recognize them as unrealistic and relinquish them.

In contrast, stepfamilies that receive little support, that are unable to speak to others about their struggles, generally take more time to complete the process.

Third, spouses who, early on, find a way to communicate with each other more fully and without judgment tend to complete the early stages more quickly. In such families, the stepparent voices her own needs and concerns from the start, and the biological parent hears those statements as heartfelt and real for his partner. Each side empathizes with the struggles of the other.

Fourth, in stepfamilies that move more quickly through the process, the children likewise attempt to express their experience and their feelings more often and more readily. They pick up on the modeling of the adults, respect each other's differing viewpoints, and actively try to get to know the new family members.

In our experience, certain characteristics specific to individual families can slow down the process.

For example, the degree to which each family member has actively and appropriately mourned the death of the parent will affect the length of time it takes to complete the process. After all, as a preschooler, if I still think Mom might return, I may need to fight to maintain her spot in the family. If as an older child, I have not yet come to grips with my anger about the death, I may take it out on the stepparent. In this case, what looks like the conflict-producing issue (household rules, different family styles or temperaments) is only part of the issue—and no one may realize it! Only after repeated failures to resolve the issue does it become clear: Something deeper is going on here. When significant pieces of mourning have yet to be completed, the stepfamily-formation process can be lengthened considerably.

Additionally, children who feel abandoned by the death of a parent may take longer to trust an incoming stepparent. As one of our kids spat out to Mary Ann, "Why should *you* care? You're not my real mom!"

Further, the age of the children can influence the speed at which the stepfamily forms. Adolescence is particularly tough: at just the time when kids naturally begin to strain against family bonds, a new stepparent asks them to devote energy to working out differences and making new connections.

Finally, temperament can play a role in stepfamily formation. Very private or quiet family members may struggle more to express their feelings or needs, lengthening the time it takes to find common ground and negotiate differences.

HOW GRIEVING STEPFAMILIES DIFFER

As the daughter of divorced parents, Justine thought she was fully prepared for her grieving stepchildren's reactions. "I knew we were in for some rough times," she says. "I remembered what a pain I was to my own stepmom when I was a kid. Now I thought I was prepared for it. What I didn't count on was the intensity of the kids' grief, how it resurfaced over time, and my own impatience with it all!"

Among the many myths about stepparenting is the myth that stepparenting after death is the same as stepparenting after a divorce. In fact, grieving stepfamilies differ in five key ways.

PEOPLE IN GRIEVING STEPFAMILIES TEND TO MISTAKE THE ROLE OF THE PERSON WHO DIED FOR THE PERSON HIMSELF

In stepfamilies after divorce, everyone starts off clear about the difference between the parent role and the person in that role. But in grieving stepfamilies, adults and children alike may not differentiate between the role of mom and the person filling that role. Everyone assumes that filling the role of mom or dad, finding someone to take on the tasks of parenting, will ease the heartache. But in truth, while you can replace the role, you can never replace the person. That loss, and the grief that follows to a greater or lesser degree, goes on forever.

Stepparents after divorce may fantasize that they can create a family that resembles a biological one. But even if they indulge in that fantasy, they know that they themselves can never be the "real" mom or dad, even though they may be called upon to emotionally support their stepchildren, pay the bills, or enforce discipline. In families that have experienced divorce, children rarely expect the stepparent to replace the biological one, and from the beginning, they resent anyone who tries. They already *have* a "real" mom or "real" dad.

After a death, over time, adults tend to modify their expectations. The biological parent can appreciate what the stepparent brings to the role of parenting, even while he grieves the loss of the person who died. The children, on the other hand, may not be sophisticated enough to do so. As a result, the parents become frustrated. As one stepparent lamented, "They only see that I'm not their 'real' mom. Why can't they see that I still have a lot to offer them—if they would only let me?"

If you're the stepparent in a grieving family, it's hard to accept that while you may be the only mom or dad your stepchildren have, you're not the one they want. As impossible as it is, they want their biological parent to return. You can never fill that gaping need. But no one else could, either. Despite what your stepchildren say, it's not your fault. Unfortunately, your children may need time to grow up a bit before they fully appreciate you as a person and what you can contribute to their lives.

GRIEVING STEPFAMILIES ARE MORE LIKELY TO GET BOGGED DOWN IN THE EARLY STAGES OF FANTASY AND IMMERSION

Caring adults often fantasize that they can "fix" the grief in their stepfamily. They may believe that their love will wash away the pain and repair the hole in their partners' and children's hearts. Likewise, grieving children often think they can replace the person who died. In grieving families, such fantasies can linger longer than in stepfamilies formed by divorce.

Before our first evening together even ended, Kate told Jim that she wanted him to marry Mary Ann. Over the course of dating, through the engagement, and even well into the marriage, Kate remained certain that Mary Ann could replace her mom, Mary. She knew Mary couldn't return from the dead. Mary Ann was her only hope for a "mom," and in her desperation, Kate held on to that fantasy for a couple of years.

Mary Ann can identify the moment when it began to shift. Kate wanted Mary Ann to help her sew a Halloween costume. Mary Ann explained that she couldn't sew and that, unlike Mary, she really didn't *like* to sew. "Making things is the only thing I really can't do with you," Mary Ann remembers saying. "I love to read with you. I'll play games and sports. I'll take you tubing and horseback riding. But I'm sorry: I really hate arts and crafts."

Kate had remained in the fantasy stage for a long time. After that discussion, it began to unravel. Mary Ann was not Mary and never would be. Realizing that at last, Kate entered a more reality-based stage and treated Mary Ann as an outsider (as indeed she was). She reasoned that if Mary Ann couldn't be Mary, then what good was she anyway? Coupled with emerging adolescence, in which Kate naturally began pulling away, the puncturing of her fantasy prevented Kate from exploring the possibilities of a relationship for quite some time.

CHILDREN IN GRIEVING STEPFAMILIES ARE PROFOUNDLY, SOMETIMES UNREASONABLY, LOYAL TO THE PERSON WHO DIED

In divorced families, children have constant reminders of both the good and bad in their step- and biological parents. Eventually, assuming a lack of rancor between the divorced biological parents, these constant reminders push the stepchildren to a more balanced perspective of all the adults involved.

Grieving stepchildren, on the other hand, tend to idealize the person who died out of a profound sense of loyalty, often assigning all positive qualities to the person who died and all negative qualities to the stepparent. One stepparent openly acknowledged this reality by referring to her husband's first wife as "Saint Martha." Another stepparent recalled, "My stepdaughter was convinced that life would be all sweetness and light if only her mom were still alive. I remember her spitting out one morning, 'You're really mean. If my *real* mom was here, she'd let me have all the sugar cereal I wanted.' "

Sometimes, these idealizations are almost laughably inaccurate. A grieving teen once cried to her biological father, "If Mom were here, she'd help me figure out how to dress and how to get along with guys." Dad replied, "Honey, if your mom were here, you wouldn't talk to her any more than she talked to *her* mom. Don't you remember how embarrassed you were to even be seen with her?"

Well-meaning relatives and friends may feed children's loyalty to an unhealthy level by "never speaking ill of the dead." And attempts to humanize the person who died, to point out their vulnerabilities as well as their strengths, may be rebuffed by grieving kids. One grieving father, after laughing about how his late wife had allowed dishes to pile up after dinner rather than miss her favorite TV show, was rebuked by his daughter. "Dad," she said, "why are you always so critical of Mom? Didn't you really love her?"

This good/bad splitting tempts some stepparents to compete with the person who died. They try to be more understanding, more supportive, more "there" for the kids. But because the children's loyalty is based on their own emotional needs (as opposed to the real facts of the situation), the stepparents will undoubtedly fail. Loyalty, like love, must find its own balance, hopefully one that ultimately includes the stepparent.

BECAUSE CHILDREN'S GRIEF RESURFACES OVER TIME, STEPFAMILY DEVELOPMENT FOR GRIEVING FAMILIES FOLLOWS A MORE CHAOTIC COURSE

Creating a stepfamily is always emotionally chaotic, regardless of whether it follows a death or a divorce. Needs compete. Conflicts arise. Styles of problem-solving clash.

And individual family members rarely follow the same timetable. Some family members give up their fantasies and enter the family-formation process more quickly. Others fight change for a longer period of time, hoping to retain the "old ways." The lucky few enjoy, early on, more significant common ground on which to build relationships.

Despite these differences, the creation of a happy stepfamily after divorce usually follows a relatively specific, predictable, linear course. Sure, it gets worse before it gets better, but finally family members forge new relationships and develop new routines. Life gets good again.

In contrast, just when grieving stepfamilies think they're moving forward as a unit, they often find that a significant change or growth spurt forces a child to regrieve the death in a new way. Now, on top of dealing with stepfamily dynamics, grief reactions get tossed into the emotional "stew"!

After six years together, the Harrigan family finally sensed they'd made some progress. Having endured many battles, they'd developed a way to negotiate through their differences.

Then Colleen hit fourteen years of age. She began to wonder about her mother, who had died when Colleen was only six. She didn't remember her very well. What was her mom like? How were they similar? Different? Like most fourteen-year-olds, she longed to explore her own identity by comparing herself with her mom.

In trying to identify with her mother, Colleen renewed her sense of profound loyalty and dumped her frustration and anger about her mom's absence on her stepmom, Helen. Once again, Helen's position as an outsider in the "real" family was reconfirmed. And the stepfamily-development dance started again.

Helen began to lose heart, feeling that the family would never heal and that her efforts were doomed to failure.

STEPPARENTS IN A GRIEVING FAMILY FACE EVEN MORE COMPLICATED FEELINGS ABOUT THE FAMILY-FORMATION PROCESS THAN THEY DO IN A FAMILY OF DIVORCE

In stepfamilies that form after a divorce, everyone expects some impatience and anger. The adults from the divorced family often frustrate each other over practical matters. Children are understandably confused while new routines develop. When stepparents feel jealous of the existing relationships, resent the alimony payments, and get exasperated with their partners' ex-spouses, they see themselves as normal.

Stepparents in grieving families likewise feel jealous sometimes. They've been so loving for so long. They tire of the constant battles. They yearn for some acknowledgment of their contribution, some measure of the loving, easy relationships that the biological family enjoys.

If money is tight, a stepparent may find himself angry that there's no life insurance to help, that he's asked to help pay off medical or funeral bills for the person who died, or that the kids need extra psychological help to deal with parts of their grief. Anger can also surface at the need to cope with two sets of "in-laws": his wife's family, as well as the family of her deceased husband!

And because parenting styles and priorities differ from person to person, stepparents often find themselves at odds with certain behaviors, rules, and values in their children. *If I had raised these children,* they think, many times accurately, *they'd have better table manners and keep cleaner rooms.* But knowing they have to pick their battles, they swallow their own irritation at certain actions.

The difference between stepparenting in a grieving family and in a family of divorce is that stepparents after divorce are *allowed* to feel these jealousies, resentments, and the like. But a stepparent in a grieving family may hold herself to a higher standard and reject those negative feelings inside. *After all, this family's been through hell,* she thinks. *The kids can't be blamed.* She may chide herself over and over again to be understanding, to rise above it all. *What right have I to be angry?* she asks herself. *I didn't suffer the loss. Am I a loving person or not?* asks a little voice inside her. *Didn't I sign up for better or for worse?* Her own feelings may conflict with her highest values of compassion.

And when her friends call her a saint, saying they could never do what she's doing, she may feel even guiltier about her feelings. She wonders if she's not a fraud after all. But how can she admit to what's truly troubling her? It's a long step down from the top of everyone's pedestal!

Finally, she may realize that she's called upon to actively support her stepkids in their grief. Now, chances are, she signed up for stepparenting with a large heart, wanting to help the family heal. Little did she know, though, that part of the job would be to help the kids remember the person who died, talk about what she was like, and continue to love her on an ongoing basis. That focus can leave a stepparent feeling like hired help. To survive, she needs a particularly secure sense of her own worth to the family.

SURVIVAL STRATEGIES FOR STEPPARENTING A GRIEVING FAMILY

Many stepparents say that a dark sense of humor helps them survive the trials and tribulations of early stepfamily life. Mary Ann, for example, comments, "Each of our three kids hated me at one point or another. The good news is that they never hated me simultaneously!" If you can't find any humor in the situation, though, how do you endure? Here's advice from others whose stepfamilies have become comfortable, nurturing places for everyone involved.

LEARN EVERYTHING YOU CAN ABOUT GRIEF (IN ADULTS AND CHILDREN) AND ABOUT WHAT STEPFAMILIES ARE REALLY LIKE

Understanding what's normal will help you put others' behavior and feelings into perspective. You realize that no one's going crazy, even though sometimes a child's actions and feelings (or those of your partner) may seem a little strange.

Regardless of what's happening, such knowledge will help you appreciate that you don't need to take it personally. When someone's feeling torn in their loyalties, when anger surfaces, when a child withdraws— it's not about you. It may be about grief. It may be about stepfamily dynamics. It may simply be about this child, at this point in her development, on this quarter acre of the planet. But although it's your "problem" to work with, it's not a problem that you caused. It's not a reflection on you.

RESPECT MULTIPLE VIEWS OF REALITY

You probably recognize that you and your partner sometimes see things differently. Now, in your stepfamily, you need to realize that the same holds true for each of the kids. The clothes on the floor in your stepchild's room may strike you as a sign of being a slob. Or you may feel that it's a direct effort to defy your authority. To her, however, it may mean "freedom." It may represent her rebellion from parental standards of neatness, or the simple fact that she doesn't have the time to both talk on the phone and keep her room neat—and talking on the phone is more important these days. Even if you decide to impose limits on certain behaviors, you'll fare better if you take the time to understand and respect the meaning your stepchild or partner assigns to her actions.

Many times, biological parents dismiss stepparent feelings about such issues, saying, "That's just kid stuff. Loosen up." But stepparents experience "kid stuff" differently from the way their partners do. If you're the biological parent, know that your partner doesn't have the memories of loving times to fall back on when the going gets rough. He doesn't have the history to know that your child is normally neat or sunny or witty or affectionate. He only knows the phase your child is in right now. And if your stepfamily is like most in the early stages, your partner never gets the small strokes that you do—the smiles, the responses that last more than one word, the greeting cards signed "Love." So when the worst moments come, he has no emotional reserves with your child on which to fall back. Knowledge can put the tough times in perspective, although it can never make them easy.

WORK ON CONNECTION VERSUS LOVE

Children in a stepfamily can't instantly love a stepparent, and it's just plain fantasy to think otherwise. But if you can't force love, you can at least work on connectedness.

That's how it works with children of your own. A baby doesn't come into the world loving his parents. Yes, he depends on them. He is comforted by their presence. After several months of life, he responds with smiles and laughter to their antics. But the ability to give? To see another person's viewpoint? Gratitude? Those come much, much later. First, it's the parents who do all the giving, who perform all the details of changing diapers, feeding, holding, and helping.

Why should stepparenting be any different? Doesn't it make sense that those bonds, too, will be woven of hundreds of thousands of thin, nearly invisible strands of daily connections? Kids are concrete thinkers. They know what they see and touch and feel. Maybe it's only after a certain number of lunches packed and soccer games attended and drills on Spanish vocabulary that your stepchild will be able to believe that, indeed, you care for her and are in it for the duration.

So if you can't force love, foster connection. It's the soil in which love grows.

COMMUNICATE HONESTLY AS A COUPLE AND AS A FAMILY ABOUT EVERYTHING—THE PERSON WHO DIED, THE KIDS, YOUR PARTNER, HOW YOU FEEL ABOUT THE INTERACTIONS IN THE FAMILY

Let's perform an experiment. Remember your single days. Imagine your finances have hit a rough spot, and you're forced to take in a roommate. What do you have to talk about? Who's going to do which chores around the house? What habits do each of you need to modify in order to live peaceably together? Who pays for which expenses? The list would seem endless early on.

In fact, that's the situation you face when your stepfamily first forms. Sure, you and your partner know each other. And the biological parent knows each of the kids. But the relationship between everyone else is that of new roommates. There's only one way to make it work better than a television sitcom: to talk, talk, and talk again, and when you're finished doing that, talk even more.

Because you're ultimately hoping to become more than roommates, you'll need to talk about more than just the practical details of life. You'll need to talk about feelings—the good, the bad, and the ugly. Many people hate "feelings work." They're uncomfortable talking about their anger or sadness or fear. But there are two excellent reasons for taking a deep breath and plunging in.

First, feelings that aren't talked about get expressed in other, often less helpful ways. Anger turns into aggression. Fear turns into withdrawal. Sadness turns into depression.

Second, talking breeds understanding, understanding breeds tolerance, and tolerance provides open space in the heart where caring can take root. One couple, knowing they needed some time alone, planned Saturday nights as "date night." Craig, a single dad for the three years after his wife died during a weekend away with her girlfriends, took the time to explain to his own six-year-old son, Ian, what would happen: Ian's favorite baby-sitter would come each Saturday at seven o'clock, play with him a bit, and tuck him in bed; and Craig would come kiss him goodnight when he and his new wife, Jenny, returned home around midnight. Ian agreed.

But for the first three weeks running, Ian came down with a stomachache each Saturday, late in the afternoon, forcing them to stay in for the evening. After the third week, when yet again no other symptoms appeared and Ian developed a hunger for pizza two hours later, Craig and Jenny suspected something else was at play. Jenny began to get angry. She accused Ian of manipulating the situation to keep Craig for himself. She faulted Craig for letting Ian get away with it. "Who's in charge here, anyway?" she fumed. "Am I always going to play second fiddle to a six-year-old boy?"

Finally, Craig confronted Ian about the situation. Ian broke down, sobbing in Craig's arms. "Daddy, but what if you don't come home?"

he said. "What if you die too?" Overhearing Ian's outburst, Jenny's anger dissolved as well. How can you be angry at a little boy who's too afraid to let his daddy go?

DECIDE WHAT REALLY MATTERS TO YOU, AND LET GO OF THE REST

You can't win every battle. And in some battles, winning simply costs too much in terms of your energy or the long-term consequences to the relationship. No relationship can withstand constant comment or correction.

One stepmother agreed with her husband on a parental strategy for their three teens that incorporated only their most cherished values. Between themselves, they stated their first goal as "Alive at twenty-five!" They wanted their children alive and healthy at that age. Second, they hoped their children would become functioning adults capable of living respectfully with other people. As for the rest, they trusted that roommates, spouses, and employers would sand down the rough edges as needed.

They articulated their position to their three adolescents by saying, "If we think you're going to do significant, irreparable damage to yourself or somebody else, we're going to stop you. We're insisting that you respect each other and our common living spaces. But for the rest, it's up to you."

The stepmother then stopped nagging them about cleaning their rooms and closed the doors. She ignored their bad table manners, and when the kids' boom boxes blasted, she plugged in the stereo earphones. At dinner, she no longer insisted that they drink milk and eat vegetables, although they were available each night. She turned off the ringer on the telephone in the master bedroom so she didn't hear when they got late-night phone calls. She stopped asking about homework and papers.

On the other hand, she and her husband established several rules. Drinking and driving would result in no more car privileges—ever. Poor grades would limit their college choices, so good grades were expected. Since everyone used the family room, kitchen, and bathroom, those had to be straightened every day. And the kids had to stop the verbal abuse so common among adolescent siblings.

These parents knew what was most important to them. Although they disagreed with some choices their kids made, they tolerated their own discomfort in the hope of building long-lasting, peaceful relationships.

SEARCH FOR AREAS OF COMMON INTEREST AND COMMON GROUND AMONG EVERYONE IN THE FAMILY

Just as constantly exercising the same muscles results in physical injury, constant *working* at stepfamily functioning will also do damage. Everybody needs a break periodically, time to just relax and enjoy, if possible, the areas of family life that are already easy and comfortable. That's why common areas of interest are so important. Can you enjoy a movie together? Do it. Is everybody in a better mood when you're camping together? Make time for it. Does a big turkey dinner soothe the savage stepfamily beast? Cook the meal. It's a respite from the tough emotional work you're involved with day to day.

IF YOU'RE THE BIOLOGICAL PARENT, SPEND SOME SEPARATE TIME WITH EACH PERSON IN THE FAMILY

Early on, you're the only common strand holding together the individual relationships in the family. Until the whole web is spun, you need to spend time with each person individually. Each one needs you to support her, to hear his point of view, to express your commitment to her through your sheer physical presence and attention.

Think of yourself as the stitches closing a cut. You're holding together the gaps in the wound until the cells themselves are knit together as a working body.

SPEND TIME ON YOUR MARRIAGE INDEPENDENT OF YOUR KIDS

According to the Stepfamily Association of America, almost 60 percent of remarriages end in divorce.[2] It makes sense: no matter how much you love your new spouse, that's still the weakest bond in a new stepfamily. You don't have enough history together for it to be otherwise. You need to spend time alone together building that relationship.

Additionally, in good relationships, being alone together recharges your emotional batteries. It's a deposit in an emotional bank account that otherwise may feel below its minimum daily balance on a pretty regular basis. It's the stream that feeds the well so that it doesn't run dry, despite the buckets of water being drawn out daily.

DON'T COMPARE SPOUSES

This advice holds both for the surviving parent and for the new spouse. In times of self-doubt, it's easy for a stepparent to wonder if the dead parent wasn't simply a better parent. When a surviving parent wonders the same thing, the stepparent's resulting jealousy and guilt are aggravated. From there, it's a downward track.

If you can't stop comparing yourself to your partner's dead spouse, let us satisfy your curiosity. We can tell you how you measure up, even without knowing you personally.

First, except in cases of neglect and abuse, your kids' original parent would *always* have been the better parent *for her own kids.* No one can step in midstream and do a better job. That doesn't mean she's a better person or has better parenting skills. It simply recognizes that the constant, loving presence of the parent who cared for a child from the start is more important than any individual parenting skill or attitude. As a stepparent, you can't do a better job with her kids than she could have— nor could she have done a better job of raising any children of yours.

Second, parenting is a patchwork of varying abilities and attitudes, with different aspects important at different stages of development. No one is perfect at all of them at all ages. No doubt your kids' original parent was better at some parts of parenting than you are, just as you are more proficient at other pieces than she could ever be. Accept it, and don't bother to try to figure it out. It doesn't help. It only saps energy from the work and enjoyment that lie ahead of you.

IF YOU'RE THE STEPPARENT, NURTURE AN INDEPENDENT SOURCE OF SELF-ESTEEM AND PERSONAL NOURISHMENT

Even in first-time biological families, parents report feeling used by their children. In the earlier stages of stepfamily growth, that sense is compounded even further as the stepkids actively fight the change involved in becoming a new kind of family. They may treat you as a "wicked" stepmother or stepfather. They may disregard you at best or scream their hatred of you at worst.

Try as he might, your partner can only take the edge off your self-doubts. He is too close to the situation and to his kids' concerns. You need to find a way to maintain a solid, internal confidence that you're a good person performing well at an extremely difficult and long-range task. For that, you need an external source that confirms your value.

Some stepparents find that source in their work life. Surrounded by a boss and colleagues, the on-the-job appreciation buoys them through the rougher seas at home. A rewarding volunteer role can achieve the same effect. A circle of close friends may also help you continue to believe in your own worth.

RECOGNIZE THAT EVEN HEALTHY, LOVING ADULTS WILL FIND CREATING A STEPFAMILY TO BE HARD WORK AND PAINFUL AT TIMES

There's a myth in this country that if you're psychologically healthy, you'll be able to weather any emotional storm that comes your way without breaking a sweat. Cancer? The right attitude will heal it. A loved one dies? Just get over it (in the three business days allotted please). Lose a job? Keep your nose to the grindstone and all that stuff.

In *Bag of Bones,* Stephen King writes of a widower attempting to overcome his anxiety after his wife's death. "The plan," King writes, "was pretty much based on that bit of New Age wisdom which says the word 'fear' stands for Face Everything and Recover. But, as I stood there and looked down at that spark of porch light (it looked very small in the growing darkness), it occurred to me that there's another bit of wisdom, one not quite so good-morning-starshine, which suggests fear is actually an acronym for F*** Everything and Run. Standing there by myself in the woods as the light left the sky, that seemed like the smarter interpretation, no two ways about it."[3]

Perhaps the reality we all need to face is this: Some struggles tax the endurance of even the wisest among us. And that's okay.

FIND OTHERS WHO HAVE WALKED DOWN THIS ROAD, WITH WHOM TO SHARE YOUR STRUGGLES

"You're not going crazy." "We went through that too." "You're going to make it." "Sounds like the kids are being real jerks right about now." "It gets better." Out of the mouths of experienced people, especially ones who have successfully finished creating their stepfamilies, such words are golden. They lend perspective. They hold out hope. They help us interpret when simple endurance will work and when expert help might prove beneficial.

Some of us find it nerve-wracking to share our pain. Doing so makes us feel weak, incompetent, or vulnerable to criticism. It takes courage for us to speak out the first time. What a relief it is, though, when you discover that virtually every other family experiences the same dynamics—some, incredibly, in even more painful ways!

If you don't know of any stepfamilies with whom you'd feel comfortable speaking, check out the Stepfamily Association of America (phone 800-735-0329; Web site www.stepfam.org). They sponsor support groups in a number of cities and can put you in touch with most of the known resources.

DON'T JUDGE THE RESULTS OF YOUR STEPFAMILY EFFORTS IN DAYS, WEEKS, OR MONTHS BUT IN YEARS AND DECADES

Most first-time biological families report that their kids begin to come around, responding more lovingly and with greater appreciation, somewhere between the ages of twenty and twenty-five. After struggling to make it on their own and after comparing *their* lives with the lives of others, young adults begin to realize the many ways in which fortune has smiled on them. When they care for children of their own, they start to understand the hundreds of daily sacrifices you made for their well-being.

Grieving children follow the same course. All along, they've been aware that they've suffered one of the greatest tragedies to befall a child. Now, however, it dawns on them that it could have been much worse. For most kids, at least *one* parent survived to love them into adulthood. Most stepparents contributed lovingly, if imperfectly, to their children's development. Many grieving kids in the Western world enjoy financial and educational resources that empower them to lead healthy, productive, rewarding lives. From seeing the glass as half empty, they shift to seeing the glass as at least half full. And many become grateful in new and, to parents, rewarding ways.

The only catch? You need to wait until the third or fourth decade of your child's life to see it happen. Expecting it earlier sets you up for frustration. Set your sights on a longer-term horizon. As they say, parenting has never been for wimps!

FOSTER A PHILOSOPHY OF LIFE OR SPIRITUALITY OF STEPPARENTING, ONE THAT VALUES GROWTH IN GIVING AND IN UNCONDITIONAL LOVE

What do you do when hope runs out? What do you do when the promises of other, surviving stepparents seem empty? How do you survive when that little voice inside says, "Well, other stepfamilies evidently come together, but not this one. We're not going to make it"?

When all your efforts appear fruitless, it's time to focus on how the experience of stepparenting may be helping you to grow as an individual. Virtually every spirituality in the world recognizes that "no man is an island." Whether you hold Gandhi or Jesus or the prophets of Hebrew scripture as your wisdom figures, you're called by those traditions to grow in giving of yourself to the world.

What better place to begin than at home? Even if nothing ever changes in your stepfamily, no better practice field for unconditional love exists. Who needs a monastery? Who needs a hair shirt? We're parenting stepfamilies!

As Mary Ann wrote to a friend early on, "Usually, I just scream inside every time one of the kids ignores me or says something hurtful. But in my better moments, I remember to look at their pain, to love them anyway. In a lot of ways, I don't consider myself a very religious person—I don't pray very often really, for example. But in those better moments, I feel like somehow I'm looking at the kids with the eyes of God. And I sense that maybe I'm growing, just a little bit, into a person I'll be really glad to call 'me' at the end of my life."

Chapter 13

CARING FOR YOURSELF

Everyone told me the first year of grieving is the worst. But to me, the second year hit me like a ton of bricks. I realized I had spent the whole first year taking care of the kids and making sure their needs were met. They're doing fine, but I'm a basket case.

—Charlie, 37 years old

ISAAC CAME INTO OUR OFFICE ONE DAY, AS HE HAD EVERY MONTH since his wife, Pat, died almost a year earlier. He checked in once a month to make sure that his reactions and behaviors were normal and to ask for help on how to raise his four grieving children. But on this visit, Isaac looked particularly ragged and worn down. He said the kids seemed to be getting worse, rather than better, and that he wasn't helping matters very much. He said he was getting really tired of working through his own grief while trying to help his children through theirs.

In addition, he prepared breakfast, made their lunches for school, cooked dinner, cleaned the house, paid the bills, and did all of the practical things that he and Pat used to do together. And on top of that, he was trying to hold on to his job as a manager at the phone company. Lately, Isaac found himself snapping at his children, losing patience when they simply acted like kids. He felt like he was at the breaking point and didn't know what to do.

We asked Isaac when was the last time he had been alone to just think and reflect. He said he hadn't had a chunk of time like that since Pat died. So we suggested that he find a baby-sitter for the weekend and check into a hotel. We instructed him to relax, take a walk, sit in the hot tub, treat himself to room service, and read a good book. Just *be* for the weekend and *do* nothing other than activities he enjoyed.

The week after he returned, Isaac called us. "My time away really did make a difference," he said. "Today I find I have more patience with the kids, I feel like I'm back in control, and I have more energy than when I left. The grief is still all around me, but I've got it in a different perspective. I just may get through this after all."

While raising a grieving child, you have to pay attention to yourself. It's hard work—it can drain you of your time and energy. So even though caring for your grieving child may be your highest priority, caring for yourself has to receive some attention if you want your child to be okay. Here's why.

IF YOU DON'T TAKE CARE OF YOURSELF, YOU CAN'T TAKE CARE OF YOUR CHILD

As Isaac discovered, a parent who neglects his own needs will eventually neglect the needs of his child. Our bodies and minds were not made to work at such a constant pace. They need to be replenished and renewed. Otherwise, they'll begin to do weird things. You may become physically ill, waking up with headaches and stomach pains. You may feel like you're losing your mind—more than in the usual grief reaction—when you can't remember things or you get confused. You may slump into a deep depression, feeling that the world is too overwhelming.

It will be all that you can handle to get through the day, much less take care of your child and be attentive to her needs. It takes an enormous amount of energy to raise a child under ordinary circumstances. The added toll of grief work can sap your strength even more severely. Over time, neglecting your own needs and refusing to care for yourself prevents you from being a helpful resource for your child.

YOUR WELL-BEING GIVES YOUR CHILD A SENSE OF SAFETY

We hear it over and over again: "I can't take care of myself until my kids are okay." And we respond: "Your kids will have a better chance of being okay if you take care of yourself." It's crucial for you to grieve as the feelings arise. If you delay your own grief and push down your feelings, they will eventually erupt and overwhelm you. Yes, your child's grief is an important factor in your life. But your grief is important too. You're a person, not just a parent, and your grief demands your attention. Care for your grieving self as well as for your grieving child.

If you're physically ill, disoriented, or can't get out of bed in the morning, you can't project dependability for your child. As you know, the first need of a grieving child is to reestablish a sense of safety and security in her life. Not that you have to be a pillar of strength all the time, never crying or showing emotion, but you do need to be reliable. If your child can't count on you to be there for her, she may feel even more alienated and alone. If she has to take care of you because you have nothing left with which to take care of her, she won't be able to be just a kid. And if you look drained, depressed, and ill all the time, it may trigger a grieving child's greatest fear: that you will be the next to die.

If you want to reestablish safety and security in the life of your grieving child, take care of yourself. Replenish your resources so you can be there for her when she needs you.

FOR PARENTS WHO HAVE LOST A CHILD, SELF-CARE CAN BE CRUCIAL TO YOUR RELATIONSHIP AS A COUPLE

Men and women grieve in different ways. Men often want to know how to get over their grief as quickly as possible and how to do it the right way. In other words, they want an instruction manual. They also want to do it alone. Women generally take their time. They feel the feelings, are more open to crying, and find support to help them. They tend to have more intimate friendships and can talk to others freely and comfortably.

When a father and mother grieve the loss of a child, their grieving styles may come into conflict. He may question why she's not getting over it more quickly, and she may think he doesn't care enough about her or their child. To nurture their relationship during this stressful time, they must nurture themselves. Both should take some time for self-care, renewing and replenishing their energy. That way, they will have more to give to each other and more patience with each other. A couple who has lost a child is not only caring for a grieving child but for one another and for their relationship as a couple.

TAKING CARE OF YOU

Here are our suggestions for caring for yourself as you care for your grieving child. But before you begin to act on strategies of self-care, it is usually helpful to take a few moments to make a plan. On a piece of paper, write down one activity of caring for yourself for every day of the week. Some self-care activities may require quite a bit of time—schedule them when you have longer periods of time available. On your busier days, try a quick pick-me-up activity.

Incidentally, planning in general can be a means of caring for yourself. Plan all of the activities for your day and week in as much detail as possible. List your dinner menu for each night, and make a shopping list of what you'll need. Write down all of the activities that your child is involved in and the times you need to bring him there and pick him up. Keep a running to-do list. Indicate on a calendar when you need to pay the bills, attend meetings at school, and schedule doctor appointments.

After Mary died, Jim began each day with a cup of coffee and a notepad. He wrote down a schedule for that day. Some days, his schedule was so detailed that he listed each event in minutes:

3:30 Pick up Kate at school
3:42 Grocery store
4:00 Drop off Kate at friend's house
4:08 Drive Greg to baseball practice
4:23 Drive Pat to dentist for 4:30 appt.

When you're in the midst of grief, making a detailed plan may seem like a lot of work (even if you are not quite as compulsive as Jim!), but having that plan in hand can make you feel much more in control of your life. And that, in turn, will make you feel better.

Here are some suggestions for self-care that we hope you'll incorporate into your routine:

STAY HEALTHY

Grieving can be hazardous to your health. If you're not careful, the increased stress and depletion of energy can do serious damage to your body. Make a conscious effort to take care of your physical needs. One reason for making a weekly plan for your dinner menu is to guarantee that you eat well-balanced, nutritious meals. When you're grieving, it's too easy to just throw a frozen dinner into the microwave or grab something at a fast-food restaurant. Eating well is critical to maintaining the energy you need in order to do all you have to do while raising a grieving child.

Exercise daily. Walk around the neighborhood, jog, bicycle, swim, or do whatever you can to stretch your muscles and pump your heart. Exercise reduces stress and gives you more energy. It will pick up your mood as well.

Avoid drugs, alcohol, and caffeine. Although there's nothing wrong with a cup of coffee in the morning or a glass of wine with friends at dinner, too much caffeine or alcohol can prevent you from sleeping well, a critical activity for replenishing your resources.

Get a physical, and check in with the doctor every few months. The doctor can give you an objective opinion about whether you're maintaining your health.

LEARN ABOUT GRIEF

Understanding what you're going through and what you can expect in the future is another way to feel more in control of your grief and of your life. You can learn about grief and its effects on adults in many ways. There are hundreds of books on the subject, from general topics of grief to specific issues of loss. (We've listed several books on grief in Appendix A.) You can also learn about grief at information sessions at your local hospice, hospital, or funeral home. Several Web sites on the

Internet are devoted to grief and loss. Again, some are general in content while others deal with more specific issues.

Learning about grief and how adults react to the loss of a loved one will not take away the pain, but it may ease the sting of surprise as you adjust to the changes in your life. Feeling in control a little more may help you be less overwhelmed in your daily life and better able to cope with the demands that you face.

ALLOW YOURSELF TO GRIEVE

As Charlie realized, ignoring grief while taking care of a child will only postpone the inevitable. And delayed grief comes back with a vengeance. So face your grief as it occurs. Feel the feelings, and express them. Find someone to talk to, and get it out. Grab a big pillow and punch it until you feel better. Cry, and know that every tear is a drop of healing.

Name each feeling as it arises. Talk to yourself about what you are experiencing. Keep a journal, and write down your feelings, reactions, and reflections each day.

Maintain connections with your loved one. Put out your favorite photos, wear his shirt, put on her locket. Go to the gravesite, and talk to him. If people think you're a little crazy, too bad. It's your grief, not theirs, and you're entitled to grieve the way you wish.

ASK FOR HELP

You can't get through this time alone. Don't even try—it will simply add to your stress. You probably had plenty to do before the death of your loved one. If you lost a spouse, you are doing everything he or she did as well as your own chores and duties. If you lost a child, you are trying to deal with your own grief, your spouse's grief, and your family's grief as you strive to put your life back together. The daily activities that you used to carry out with some sense of control and competence may now seem absolutely overwhelming.

To take care of yourself through the months of active grieving, you need to ask for help. Seek out friends and relatives whom you can count on, and ask them to help you with some of the tasks that burden you.

Most friends want to help after someone experiences a loss, but they don't know what to do. Often they refrain from calling to offer help because they don't want to bother you or they assume you're receiving enough help from others.

When someone offers to take your child somewhere for you or to go shopping for some groceries or to help you make sense of hospital bills, by all means take her up on it. Those offers won't happen for long; take advantage of them while you can. Everything that someone else does for you is one less thing that you have to do, and that means you have more time to care for yourself. Allow others to help and relieve some of the burdens of your grief.

TAKE A BREAK FROM RAISING A GRIEVING CHILD

As important as it is to be present to your grieving child and to make sure he's okay, you won't be a helpful presence for long if you don't take a break once in a while. You need to take a break from your own grief periodically just to get away from the intensity of the feelings. When you're helping a child get through his grief as well, it's even more important to find some relief both from your grief and from his.

If your life consists of work, cooking, cleaning, and taking care of the kids—constant chores and obligations—you will likely end up like Isaac. You'll lose your patience and your temper, and you'll be more of a hindrance than a help to your grieving child.

Get away. Go somewhere for a weekend if you can. Just relax and recharge your batteries. Do nothing for a change. Let all of your worries and tensions disappear for a while. If you can't get away for an entire weekend, take a day. Go to the beach or the mountains. Find a retreat center. Get a massage. Just hang out. But get away from the house. At home, there are too many distractions and temptations to do things instead of relax and replenish yourself.

Taking a break does not mean escaping the pain or avoiding your grief. It simply means getting away from the intensity of the grief work that you and your family are doing. You'll be amazed at what a difference getting away can make. You'll return a little more relaxed and refreshed, and you'll have more resources to deal with your own grief and that of your child.

FIND A SUPPORT GROUP

As much as friends and relatives can lend an ear and be with you through the acute grieving period, there's no substitute for a good support group. Getting together with a group of people who are experiencing the effects of loss can be very powerful and healing. In a support group, you realize you're not alone in your grief, and you feel supported by others who are traveling many of the same paths that you are. Often an instant bond is formed as people in similar circumstances comfort one another.

There are many types of support groups. Find one that is closest to your loss and to your needs. You may find a young widows or young widowers group that discusses issues of single parenting while it processes grief. If your child died, look for a group of parents who have lost a child and are dealing with the specific aspects of that type of loss. If you join a support group for grieving children, you may participate in the parent group as they learn about how children grieve and how to work on their own feelings.

To find a support group, contact your local hospice or hospital. They may have their own groups, or they can refer you to a group nearby. If all else fails, consider starting your own peer support group. Put a notice in the newspaper that you are starting a group, and indicate the specific loss that the group will focus upon.

The power of any group resides in the gathering of people in similar circumstances and the expression of feelings. There's a comfort in knowing that you are not the only one to whom this terrible tragedy has happened, and it's a great relief to talk about how you feel to people who really understand.

Joining a group helps you care for yourself as well as your child. Rather than burden yourself or your family with the all-consuming expression of your grief, you can let it out in the safety and comfort of a support group. Almost everyone feels better after attending a group, and it can help to mark your progress as you travel the unknown.

BE PATIENT WITH YOURSELF

Caring for yourself in the midst of grief involves a great deal of patience. The effects of loss take a long time to heal. Don't rush it. No one wants to be in pain, but the pain of grief is a necessary part of the healing process. Take one day at a time. At the end of each day, congratulate yourself for making it through. Grief is exhausting and arduous. Be gentle with yourself.

Don't let anyone else tell you how to deal with your grief. Everyone's grief is unique, and what worked for someone else may not work for you. Do what you feel is right and what's helpful to you.

Once again, a journal may be a useful tool for you. Write down your thoughts and reflections each day. Talk about your loved one, and express your anger, fears, and anxieties in the safety of your journal pages. Write your poems, memories, and any other thoughts that you find comforting. Keeping a journal can help you maintain a rhythm to your grief and give it some definition. You may feel less pressured to rush it and more open to letting it run its course patiently.

NURTURE YOUR SOUL

Once you have taken care of your physical needs by eating right and exercising and your emotional needs by expressing your feelings, it's time to feed and nourish your soul. We cannot stress enough how important it is to take a break from your grief and nourish yourself.

Think about what it is that makes you feel warm and cozy on the inside. Then plan a time to do it. The activity can be as simple as taking a warm bath or enjoying a cup of herbal tea. You might enjoy going to a play or concert. Take a long walk, ride your bike along a route you've never traveled, or hike through the woods. Curl up and read a good book. Take a course at the local university or adult education program. Become involved in activities at your church or synagogue. Put on the headphones and listen to your favorite CD. Rent a video and get lost in a good movie.

Nurturing yourself in these ways has a dual purpose. It provides a break from the burden of your grief, and it massages your mind and renews your spirit. As a result, you'll have more energy for yourself and for your child.

REWARD YOURSELF

Reward yourself anytime you can for getting through your grief. At the end of the day, say, "I did it!" and make yourself an ice cream sundae. Celebrate making it through another week by going out to dinner with a friend. Look back on how far you've come, and revel in your resilience. At the beginning of your grieving, you probably thought you'd never be able to get through it, but you *are* getting through it. Give yourself a pat on the back. You're probably doing chores, duties, and obligations that you thought you'd never be able to do. Congratulate yourself.

On the first anniversary of Mary's death, Jim took the kids to the cemetery to acknowledge the day's significance. Then he invited some close friends over for dinner. He told them they were invited for two reasons: first, to thank them for their support and, second, to celebrate the fact that he had made it through the first year of raising three kids on his own.

REDUCE YOUR STRESS

No other phenomenon in life is as stressful as the loss of a spouse or a child. It will eat you up if you're not careful. Often you will feel frazzled by too much paperwork, too many new skills to learn, and too few financial resources. It's too much change all at once, and the tension and anxiety just compound the problem. To reduce your stress, try the following:

• Establish routines at work, school, and home, including routines for meals, relaxation, and sleep.

• Examine your assumptions about what needs to be done, to what level of perfection, and by whom. Check to make sure your assumptions are real. Eliminate or postpone tasks as much as you can.

• Of those tasks that must be done, figure out which ones you might be able to delegate to someone who has offered to help.

• Reduce the noise level in your environment. Close doors. Turn off or turn down the television and stereo. Unplug your phone for a while—or screen your phone calls to eliminate stressful conversations.

• Use the following breathing exercise at least five times each day to break the stress cycle.

Step 1: Lie on your back with the palm of your left hand over your navel. Rest your right hand over your left. Keep your eyes open.

Step 2: Imagine a balloon lying inside your stomach beneath your hands. Begin to inhale through your nose, imagining as you do that the air is filling the balloon in your stomach. Picture the balloon filling completely as you continue to breathe in. Notice your rib cage and chest expanding. As you practice this breathing exercise, inhale for at least three seconds. Over time, lengthen your inhalation to five seconds.

Step 3: Slowly exhale, completely emptying the balloon. As you do so, repeat to yourself the word *relax.*

Repeat the breathing exercise twice, then breathe normally for five to ten breaths. Be sure to exhale fully each time. Then repeat the entire process again. Stop if you begin to feel light-headed or uncomfortable in any way. As with any exercise program, it may take a week or two to feel any immediate relaxation. Practice is critical to achieving the full benefit.

DO YOU NEED EXTRA HELP?

If you're caring for yourself and working on your grief but don't seem to be making much progress after several months, you may need some extra help. Although grief is a natural response to loss that doesn't normally require professional assistance, certain types of losses or specific circumstances may complicate your mourning. How do you know if you need extra help from a grief specialist?

Here are some questions to ask yourself about various aspects of your grief. Any grieving person might experience them briefly, but if you sense them continuing, it's probably time to talk to someone knowledgeable about grieving—if only to reassure yourself that you're on the right path.

1) Are you *always* irritable, annoyed, intolerant, or angry?

2) Do you experience an *ongoing* sense of numbness or of being isolated from your own self or from others? Do you usually feel that you have no one to talk to about what's happened?

3) Since your loved one died, are you *highly* anxious *most* of the time about your own death or the death of someone you love? Is it beginning to interfere with your relationships or your ability to concentrate or live as you would like?

4) Do you feel that you are *always* and *continually* preoccupied with your loved one, his death, or certain aspects of it, even though it's been several months since his death?

5) Do you *usually* feel restless or in "high gear"? Do you feel the need to be constantly busy—beyond what's normal for you?

6) Are you afraid of becoming close to new people for fear of losing again?

7) Do you find yourself active in ways that might prove harmful to you over time: drinking more than you used to; using more prescription or nonprescription drugs; engaging in sexual activity that is unsafe or unwise; driving in an unsafe or reckless manner (beyond what's normal for you); or entertaining serious thoughts about suicide?

8) Are you taking on too much responsibility for surviving family members or close friends? (What's too much responsibility? That varies greatly and depends on the situation, but if you're feeling heavily burdened by it, angry, or like the situation is "suffocating" you, it may be time to speak with someone.)

9) Do your grief reactions continue, *over time,* to be limited in some

way? Are you experiencing only a few of the reactions or emotions that usually come with grief? Are you unable to express your thoughts or feelings about your loved one and her death in words or actions? Do you remember only certain aspects of your loved one or your relationship together—for example, only the good parts as opposed to a more complete and balanced view of her?

10) Is there some aspect of what you're experiencing that makes you wonder whether you're normal or going crazy? Do you feel stuck in your grief in some way, unable to move on, even though it's been quite some time since your loved one's death?

Beyond looking for these ten signs, trust your own judgment. If you think that talking to a professional might help, talk to one or more to see whom you are comfortable with. Take advantage of one who seems helpful to you. After all, grief is painful enough without trying to do it all by yourself.

As you grieve the loss of your loved one, take the time to care for yourself. If you want to make sure that your grieving child is okay, make sure that you're okay. The process of raising your child will go much more smoothly, and you will come through the experience with strength and a renewed sense of spirit.

Chapter 14

FREQUENTLY ASKED QUESTIONS

I can talk to my kid about anything. I never held anything back, not all through his mom's illness. But how do I tell him that we cremated her? I mean, you can't just say, "We burned your mom like a pot roast!"

—Pete, 38 years old

AFTER A DEATH, THE QUESTIONS YOUR KIDS CAN ASK CAN STUMP you even as they rip out your heart. You may worry that your child can't handle a certain topic or situation, or that you yourself can't. We share suggestions for answering the most common questions that you may encounter.

WHEN DEATH IS APPROACHING

MY HUSBAND IS DYING NOW. WHAT DO I SAY TO THE CHILDREN? WHAT DO I DO?

When a loved one is dying, life seems unreal, chaotic, and overwhelmingly complex, so let's keep this simple. What's most important is that you help your children feel safe, explain what's happening, and be gentle with yourself.

Help your children feel safe. Be present, hold them, and cuddle together. Increase the number of long hugs. Tell your children more often than usual that you love them. And don't be put off by adolescent shrugs and nonresponsiveness. Do it anyway. They need your warm presence every bit as much as younger children do.

As we've said before, be predictable. Tell them what's happening and why. Explain to them what they can expect as your family member dies. Hospice nurses and social workers can guide you through this sharing.

Likewise, anticipate their concerns about what will happen after your loved one dies. In the short run, what will the wake, funeral, graveside ceremony, postfuneral gathering be like? In the long run, how will you get through this? (Of course, you yourself may be wondering about the answer to this one, but your kids don't need to know about your emotional anguish. They need to know the concrete details: where you'll live, who will drive them to school and Scouts, who will fix meals and do laundry. And they need to know that *you* believe you'll all survive.)

Give them options. They can choose meals and baby-sitters. They can decide how they might like to help care for the person who is dying. Many children report feeling comforted themselves by helping out: it gives them a sense of self-esteem, some small measure of control over what's happening, and a concrete way of showing their love for the person who is dying. Even the smallest child can carry a glass of water, bring a flower, draw a picture, or visit with a person who is dying.

Explain what's happening. Don't wait for the perfect time. Begin now to explain to your child how very, very sick your loved one is. Help him understand the specific causes of the illness. Talk about what *dead* means: that the body stops working, and that once a body stops working, it can't start working again.

Expect that your child will be able to absorb only a little bit at a time—and that you yourself may be able to talk about it only in brief spurts. That's okay. Revisiting the topic actually helps children digest it on their own timetable.

Don't worry if you tear up or cry. Your child, of course, won't like it. None of us likes to see someone we love in pain. But if you are free to show your tears, your child will learn that she can cry too. If you think you may start sobbing uncontrollably and scare your child, ask someone to help you.

Explain to other close friends and family members what you're trying to accomplish with your child. Ask for their support and reinforcement in their conversations with your child. Expect that some may resist your efforts out of their own discomfort with the topic. Hold firm. Ask them not to undermine your efforts to be truthful but loving with your child.

Be gentle with yourself. Don't expect yourself to be a superparent. You're going through one of the hardest experiences life ever hands us. Cut yourself some slack. Pare back what you do to the barest of necessities. Of these, do what you can. Know that you'll have time to do the rest later.

SHOULD MY CHILD ATTEND THE WAKE AND FUNERAL?

Children of every age should be encouraged to attend wakes and funerals, for several reasons. First, it enables them to stay close to their surviving parent or caretaker. At a very scary time, this presence is crucial to their comfort. Second, seeing the body helps children begin to realize that the person is really dead, and it provides a concrete experience of a dead body not seeing, feeling, or breathing. Third, if you exclude your child, he may conclude that it's too scary or "bad" to be dealt with or even discussed.

Of course, no child should be forced to go. Coercion, in and of itself, would be scary to a child. But usually, your child will go if you explain the following to her:

1) That you'll be there all the time.

2) What your child can expect to see and feel, including who else will be there; what all the people will be doing; where the body will be; and what the body will and won't do (it won't move, feel warm, or talk because it is dead).

3) That she has options: She can stay for the whole time or just a while; she can view the body or not (most will, with a little encouragement and your presence); she can stay in the viewing room, or she can

go into another room at the funeral home, to which she can bring her own toys, books, or coloring materials.

4) That she can always change her mind about her choice. For example, if she decides she'd like to view the body, but when she gets to the funeral home, she decides against it, that's okay.

Sometimes parents encourage their children not only to attend, but to place cards, letters, or special mementos (a catcher's mitt or doll, for example) in the casket with the person who died. That's fine, as long as your child realizes that the person doesn't need it and won't use it because the body doesn't work anymore. When four-year-old Ana placed her own favorite blanket in her sister's casket, everyone welled up over her loving gesture. Three months later, after the first snowfall, Ana asked her mom to take her to the cemetery. "My blanket won't be warm enough," she explained. "We need to help her put on her winter coat."

What if you've already held the wake and funeral and your children didn't attend? Don't beat yourself up over your choice. You can always help your children plan and hold another memorial service or graveside ritual. Let them decide which readings, songs, and symbolic gestures they'd like to include. Ask them who they'd like to invite. Help them express their feelings in ritual just as you may have at the funeral itself.

SHOULD A CHILD ACTUALLY VIEW THE BODY?

In general, if you've prepared your child for the experience as discussed above, viewing the body is helpful. By doing so, children and adults can get a picture (not pleasant, certainly, but not necessarily horrifying) of what the person looks like dead. Not only can it help make the death real to the child, but it shows the child that the person's body is no longer in pain.

Funeral directors work wonders these days in making bodies viewable. And from their long experience, they generally can and will tell you when a body is too nightmarish to view. In such cases, most grief counselors suggest two approaches. First, if some part of the body is viewable (the face, for example), the funeral director may be able to cover up the more disturbing parts of the body while still giving family members a chance to take a final look at the person who died. Similarly, if one side of the face or body has been severely damaged, it may be possible to position the body and face so that the damaged parts are hidden.

If no part of the body is viewable, it's sometimes helpful to ask the funeral director to take pictures of the body and identifying birthmarks and then to find a safe, obscure spot to store them. (The funeral director or a brave family member might perform this task.) Pictures can help years later if an adolescent or young adult starts to wonder whether the person who was buried was really her parent or sibling. Pictures may remove that doubt and allow the young person to proceed with healthy grieving. A mental health professional specializing in grief can help you walk through this process if necessary.

HOW DO YOU EXPLAIN CREMATION TO A CHILD? CAN THEY HANDLE IT?

Each year at The Cove, we bring in the ashes of an animal to start a discussion about cremation. The kids find it riveting; they ask a million questions. Parents are the ones who find it "disgusting" and "gross."

Clearly, kids can handle the topic of cremation with the appropriate preparation. In our culture, burial remains more common than cremation. But in other countries (Japan, England, and India, for example), cremation is the usual choice. Children in these cultures learn that that's just what happens when someone's body dies.

So how do you explain it to your child? First, you need to make sure he understands what *dead* means. If he still thinks that his dad's body can feel heat and pain, the concept of cremation will be frightening to him. It's worth spending plenty of time to make sure this concept is rooted in the young child's mind before you talk about cremation. For an older child of ten or more, review what *dead* means before broaching the topic of cremation.

Once you're sure your child has a grasp of *dead*, you might open a discussion about cremation by asking her what she thinks happens to things once they die. Using dead leaves or trees as examples, you can talk about how when plants die, they break down into little, tiny, itsy-bitsy pieces. (If you live near a woods or have a garden in your yard, look for decaying plants, trees, or leaves to illustrate your point.)

Explain that the weather—when it gets really hot or rains a lot—helps to make it all happen.

Next, discuss the fact that people's bodies break down, too, after they're dead. Some parents take this time to explain that eventually bodies become part of the earth and the earth helps plants grow. Older kids might appreciate that it's nature's way of recycling on a grand scale!

Only now is it time to introduce the topic of cremation. "Sometimes," you might say, "people choose to make this process happen faster. They take a dead body, a body that doesn't feel anything anymore, and make it really hot so that it breaks down more quickly. That way, it can become part of the earth faster. When we make a body break down by adding lots of heat, we call that process *cremation*. That's what we decided to do with your brother's body."

For young children, this may be enough of an explanation. Older kids may ask more questions, all of which you should answer factually. Again, before supplying the details, you may want to remind them that dead bodies don't feel heat or pain. But if you don't tell the truth, your child will draw one of two conclusions. Either she'll decide the truth is too horrible to talk about and concoct a potentially terrifying scene in her head. Or she'll decide that you yourself are not trustworthy and stop sharing her questions with you.

Follow your child's lead in deciding how much information to share. Answer her questions, but don't go into more detail than she asks for.

Don't know much about cremation yourself? Here's a short primer. Cremation takes place in a building called a crematorium. Inside the crematorium is a stainless steel vault called a cremation chamber or retort.

When a body is to be cremated, a worker at the crematorium carefully places the body in a casket or container, puts it inside the cremation chamber, and seals the vault tightly. He turns on the gas heat, which reaches a temperature about three times that of the highest temperature of your oven at home. It burns the body until only bone fragments are left. The process doesn't smell. There's no smoke. And from start to finish, it takes two to three hours (depending on the size of the body).

After the cremation, the operator gathers the remains (small pieces of bone) in a metal tray. These pieces are further broken down in a processor until they're the size of coarse sand or kitty litter. At this stage, the white or gray remains are called ashes.

The ashes are then sealed in a clear plastic bag and tagged for identification. Each bag weighs about five pounds and is about the same size as a five-pound bag of sugar.

Children will want to know what an urn is: it's a special box or container for the ashes. You'll need to teach them that urns can be buried, kept at home, or used to scatter the ashes in a place that's special to the family or the person who died.

DISCUSSING SPECIFIC TYPES OF DEATH

HOW DO I EXPLAIN DEATH FROM CANCER TO MY CHILD?

For young children, you can explain that everybody's body is made up of teeny, tiny parts called cells. You might say, "They're so small, you can't even see them except with a special machine called a microscope. Each cell has a special job in your body. Some cells are muscle cells and help you to be strong. Some help your heart to pump blood through your body. Some help you eat. Some help you breathe.

"But sometimes some of these cells become bad cells. They don't grow right: they grow too fast and the wrong way, and they stop the good cells in the body from doing their jobs. When that happens, we call it cancer."

Next, you can explain the particular kind of cancer you're dealing with and what kinds of problems it's causing. For example, for lung cancer, you might say, "Good lung cells help the body get air in all its different parts. But when lung cells have cancer, then the body can't breathe right. It can't get all the air it needs, and it gets really, really sick."

Finally, you can say that there are special kinds of medicine that help the good cells fight the bad cells (chemotherapy and radiation). Reassure your child that in most cases, these medicines work and people's bodies get better. "But in this case," you explain, "the bad cells were too strong. Even the special medicine couldn't help. Your mom's (or dad's or sister's) body was too sick—it couldn't work anymore, and so it died."

Older children can handle more detail, including an explanation of how cancer spreads to the rest of the body. Adolescents and many preteens can hear and understand explanations similar to those for adults, especially if someone is available to answer questions as they arise over the months that follow.

As always, it's best to be honest and to follow your child's lead. And at whatever age, make sure to let him know that cancer is not contagious, that neither you nor he has it now, and what he can do to help prevent it in his own body.

HOW DO I EXPLAIN DEATH FROM A HEART ATTACK TO MY CHILD?

Young children often understand muscles, so that's the place to start. You might say, "Inside your body, you have a special muscle called a heart muscle. It has a particular job to do: it pumps blood throughout the body. That blood carries air and food to all the rest of the parts so that they can do their own jobs like breathing and hearing and seeing. When a heart muscle isn't strong and stops pumping blood around the body, that's called a heart attack.

"Sometimes doctors and nurses can help a heart muscle start working again and keep it stronger with special medicines and exercises. But sometimes the heart is just too weak to work at all anymore. Then the body dies because it can't get food and air to the rest of the body."

Older children may understand blocked arteries, enlarged hearts, and irregular rhythms. Match your explanation to your child's ability to understand and to the extent of her questions.

As with other diseases, make sure to explain that both you and your children have strong hearts, as well as what you can do to keep them strong.

WHAT ABOUT SUICIDE? HOW CAN I EXPLAIN THAT TO MY CHILD?

It's a brave parent who openly speaks to his child about death. Talking about suicide, however, requires a special brand of courage. Its violence and its stigma may tempt you to remain silent, in the hope that your children won't find out about it.

Unfortunately, word usually leaks out. Your child sees a newspaper report or overhears a conversation. Then she may feel forced to deal with all of the terror of suicide on her own. *What really happened?* she may wonder in silence. Or he speculates to himself, *It must have been my fault. That's why no one will talk to me about it.*

Instead of remaining silent, it's much better to explain the situation honestly. Since most often clinical depression precedes suicide, you might start by explaining, "Sometimes people's brains get sick and stop working right. We call that clinical depression." Older kids might understand the concept of a chemical imbalance in the brain as well as the link between suicide and substance abuse or other forms of mental illness.

Next explain, "People with the sickness called clinical depression are really, really, really sad about almost everything just about all the time— not just a *little* sad, like all of us are some days, and not sad about some-one dying (everybody gets sad when someone dies). Sometimes people who are clinically depressed gain or lose a lot of weight. They almost never have very much energy, and usually they don't want to play or talk very much at all. Sometimes they sleep a lot or not very much at all. They may not want to be around other people, not because they don't like other people, but because the sickness called clinical depression makes them want to be alone a lot.

"Almost everybody who is sick with clinical depression can take spe-cial medicine to help their brains get better. But sometimes the brain is just too sick. Or sometimes, because a person has clinical depression, they stop taking their medicine. Then that person's brain *might* tell her to make her body stop working. When someone chooses to make their own body stop working, we call that suicide."

After this general explanation, tell the child simply, briefly, and hon-estly how his loved one killed himself. You might say he took lots and lots of pills all at once or that he shot himself with a gun. After that, you might explain, his body was too broken to be fixed, and it stopped working. His body died.

That may be enough for your child now. Later, though, he's likely to want a fuller explanation. Children of families who have experienced suicide, like adults, often want to know all the details over time. Questions haunt all the family members: What knife did he use? How deeply did she slit her wrists? Where did he get the rope? How many pills did she take?

As always, it's best to let your child decide how much he wants to know and at what time. So after the initial explanation, wait for his questions.

Many well-meaning friends and family members will try to squelch these kinds of questions. "Just leave it alone," they advise. "What's the point in bringing it all up again?" But details of the death, though profoundly troubling, can help make sense out of what seems like an unbelievable story.

Compare it to your thoughts after a car accident or the breakup of a longstanding marriage or relationship. After it happens, you don't simply brush it off saying, "Well, what's done is done." You don't simply forget about it right away. No, instead you examine the details, trying to figure out what happened, what went wrong, how, and why.

A study in the 1980s supports this phenomenon. Researchers found that 30 to 85 percent of adults who lost a spouse or child to death in a motor vehicle crash were still dealing with thoughts, memories, or feelings four to seven years later.[1] Further, most reported that they were still searching for some meaning in what had occurred. Far from being pathological in some way, working with the details is normal for kids as well as for adults.

In any case, make sure to drum home three ideas over time:

1) Suicide is the result of a disease—and nothing your child thought, wished, or did caused it. Next to the violent aspects of the death, a sense of responsibility is the problem that families of people who have killed themselves struggle with most frequently. You may need to work with your child repeatedly on his own innocence in the death.

2) Although you and he will be sad a lot after the death, his brain and yours are healthy, neither of you are clinically depressed, and you will not kill yourselves (even if grief causes you to be sad some days).

3) People with the disease of clinical depression (and other mental illnesses) can almost always be helped with medicine from a doctor.

HELP ME EXPLAIN MURDER TO MY CHILD

All of us struggle with the presence of evil in the world, so it's no wonder that we wrestle with how to explain crimes like murder to our children. Usually, it's best to stick with the facts. You might start with a cushioning statement such as "Sometimes people do bad things to people we love, things we have no control over, things that hurt them."

Follow this statement with a brief description of what happened: A man shot Daddy in his chest, his heart stopped working, and he died; Suzie's boyfriend, Tom, pushed her off a wall, and her body was so badly hurt that it couldn't be fixed and stopped working.

Of course, you'll emphasize that the murderer did a really bad thing. Because children will naturally want (and even fantasize about) revenge, it's important to stress how the police and the justice system are designed to capture and punish the murderer.

Children who experience the murder of a loved one are sometimes also angry at the person who died. They often ask why the person didn't fight harder or run away. Sometimes this question is an attempt to figure out how they themselves could avoid a similar fate. It also reflects the normal anxiety that families of homicide victims face.

You can help your child by making him feel he has some power in the face of violence. Point out any distinctions between his life and the circumstances of the murder. For example, if your child's sister was murdered in an unsafe neighborhood or by walking alone in the middle of the night, you might discuss the riskiness of her behavior and help him understand how to protect himself from those risks. If the murder was in your own neighborhood, you might add extra locks to the door, or teach him how to call the police in an emergency—in short, give him tools to help him feel more safe and more in charge of his own well-being.

Over time, like families that have experienced suicides, families of homicide victims often want to know the details: Where did the weapon come from? How long did it take to die? Again, it's common to ask such questions, even though others may not appreciate the reasons you or your children want to know the details. The answers can help you develop an interpretation that you and your family can live with. Of course, you'll need to be honest with your child, matching your answers to his ability to understand and cope with the information.

Beyond the techniques you use in the family, children who have lost someone to murder often require professional help to deal with the traumatic elements of the death and the anger that they feel.

RECENTLY, I SUFFERED A MISCARRIAGE. DO WE NEED TO TELL OUR FOUR-YEAR-OLD ABOUT IT?

Unless you miscarried very early in your pregnancy, chances are your child knew you were pregnant. You may have shared the news directly, or she may have overheard you talking to someone. Also, she may have noticed changes in you—nausea, tiredness, changes in eating and dress—and guessed something was up. Leaving her in the dark sows the seeds of mistrust and misunderstanding about the death. Beyond that, your miscarriage represents a real death to you, a loss that you need to mourn.

You may wonder, *Is it a loss to my child?* The answer is absolutely yes! Children lose a lot when an unborn child dies. Your child may miss the possibility of a new playmate. She may mourn the loss of the big sister "job." And in your grief, you're "lost" to her for a time, less available as a resource and playmate. Don't minimize her grief—or your own, for that matter. Address it as you would the other types of death described in this book.

WHAT CAN I DO TO HELP MY CHILD AFTER A DISASTER OCCURS?

Of all the grief reactions after a disaster strikes, fear is the most common. So in addition to all the measures we've already recommended to enhance a child's sense of safety, try these five as well.

First, work with your child to figure out what happened, why, and what can be done to prevent or avoid being part of a similar disaster in the future. For example, if your child experienced a hurricane, help him learn about what causes the weather patterns that spawn hurricanes. Explore together how weather forecasters predict them. Research together what to do when a hurricane approaches.

Second, discuss relevant safety rules with your child, and practice emergency procedures. Recently, when fire claimed the life of a family in a nearby community, one wise mother purchased a rope ladder for each of her children's windows and helped them practice how to escape. She installed a fire and smoke detector in each room, and each child learned how to check the detectors to make sure they were working. That check became part of each child's bedtime routine.

Third, take your child to talk to the emergency professionals (police, firefighters, emergency response personnel) who respond to a disaster. Help her learn how those professionals bring disasters under control.

Fourth, read stories about disasters similar to the one your child experienced or observed. Figure out together how the victims dealt with the tragedy. What helped? What words of wisdom do they share? Use the library's resources to find out about the floods in California or the Midwest, hurricanes in Florida and the Carolinas, or the Oklahoma City bombing.

Fifth, help your child help others. In this way, she experiences herself not only as a victim but as one who still has the ability to affect the world.

SHORTLY AFTER MY WIFE DIED, MY CHILD'S PET DIED. HE SEEMED TO GRIEVE OVER THAT MORE THAN OVER HIS MOM! WHAT DOES THIS MEAN?

Many children hold in their grief reactions, protecting themselves and their surviving parents from those scary feelings. It's not that they're not feeling—they're just not expressing it.

When a pet dies, however, the accumulated grief puts them over the top. They can't hold it in anymore, and the tears they shed reflect their deep sorrow over both the person and the pet that died.

In addition, the death of a pet itself means a great deal to a child. For many children, pets are true companions, fast friends. They provide unconditional love. They never demand that you clean up your room or finish your homework or do the dishes. They simply run and play and cuddle with you. So after the loss of a loving parent or sibling in a child's life, the loss of a pet can be devastating. As with any other death, the death of a pet needs to be understood and mourned.

You can help by supporting your child's grief. Talk about the pet, what caused the death, and how it feels to have the pet dead. Tell the stories about when the pet first joined the family, the house-training disasters, the times when the pet did something particularly funny or helpful or, on the other hand, frustrating or worrisome (like running away). Work with your child to develop and carry out a memorial or burial service for his pet.

Whatever you do, don't attempt to soften the blow by quickly buying another pet of the same kind. That simply teaches kids to avoid their losses, to distract themselves from the normal pain of grief.

As awkward as it may feel to you to spend so much energy on the death of your child's pet, know that it provides a wonderful teaching opportunity about death and grief. Often children are more open to death education at these moments than they are when people die. It's less scary, less threatening. So don't overlook the chance to educate your child during one of life's more tender moments.

DIFFERING CHILDREN, DIFFERING NEEDS

DO GIRLS MOURN DIFFERENTLY FROM BOYS? IF SO, HOW?

In his book *Children and Grief* and in his workshops, William Worden of the Child Bereavement Study notes a number of differences between boys and girls in how they grieve a parent's death.

Boys tend to talk less and act out more. More often, boys express their grief as anger or aggression. They evaluate their own behavior as worse than that of their peers and are more prone to concentration and learning difficulties in the first year after the death.

Girls tend to talk more and cry more. Girls show more anxiety in grief. They are particularly concerned about their own safety and health as well as the safety and health of the surviving parent. This can show up as physical complaints and symptoms or in family disagreements and fights.

Finally, girls remain more attached to the person who died. They may idealize the person more. They certainly are more likely to hold on to items that connect them to their loved one.

However, each child will grieve in his or her own way, based more on the specific situation than on gender. Rather than expect your child to react in a "boy's" way or a "girl's" way, you're wise to simply tend to his or her own particular style.

AT WHAT AGES ARE CHILDREN MOST VULNERABLE TO EMOTIONAL OR BEHAVIORAL PROBLEMS AFTER THE DEATH OF A FAMILY MEMBER?

In our experience, adolescence seems to be a particularly vulnerable time for children to lose a mother. This makes sense since teenagers naturally test the limits, and mothers are typically the ones to hold them in line. When a mother dies, then, adolescents may act out more. Likewise, since adolescence is generally a time of such emotional upheaval, to lose a mother is to lose the person most likely to help a teen through the ups and downs.

Beyond that, so many experts have advanced so many theories about this question that no good answer seems readily available. Much depends on the child himself: how his strengths and coping skills, at his particular age, match up with the challenges the family faces. Other influences include the role flexibility of the surviving parent, the child's relationship with the person who died, and the level of support among friends and extended family.

WHAT ABOUT A CHILD WHO IS VERY YOUNG WHEN A FAMILY MEMBER DIES?

Contrary to what most people think, even if your child never knew her mother or father, she'll mourn her loss. Just by watching other families, she'll know she's missing someone important. She may be sad or angry that her mother or father is gone. Likewise, she may feel left out of the family story because she doesn't enjoy the same family memories.

Don't wait for your child to bring up these feelings. Initiate conversations about how she might feel, always being careful not to project your own feelings onto her.

Then help her to create a history for herself. Tell her stories about her birth and childhood and how the person who died was involved. What lullabies were sung? What nicknames were used? What were her first words? What was the reaction of the person who died?

Give her concrete examples that show how much the person who died loved her. Talk about how Dad rocked her every night until she fell asleep. Tell how he snuck in every morning "just to check on her," more often than not waking her up. Relate his awkward attempts to bathe, clothe, or feed her.

Watch home videos. Look at pictures. Ask other friends and family members to reminisce with the child. Give your child pictures of the two of them together. Make sure she has something special to hold on to from the person who died.

When your child says that she remembers something that she couldn't possibly remember, don't correct her. Instead, congratulate yourself. You've made your loved one so real to her, the memories so vivid, that she is able to claim them for her own. This is likely to be comforting to her in an important way over time.

WHICH LOSS IS WORST FOR A CHILD—LOSING A FATHER, A MOTHER, OR A SIBLING?

Each of these losses brings its own brand of heartbreak. No type is worse than another. Each is simply different.

If your child's mother died, he'll miss the emotional processing that mothers so often provide. Sometimes this leads to a lowered sense of self-esteem, as children feel more and more confused, emotionally out of control, different from peers, and therefore more isolated. Mother loss may also lead to behavioral problems for some children since mothers often set behavioral boundaries and enforce house rules. Finally, after a mother dies, some young adults mourn the loss of the family historian. Moms typically remember more of the details of birth and growing up.

When fathers die, children experience more ripple effects. Because they may lose financial security, many families experience significant changes in home, school, recreation, and lifestyle.

Sometimes when a father dies, children also lose their cheerleader and coach for healthy risk-taking. As sixteen-year-old Elyse explained, "Dad was always the one to encourage me to try new sports. He believed I could make the debate team if I wanted. He thought it'd be great for me to spend a semester in South America on a Rotary exchange program. Mom worried more. Dad convinced her I'd be okay."

Many parents want to know if children who lose their same-sex parent (a girl losing her mom or a boy losing his dad—what researchers call *gender match*) differ from children who lose the parent of the opposite gender (*gender mismatch*). Unfortunately, there's little research on the subject. Again, most of what we know comes from the Child Bereavement Study:

1) The gender of the parent who died defines the experience for children much more than gender match or mismatch.

2) Children who lost a same-sex parent tend to identify more with the parent who died. They are more likely to take on their traits and habits and to surround themselves with that parent's belongings.

3) During the first year after the death, children who lost a same-sex parent tend to see themselves as more mature than other kids.

4) Similarly, during the first year after the death of the opposite-sex parent, children tend to worry more about the health and well-being of the surviving parent. These children themselves also seem to experience more health concerns early on.

After a sibling dies, many children feel more alone because everyone seems to be focused on the child who died. Additionally, they may feel overprotected by parents or the need to take on roles, personality traits, or activities of the person who died.

Fortunately, many children who lose a sibling also grow in self-esteem, maturity, and a sense of moral values. And many families believe that, in the long run, they are closer, value each other more, and have refocused their priorities to be less achievement-oriented and more centered on the simple things of life.

Gender plays a role in the loss of a sibling as well. The loss of a brother or sister seems to affect girls more than boys. This is especially true for adolescent girls, who according to the Child Bereavement Study showed higher levels of anxiety, depression, and attention difficulties than adolescent boys who lost parents. In contrast, boys experienced more depression and anxiety when a parent died than when a sibling died.

HOW WOULD YOU CHANGE YOUR APPROACH IF YOU'RE WORKING WITH SOMEONE WHO IS MENTALLY RETARDED?

If the child in your care is mentally retarded, his grief process may be affected in five primary ways. First, if he is profoundly mentally retarded, his intellectual capacity may limit his ability to understand the meaning of the death. But if he is mildly mentally retarded, he will probably be able to grasp the concept of death and its irreversibility— it may simply take more time for his concrete experience to develop into mental understanding. For example, he may need more than a few months to realize that the person who died is not returning. Only through the long-term experience of "gone-ness" might he be able to grasp the irreversibility of death.

Adults who discount the feelings of a grieving mentally retarded child because she can't currently understand what's happening make a huge mistake. Simply put, you don't need to understand in order to feel. Instead, understanding acts as one tool to help people cope with the feelings they're encountering. Helping your mentally retarded child to gradually understand the experience provides a strong support to her over time.

Second, once your child understands the concepts surrounding death, his more limited verbal skills may force him to struggle more than other kids with expressing his feelings. Sometimes this shows up as even more repetitive speech and behavior patterns than you may be used to. Rather than interpreting this repetition as "more of the same," it may help to realize that he may be trying to master some difficult concepts and feelings without all the verbal and cognitive skills to help. His repetition may be his way of continuing to work on something he feels he's stuck on.

You can help your child compensate for his more limited verbal skills by providing him with alternative ways of expressing his grief. Music, drawing and art, physical exertion—all of these work particularly well in helping the mentally retarded release their emotions.

Participating in simple rituals (taking flowers to the graveside, for example) provides powerful emotional outlets as well. One young woman we know developed her own nightly ritual after both her parents died in a car crash. "Every night I take out two candles," she said, "and I light one for Dad and one for Mom. Then I just sit there for a while. It makes me sad, but it also makes me feel close to them, and I know they're looking down on me and helping me figure out what to do during the day."

Third, if your child is mentally retarded, the realization of his own dependence may prove more frightening after a death. If the person who died was a significant caretaker in his life, he may feel particularly vulnerable and defenseless.

For these reasons, your child will benefit even more strongly than other children from your presence, from routine and predictability, from your ability to tell him what to expect, and from your reassurance that he will be cared for in the concrete ways that concern him.

Fourth, because your child's social skills may be more limited, she may not enjoy the broad base of support that so often helps children through crises. Especially if you yourself are grieving, you may need to more actively solicit others to help her process her grief. This holds true especially if your child, like so many folks with mental retardation, tends to respond in a positive, happy manner to whatever is said to her. Often adults who see such behavior in a grieving mentally retarded child conclude, "She's doing fine! She must not really get it, or maybe she's not really grieving because she seems so happy." If this is the case, you need to educate your child's holding community to look at her behavior instead of her facial or verbal expressions and to work with her to express her grief.

Fifth, the smaller your child's social world, the more powerful any single death may be. Even the death of a seemingly less important person in his life may hit him more profoundly simply because his world is so small: each person, no matter how distant, may provide some anchor for her, some comfortable corner in your child's world.

This means you need to be more aware than other caregivers of the losses your child experiences, losses due not only to death but to changes or moves by teachers, aides, cafeteria people, neighbors, and others. Each loss, from whatever source, needs to be appropriately mourned, or together they can mount up quickly, overwhelming your child.

Overall, then, your mentally retarded child can cope with death just as well as any other child. It simply takes more awareness of his uniqueness and his life story, as well as more long-term support for his grieving process.

DOES LOSING A FAMILY MEMBER TO DEATH MEAN MY CHILD WILL SUFFER FROM MENTAL ILLNESS?

Despite years of research, no consistent link has been found between childhood grief and any specific mental illness. But in some cases, where biology coincides with negative viewpoints (about self, the world, the future) following a death, an adult who has experienced young death may be more prone to depression. Sometimes, too, a traumatic death or traumatizing circumstances after a death can promote anxiety issues in children that last into adulthood.

Some grieving children or adolescents end up using drugs or alcohol in an attempt to cope with their grief. Many will eventually give up the practice and move on to more healthy coping styles, but some may end up with long-term difficulties.

Other grieving adolescents may attempt to assert control in an otherwise chaotic grief situation by strictly controlling their weight through dieting, exercising, and the like. Very little research has been conducted in this area, but it may be that in extreme cases, such coping attempts could coincide with an eating disorder.

Childhood grief is not linked to any other adult mental disorders. As you can surmise from the above discussion, the best way to help your child avoid future problems with depression, anxiety, substance abuse, and eating disorders is to follow the suggestions outlined in this book.

YOU PLACE SUCH AN EMPHASIS ON HOW WELL THE SURVIVING PARENT FUNCTIONS AFTER A MAJOR LOSS. WHAT IF I'M REALLY NOT FUNCTIONING WELL? HOW CAN I MAKE SURE MY KIDS ARE OKAY?

You've identified one of the key variables in how children cope with a death in the family: how well their parents cope. But gauging the quality of parents' functioning remains the tough part of the equation.

At any given time, grief looks chaotic, numbing, traumatic, overwhelming. Many people feel they're going crazy—and their friends and family fear they're right! But before you judge how well or poorly you're coping, make sure that what you're seeing aren't just the lows of normal grief. Read books about grief. Talk to others who have been through it. Compare notes.

Next, be certain that you're not mistaking a different personal style or values for poor functioning. Three months after her sister died, Carla called about her brother-in-law, Bryce. "I'm worried," she said. "Every time I go there, I find the beds unmade, the clean clothes laying heaped in a basket, and the dishes heaped in the sink. If this is how he's caring for the house, how's he ever caring for the kids?"

Bryce saw it differently. "Since my wife died," he explained, "there are only a few things that really matter to me—mostly my kids. When I get home from work, I focus on spending time with them. We eat, do homework, play a game, or watch TV. Sometimes we go to Scouts, a sports practice, or a music recital. If I get to the dishes or laundry, that's an extra. Frankly, I don't really care. That's what I learned from this experience: It's only the people in my life that count."

Finally, look for patterns in your behavior. As long as the kids are cared for, don't worry about one or two days of sitting on a couch and staring out the window. You need to be concerned only when your kids are clearly left to their own devices, when they're not getting what they need, or when the sadness, withdrawal, anger, or nonfunctioning at work or home continues persistently and unrelentingly day after day, week after week.

Let's say you've carefully evaluated what you're experiencing, and you're still questioning how you are doing. What can you do? First, ask someone to help you find a mental health professional who specializes in grief. Don't expect to do it all yourself. Chances are you just don't have the extra energy to call around and identify resources. If you wait until you do it, getting help may be postponed indefinitely.

Next, suggest concrete ways that your family members and friends can provide structure and support for the family while you get back on your feet.

Finally, open up discussions with your children. Ask them what they need. Let them know you're available to help, as are others. Teach them to call members of the holding community as necessary.

THOUGHTS FROM DOWN
THE ROAD

As we finish this book, our youngest child, Kate, is finishing her first semester at New York University. Just yesterday we drove into the city to visit her, and on our way home, a wave of memories hit us.

We had moved Kate into the dorm on a hot, sticky day this past August, trudging with box after box up eleven flights of stairs with dozens of other panting parents. Finally finished, tired and sweaty, we hugged her good-bye and headed back to the empty nest in Connecticut. We hit the border and realized, with a dawning sense of awe, that we'd made it! After ten years of raising three grieving kids, all of them were launched in positive directions. Most important, they seemed happy.

It didn't always seem that it would work out that way. We remember more than one night of lying awake in bed in a darkened room, troubled about lingering moods or the latest stunt one of them had pulled. We worried. We brainstormed. We cried. And then we did something. Sometimes that something worked. Sometimes it didn't, and we were back to where we started.

More than once, we looked at photographs of the kids taken before Mary died, and we compared those faces with the faces we saw at the dinner table each evening. We wondered, *Will we ever see real, true joy in our kids again?* We lived with real doubt.

Now we feel a sense of accomplishment. Our oldest, Pat, works at a bank in Boston by day and plays music by night (and is in love with a wonderful young woman). Our middle child, Greg, attends college in Boston, working toward a career in business. And Kate, as we've mentioned, is studying and exploring and growing in New York.

We certainly weren't perfect parents. (Our kids could tell you the specifics, we're sure.) And looking back, even we wince at the mistakes we made out of ignorance or sheer fatigue. But we did *enough*—enough to get them back on track to satisfying, contributing lives.

Nestled next to that feeling of accomplishment, of course, is a perennial sorrow: sorrow that they had to grow up without Mary—sorrow that she'll never be here to share all the good times we believe lie ahead. What more can we say about that? It's a hole no one will ever really fill.

Finally, we feel profound gratitude. We're grateful that we all made it through. We're grateful to all the folks who helped us and who helped our children—our family; our friends and, equally important, *their* friends; teachers and mentors; and countless others. And we're grateful for the opportunity to have made a difference in the world through these three very precious individual lives. Parenting these three kids didn't always make us happy, but at the end of our lives, we're convinced we'll look back and say, "That was the most meaningful work we've ever done, the best way we could ever have spent our lives."

We share our story and this book with you out of the conviction that if we can make it, you can too. We've lived it, and so we know: After darkness comes dawn; after winter, spring; after death, new life—a new life that's feeble perhaps, at first, but there after all, certainly there.

Jim and Mary Ann
Fall 1999

SUGGESTED READING

WE ASKED FOLKS FROM THE DOUGY CENTER IN PORTLAND, Oregon, and The Center for Grieving Children in Portland, Maine, for books that they would recommend to parents and other caregivers working with grieving children. In addition to our own recommendations, here are some of their favorites.

FOR AGES 2–5:

Brown, Laurie K. M. *When Dinosaurs Die: A Guide to Understanding Death.* Boston: Little Brown & Co., 1998.

Brown, Margaret W. *The Dead Bird.* New York: HarperTrophy, 1995.

Mellonie, Brian, and Robert Ingpen. *Lifetimes: The Beautiful Way to Explain Death to Children.* New York: Bantam Books, 1983.

Viorst, Judith. *The Tenth Good Thing About Barney.* New York: Atheneum, 1971.

FOR AGES 6–9:

Cohn, Janice. *I Had a Friend Named Peter: Talking to Children About the Death of a Friend.* New York: William Morrow & Co., 1987.

Saltzman, David. *The Jester Has Lost His Jingle.* Palos Verdes Estates, CA: The Jester Co., Inc. 1995.

Varley, Susan. *Badger's Parting Gifts.* New York: Lothrop, Lee & Shepard Books, 1984.

Vigna, Judith. *Saying Goodbye to Daddy.* Morton Grove, IL: Albert Whitman & Co., 1991.

FOR AGES 10–12:

Babbitt, Natalie. *The Eyes of the Amaryllis.* New York: Farrar, Straus & Giroux, 1986.

Krementz, Jill. *How It Feels When a Parent Dies.* New York: Knopf, 1981.

Little, Jean. *Home from Far.* Boston: Little Brown & Co., 1965.

MacLachlan, Patricia. *Cassie Binegar.* New York: HarperTrophy, 1987.

McLean, Susan. *Pennies for the Piper.* Sunburst, 1993.

O'Toole, Donna. *Aarvy Aardvark Finds Hope.* Burnsville, NC: Mountain Rainbow Publications, 1988.

Paterson, Katherine. *Bridge to Terabithia.* New York: HarperTrophy, 1987.

Powell, E. Sandy. *Geranium Morning.* Minneapolis: Carolrhoda Books, 1990.

Rofes, Eric E., ed. *The Kids' Book About Death and Dying.* Boston: Little Brown & Co., 1985.

FOR TEENS:

Deaver, Julie R. *Say Goodnight, Gracie.* New York: HarperTrophy, 1989.

Ellsworth, Barry. *The Little Stream.* Los Angeles: Bonneville Worldwide Entertainment, 1995.

Grollman, Earl. *Straight Talk About Death for Teenagers: How to Cope with Losing Someone You Love.* Boston: Beacon Press, 1993.

Grollman, Earl, and Max Malikow. *Living When a Young Friend Commits Suicide: Or Even Starts Talking About It.* Boston: Beacon Press, 1999.

Krementz, Jill. *How It Feels When a Parent Dies.* New York: Knopf, 1981.

O'Toole, Donna. *Facing Change: Falling Apart and Coming Together Again in the Teen Years.* Burnsville, NC: Mountain Rainbow Publications, 1995.

FOR ADULTS HELPING CHILDREN:

Fitzgerald, Helen. *The Grieving Child: A Parent's Guide.* New York: Fireside, 1992.

Goldman, Linda. *Life and Loss: A Guide to Helping Grieving Children.* Levittown, PA: Taylor & Francis, 1994.

Grollman, Earl. *Bereaved Children and Teens: A Support Guide for Parents and Professionals.* Boston: Beacon Press, 1996.

Grollman, Earl. *Talking About Death: A Dialogue Between Parent and Child.* Boston: Beacon Press, 1991.

Harris, Maxine. *The Loss That Is Forever: The Lifelong Impact of the Early Death of a Mother or Father.* New York: Plume, 1996.

Jarratt, Claudia J. *Helping Children Cope with Separation and Loss.* Cambridge, MA: Harvard Common Press, 1994.

Schaefer, Dan, and Christine Lyons. *How Do We Tell the Children?: A Step-by-Step Guide for Helping Children Two to Ten Cope When Someone Dies.* New York: Newmarket Press, 1993.

Schuurman, Donna. *Helping Children Cope with Death.* Portland, OR: The Dougy Center, 1998.

Silverman, Phyllis R. *Never Too Young to Know: Death in Children's Lives.* New York: Oxford University Press, 1999.

Worden, J. William. *Children and Grief: When a Parent Dies.* New York: Guilford Press, 1996.

FOR ADULT GRIEVERS:

Fine, Carla. *No Time to Say Goodbye: Surviving the Suicide of a Loved One.* New York: Doubleday, 1997.

Grollman, Earl. *Living When a Loved One Has Died.* New York: Beacon Press, 1977.

Kushner, Harold. *When Bad Things Happen to Good People.* New York: Avon Books, 1988.

Lewis, C. S. *A Grief Observed.* San Francisco: Harper, 1995.

Rando, Therese R. *How to Go On Living When Someone You Love Has Died*. New York: Bantam Books, 1988.

Sanders, Catherine. *Surviving Grief and Learning to Live Again*. New York: John Wiley & Sons, 1987.

Tatelbaum, Judy. *The Courage to Grieve*. New York: HarperCollins, 1980.

SUGGESTIONS FOR SCHOOL PERSONNEL AND HEALTH CARE PROFESSIONALS

TIPS FOR SCHOOL PERSONNEL

School personnel interact with grieving children at least as much as parents, and in some cases, more. Often school is the place that kids feel most safe, outside of their own home. As such, schools are in an excellent position to help in these concrete ways.

RECOGNIZE THAT CRISIS INTERVENTION PLANS MEET ONLY THE NEEDS OF THE MOMENT

Many grief-related reactions begin surfacing months after the death itself. By then, crisis intervention plans are ancient history. To support kids who have lost someone close, schools need plans that reach out for a year or two, especially for children at risk for complicated mourning.

Some schools argue, "That's not our role! Our job is education." We respond by comparing grief support to federally subsidized school lunch programs. In the 1960s, educators realized that hungry kids don't learn. They don't have the mental energy. So, too, with grieving kids. They're so focused on their grief that, at any given moment, they may not be able to learn. But if skilled educators and pupil support personnel can help grieving kids learn to cope with their grief, then teachers can teach and students can learn.

CREATE SAFETY THROUGH MAINTAINING PREDICTABILITY AND CONSISTENTLY ENFORCING RULES

Kind-hearted school personnel who cut kids slack because they're grieving do them no favors. Kids need routine, predictability, and boundaries to anchor them in a world that feels suddenly chaotic and frightening. It's important to be sensitive to grieving kids, but they should be held accountable to the same interpersonal standards as their peers.

PROVIDE OPPORTUNITIES FOR VENTING EARLY IN THE DAY

If a grieving child in your school appears anxious or angry, give her a chance to get it out physically early on so that she can move through the day concentrating on her schoolwork rather than her grief. If possible, move gym to an earlier time slot. Have him clap the erasers together, aggressively and quickly, whether they need cleaning or not. Move art class to earlier in the day, and implement a project in clay that requires working the clay assertively. When normal classroom activities provide no outlets, encourage the social work office to stock old phone books for ripping, paper cups or bubble wrap for stomping, pillows for punching. Introduce the child to the folks in the social work office, and help her feel comfortable accessing these activities.

EDUCATE YOURSELF ABOUT GRIEF IN CHILDHOOD

Learn what the experience of grief is like for the children in your care. Explore how you can help on an informal basis, in your everyday interactions. Consult *Guiding Your Child Through Grief* and the resources listed in Appendix A.

Importantly, use accurate language and especially the *"d"* words: *Death, Died, Dying*. Practice using these words in conversation instead of phrases like *lost* or *passed away*, which may be more comfortable for you but can cause confusion in younger minds and may signal to older ones that you yourself are uncomfortable talking about the subject.

WEAVE DEATH EDUCATION INTO THE NORMAL CURRICULUM

In preschools and kindergartens, use the change of seasons to talk about what death means. Autumn leaves are dead, not alive. They don't work anymore. Talk about the cycle of seasons, explaining that everything that is living dies, and once something is dead, it can't return to life again. Even if no one in your class experienced a death, such information will prepare them for the time when it happens to them. And if you have a grieving child in your midst, he or she needs such information in order to process their grief.

In older grades, use guidance and health classes to talk about normal grief reactions, just as you presently use them to talk about sex education, smoking, cancer prevention, and self-esteem. Like adults, kids often worry that they're going crazy. They hesitate to express their grief for fear that it will take them over.

Some teachers with grieving children in their classrooms have used social studies classes to talk about funeral and mourning practices. That gives them an entry into talking about grief itself. Others, with the same purpose, have visited funeral homes as part of a career exploration module. Language teachers might explore death customs or death-related holidays like El Dia de los Muertes. Endless opportunities exist for opening up the topic. Use your imagination.

EDUCATE YOUR CLASSES ABOUT FEELINGS

Knowing that feelings are neither good or bad, that they just indicate how we interpret what happens in life, partially prepares children for grief when it happens. Validating anger, fear, relief, and guilt as normal (if not realistic) can give permission for grieving kids to vent those feelings when they arise.

IF A CHILD IN THE SCHOOL DIES, MEMORIALIZE HIM

Don't simply rearrange the desks in hopes that the kids will forget he ever died. It won't happen. All they will learn is that when you die, you're not important enough to remember.

Instead, keep his desk unoccupied for a few months or the rest of the year. Let the kids decorate it. Invite them to take turns each week bringing in a flower to set on the desk. Create a memory wall of blank paper on which kids can write notes to the child who died or draw pictures of their memories. Plant a garden in his name. Dedicate a school concert or play to him.

Remember, too, that a child's death may affect more than those in her immediate classroom. Other children in the same grade may have been in class with her in prior years. Other teachers taught her. And even children in other grades may have known her through church, sports, play groups, or other community activities.

CONSTRUCT ASSIGNMENTS SO THAT GRIEVING KIDS CAN GIVE EXPRESSION TO THEIR OWN EXPERIENCE

If you have a grieving child in your classroom, assign reading that deals healthfully with grief. Create essay questions that ask him to plumb his grief experience as well as practice his writing skills. Foster ongoing connections with the person who died through show-and-tell activities or essays about his own personal heroes.

If you teach music, explore percussion! Create drums. Play them. Have a classroom drumming event. If you teach art, use techniques that encourage self-expression. Art therapy books and manuals offer hundreds of possible activities. If you're a physical education teacher, work on sports that require significant physical exertion as opposed to finesse. Weight training, running, boxing, and the martial arts have been successfully used to work through tough emotional situations. "When I'm running up a steep hill," said one griever, "I feel like I'm pulling up all the anger out of me. Sometimes I think, 'If I can survive this hill, I can survive my grief.' "

Be careful about holidays. Grieving kids struggle with activities such as creating cards for Mother's Day and Valentine's Day or writing essays about what they're thankful for at Thanksgiving. While these activities may look like they're simply helping children face their grief, too often grieving kids end up feeling different and embarrassed. Activities that help are those that invite kids to explore their grief experience, at whatever depth they're comfortable with. Forcing the issue rarely works.

OFFER EXTRA HELP IF GRIEF INTERFERES WITH LEARNING

Kids rarely suffer long-term learning consequences after a death. Periodically, though, they may wrestle with attention difficulties that can affect their academic performance. In your classroom, these difficulties may show up as distractibility, daydreaming or staring off into space, not working on the task at hand, memorization difficulties, struggling with completing multistep projects, restlessness, procrastination, disorganization, difficulty following directions, or decreased reading comprehension.

Rather than dramatically reduce your expectations (and leave the child vulnerable to feelings of inadequacy on top of her feelings of grief), utilize these techniques:

- Reduce the length of each assignment.

- Break up tasks into small, specific steps.

- Allow extra time for completion.

- Work one on one with the student to focus his attention.

- Use your physical proximity to bring the child back to current tasks. Use a gentle touch on the shoulder or a secret signal to remind the child to refocus.

- Encourage group work. Other children may be better able to keep a grieving child engaged in the work at hand.

• Reward attention and the timely completion of tasks. Increase the frequency of positive reinforcements.

• Give the child some time each day to express her grief so that she need not focus on suppressing it.

COMMUNICATE WITH PARENTS AND REFER TO OUTSIDE RESOURCES AS APPROPRIATE

Parents of grieving children usually welcome the thoughts and observations of teachers. It helps them decipher their children's grief. When grief becomes complicated, they appreciate guidance on where to turn. Even if they're aware of competent mental health professionals, they hunger for the names of those who have experience working with normal kids overwhelmed by grief. If you yourself don't know of resources, contact the social work departments of your local hospice, children's hospital, or grief support center.

TIPS FOR HEALTH CARE PROFESSIONALS

Like teachers, police officers, and parents, nurses, pediatricians, and other health care professionals enjoy a position of power in the minds of many children. So what you say (or don't say) becomes the definitive truth.

Two years after Mary took a few irregular breaths and died of heart failure, our Kate experienced difficulty breathing. We suspected that Mary's death and Kate's breathing problems might be linked, but we decided to reassure Kate with a checkup. Her pediatrician performed the appropriate tests, assured Kate that her breathing was normal, and gave her a plastic tube that enabled her to test her own lung capacity whenever she was concerned. Kate never complained of breathing difficulties again, even after repeated bouts with seasonal allergies!

As a pediatrician or nurse, your opportunities for support are limited. Nonetheless, they are crucial. Here's what you can do.

EDUCATE YOURSELF ABOUT GRIEF IN CHILDREN

Learn what the symptoms look like, what language is best to use. Read *Guiding Your Child Through Grief* and basic resources listed in Appendix A.

ASSUME THAT THE GRIEVING CHILD IN YOUR CARE HAS QUESTIONS ABOUT WHY AND HOW THE PERSON DIED

Often adults don't tell children the whole story (because they don't know how or fear the consequences), or they use language and concepts beyond the child's capacity to understand. The next time you see the child, take the initiative. Don't ask if he understands what happened. Like the rest of us, he's likely to say yes only because he hates appearing stupid. Find out what happened beforehand, then tell the child you'd like to talk about how the person died. Explain what you know in accurate but child-friendly language. Use the *d* words—*dead, dying, death*—instead of phrases like *passed away* or *lost,* which may be confusing to young minds. Don't dodge the tough issues. Your patient is looking to you for the truth.

REASSURE YOUR PATIENT THAT HE'S HEALTHY

If you can, talk about what evidence you have that your patient doesn't share the condition of the person who died. And if you have permission to talk to his parent's own personal physician, check out his parent's health so that you can reassure the child that his parent is likely to live for a long time. Just don't overpromise.

After Moira's dad died, her pediatrician reassured her that everyone else in her family was safe. "Don't worry," he said. "God knows what we can handle, and he wouldn't let it happen to you twice." Nine months later, when her aunt and uncle died in a car crash, Moira sobbed behind closed doors. Her mom went to hold her, and Moira blurted out, "The doctor said this wouldn't happen. Why is God doing this to me? What am I doing wrong?"

EXPLAIN THAT MOST PEOPLE HAVE LOTS OF QUESTIONS WHEN SOMEONE DIES

Note that sometimes questions arise right away, sometimes later on. Ask the child which ones she might have right now. Over the years, touch on the subject periodically. Since kids often hesitate to discuss the death in front of surviving parents, ask the parent to wait in the lobby. Continue to invite your patient to discuss what she's wondering about now. Remember, children reprocess death as their intellectual capacities develop. New questions will surface over time.

MAKE IT PART OF YOUR PRACTICE TO MONITOR GRIEVING KIDS FOR THE SIGNS OF COMPLICATED MOURNING

Refer to Chapter 10 of *Guiding Your Child Through Grief* for indications that a child is struggling more profoundly with the consequences of a death. Consider emotional causes for physical symptoms when no other cause seems apparent, and refer to grief experts as appropriate.

NOTES

CHAPTER 2: HOW CHILDREN GRIEVE

1. David Schonfeld, M.D. "Talking with Children About Death," *Journal of Pediatric Health Care 7* (1993): 269–274.

2. J. William Worden, *Children and Grief: When a Parent Dies* (New York: The Guilford Press, 1996). *Children and Grief* presents the findings of the Child Bereavement Study, research conducted by Drs. Steven Nickman, Phyllis Silverman, and J. William Worden among seventy Boston-area families with children ages 6 to 17 who experienced the death of a parent. Funded in part by the National Institute of Mental Health, the Child Bereavement Study is one of the very few published studies to track grieving children over time and compare their behavior and attitudes to those of non-grieving children. J. William Worden holds academic appointments at Harvard Medical School and the Rosemead School of Psychology. Throughout *Guiding Your Child Through Grief*, we draw on the statistical findings of the Child Bereavement Study, which can be found in *Children and Grief*.

3. For more information on Compassionate Friends, please call 630/990-0010 or visit the website (www.compassionatefriends.org).

CHAPTER 3: WHAT GRIEVING CHILDREN FEEL AND DO

1. Worden, *Children and Grief*, p. 63.

2. W. D. Rees, "The Hallucinations of Widowhood," *British Medical Journal* 4 (October 2): 37–41.

3. These statistics are from the website of the American Foundation for Suicide Prevention (www.aafsp.org).

4. Russell Baker, *Growing Up* (New York: New American Library, 1991), p. 60.

CHAPTER 4: HOW GRIEF AFFECTS FAMILIES

1. Murray Bowen, "Family Reaction to Death," in P. Guerin (ed.) *Family Therapy* (New York: Gardner, 1976): 335–348.

CHAPTER 5: FIVE CHALLENGES OF A GRIEVING CHILD

1. Personal communication with Therese Rando during a workshop entitled Advanced Treatment Protocols for Complicated Mourning held in Warwick, Rhode Island, September 1996.

CHAPTER 6: HOW TO COMMUNICATE WITH A GRIEVING CHILD

1. Russell Baker, *Growing Up,* p. 60.

2. William Kroen, *Helping Children Cope with the Loss of a Loved One* (Minneapolis: Free Spirit, 1998), p. 34.

3. Thomas Gordon, *P.E.T.: Parent Effectiveness Training* (New York: David McKay, 1970).

4. Gordon, *P.E.T.,* p. 46. For more practice and further information on this style of communication, we strongly recommend *How to Talk So Kids Will Listen and Listen So Kids Will Talk* by Adele Faber and Elaine Mazlish (New York: Avon, 1980). It is written in an informal, easy-to-understand format with examples and exercises to practice your skills.

5. Maxine Harris, *The Loss That Is Forever: The Lifelong Impact of the Early Death of a Mother or Father* (New York: Plume, 1996), p. 22. This book is based on her interviews with sixty-six men and women aged 24 to 66, all of whom experienced the death of a parent before the age of 18. It is an extensive look at the long-term impact of the early death of a mother or father on such issues as identity formation; intimate relationships in adulthood; parenting; and issues of mortality and meaning-making. Dr. Harris is a clinical psychologist and co-director of Community Connections, a community-based mental health agency in Washington, D.C.

6. Quoted in Jennifer Cadoff, "How Kids Grieve," *Parents,* April 1993, p. 144.

7. Dan Schaefer, *How Do We Tell The Children?* (New York: Newmarket Press, 1993), p. 142.

8. T. Berry Brazelton, *Families: Crisis and Caring* (Reading, MA: Perseus, 1989), p. 73.

CHAPTER 7: HOLDING COMMUNITIES: CREATING AND USING THEM

1. Therese Rando, *Treatment of Complicated Mourning* (Champaign, IL: Research Press, 1993), p. 496.

2. Hope Edelman, *Motherless Daughters: The Legacy of Loss* (Reading, MA: Addison Wesley, 1994), pp. 107–108.

3. Edelman, *Motherless Daughters,* p. 186.

4. *Inside Fernside,* Vol. 13, No. 4 (July/August 1999).

CHAPTER 8: DEALING WITH HOLIDAYS AND OTHER SPECIAL DAYS

1. Evan Imber-Black, "Using Ritual in Grief Work," *Grief Letter*, No. 4 (Guilford, CT: New England Center for Loss and Transition, 1997).

CHAPTER 9: TEENS AND GRIEF

1. Ilene C. Noppe and Lloyd D. Noppe, "Ambiguity in Adolescent Understandings of Death," *Handbook of Adolescent Death and Bereavement*, David E. Balk and Charles A. Corr, eds. (New York: Springer, 1996), p. 36.

2. John B. Mordock and William Van Ornum, *Crisis Counseling with Children and Adolescents: A Guide for Nonprofessional Counselors* (New York: Continuum, 1990), p. 76.

3. Leslie Balmer and Stephen Fleming, "Bereavement in Adolescence," *Handbook of Adolescent Death and Bereavement*, David E. Balk and Charles A. Corr, eds. (New York: Springer, 1996), p. 152.

4. David Elkind, *All Grown Up and No Place To Go: Teenagers in Crisis* (Cambridge, MA: Perseus Press, 1997).

CHAPTER 10: WHEN GRIEF GOES WRONG

1. Rando, *Treatment of Complicated Mourning*, p. 194.

CHAPTER 11: LONG-TERM EFFECTS OF CHILDHOOD GRIEF

1. Rosie O'Donnell, quoted in Gail Shisier, "Motherhood, new talk show take Rosie O'Donnell's life on a different course," May 31, 1996 (c) Knight-Ridder Newspapers.

2. "Transformative Grief—Loss as an Opportunity for Growth," *Grief Letter*, Vol. 2, No. 1 (Guilford, CT: New England Center for Loss and Transition, winter 1996).

3. R. S. Smith and E. E. Werner, *Overcoming the Odds: High Risk Children from Birth to Adulthood* (Ithaca, New York: Cornell University Press, 1992).

4. The quotes in this chapter are from an interview Mary Ann Emswiler conducted with Maxine Harris for the article "Will My Kids Be OK?," *Grief Letter*, No. 1 (Guilford, CT: New England Center for Loss and Transition, 1997). See also Maxine's book *The Loss That Is Forever: The Lifelong Impact of the Early Death of a Mother or Father*, cited in the Chapter 6 notes.

5. Quoted in Edelman, *Motherless Daughters*, p. xix.

6. Gilbert A. Harrison, *The Enthusiast: A Life of Thornton Wilder* (New York: Fromm International Publishing Corporation, 1986), p. 8.

7. Quoted in Edelman, *Motherless Daughters*, p. 261.

8. Marvin Eisenstadt, A. Haynal, P. Rentchnick, and P. Senarclens, *Parental Loss and Achievement* (Madison, CT: International Universities Press, 1989).

9. Edelman, *Motherless Daughters*, pp. 274–275.

CHAPTER 12: STEPPARENTING A GRIEVING CHILD

1. Patricia Papernow, *Becoming a Stepfamily: Patterns of Development in Remarried Families* (Hillsdale, NJ: Analytic Press, 1993). This book is based on Dr. Papernow's

extensive interviews with more than one hundred stepfamilies as well as her extensive research and counseling with stepfamilies. The book explores the stages of stepfamily development and intervention possibilities for mental health professionals working with stepfamilies.

2. For more information on the Stepfamily Association of America, see the website (www.stepfam.org).

3. Stephen King, *Bag of Bones* (New York: Scribner, 1998), p. 111.

CHAPTER 14: FREQUENTLY ASKED QUESTIONS

1. D. Lechman, A. Williams, and C. Wortman, "Long-term effects of losing a spouse or child in a motor vehicles crash," *Journal of Personality and Social Psychology*, 57: 218–231.

ACKNOWLEDGMENTS

So many people own a piece of this book. In particular, we'd like to thank:

All those who taught us about children and grief through their professional work, especially Phyllis Silverman and William Worden.

Our colleague and friend, Terrie Rando, who encouraged us to write this book and who inspired us by her incredible amount of knowledge and experience in the field.

The pioneer and guru of the field of children's grief, Earl Grollman, for his support and friendship from the start.

The grieving children and families of The Cove, who hold our hearts every day by courageously sharing their stories, giving of themselves to each other, and choosing life.

Renée McIntyre, co-founder of The Cove, who dreamt with us when all we had were blank easel pages and hearts full of ideas.

All the leaders of children's grief groups across the country, especially Donna Schuurman of The Dougy Center in Portland, Oregon; Rachel Burrell and Barb Coe at Fernside Center in Cincinnati; and Gail Cinelli at Portland, Maine's Center for Grieving Children. It's your work on which we've built.

Our colleagues in children's grief and grief programs across the country, who pushed us to keep going by reminding us of the great need for this book, especially Dr. David Schonfeld of Yale New Haven Hospital; Dr. Laura Basili at Children's Hospital in Boston; Gabbi DeWitt at

Cedar Valley Hospice; Mary Keane at Mary's Place; Linda Cunningham at Teen Age Grief; Danny Mize and Charlotte Burrough of The Kid's Place; Becky Byrne at the St. Louis Bereavement Center; Ben Wolfe at St. Mary's Grief Support Center; Debra Collins at Comfort for Kids; Steve Merwin at Courageous Kids; Stefanie Norris at Willow House in Lincolnshire, Illinois; Barbara Weiner and Mark Dubek at The Garden in Northampton, Massachusetts; Gail Hanson in Champlain Valley, Vermont; Andre de Lisser at The Den in Greenwich, Connecticut; and all of our colleagues at The WARM Place in Texas, Ann Arbor Hospice, Children to Children in Tucson, Erin's House in Ft. Wayne, The Caring Place in Pittsburgh, Ele's Place in Lansing, Michigan, Bo's Place in Houston, and The Front Porch in Atlanta.

Our editor, Robin Michaelson, and our agent, Betsy Amster, who both believed in the value of this book and then worked to make it happen. We hope you know how many lives you've touched.

Mary Riley Emswiler, Barb Emswiler, and Bill Emswiler, who, by their deaths, taught us more than we ever wanted to know about grief and who left behind the young people who inspired this book.

INDEX

ABOUT THE AUTHORS

JIM EMSWILER holds master's degrees in counseling and education. He is the executive director of the New England Center for Loss and Transition and co-founder of The Cove, a support program for grieving children and their families. He speaks nationally on the subject of grief in both adults and in children. Before entering the bereavement field, he worked in publishing. Jim's first wife, Mary, died at the age of thirty-nine, leaving him with three children aged 8, 11, and 14.

MARY ANN EMSWILER is a licensed mental health counselor with master's degrees in clinical psychology and pastoral studies. She co-founded The Cove and managed its growth throughout the state of Connecticut. In 1997, she organized the National Symposium on Children's Grief Support, pulling together more than 100 professionals nationwide who work in children's grief. Before working in bereavement, she held executive-level marketing jobs with Fortune 500 companies. After Jim's first wife, Mary, died, Mary Ann helped Jim to raise his three grieving children.

The Emswilers can be reached at P.O. Box 292, Guilford, CT 06437 or www.neclt.org

New England Center for Loss & Transition

A non-profit organization dedicated to creating hope in the midst of loss through training, education, and outreach on loss and transition issues.

Since its inception in 1993, NECLT has acted as a consultant to media sources such as *Newsweek* and the television news magazine *20/20*. The staff of NECLT has provided training to over 10,000 human service professionals in school systems and universities, hospitals and hospices, government organizations and other community groups across the nation.

The Cove Center for Grieving Children

This outgrowth of the New England Center for Loss & Transition creates safe harbors for grieving children and their families throughout Connecticut. In family-based support groups, children find a place to begin to explore what the death of a family member has meant to them while their parents learn how to support them in their grief.

For more information about NECLT or The Cove, please contact:

P.O. Box 292
Guilford, CT 06437
www.neclt.org

For more information about The Cove's annual training on starting your own support group for grieving families or for a listing of children's grief support groups across the country, please go to www.neclt.org/cove.htm